Extra Time
My Autobiography

D0542152

Extra Time
My Autobiography

David Weir

with Douglas Alexander

HODDER

First published in Great Britain in 2011 by Hodder & Stoughton
An Hachette UK company

First published in paperback in 2012

1

Paperback ISBN 978 1 444 72422 6
Ebook ISBN 978 1 444 73377 8

Typeset in Nexus Serif by Hewer Text UK Ltd, Edinburgh

Printed and bound by CPI Group (UK) Ltd, Croydon, CR0 4YY

Hodder & Stoughton policy is to use papers that are natural, renewable
and recyclable products and made from wood grown in sustainable
forests. The logging and manufacturing processes are expected to conform
to the environmental regulations of the country of origin.

Hodder & Stoughton Ltd
338 Euston Road
London NW1 3BH

www.hodder.co.uk

For Fiona, Lucas, Jensen, Kenzie and Ruben.
Your make it all worthwhile.

Contents

Acknowledgements

David Weir's Acknowledgements

I was not sure whether to write this book as I thought I was a private person but decided to do it after persuasion from my friend David Ball, who felt it was too good a story not to tell – I am so glad he convinced me.

When I first met up with Douglas to ask him if he would be interested in writing my book and, simultaneously, he asked me if I was interested in writing a book, it felt like the decision was made. From start to finish, Douglas has been a pleasure to work with and my admiration for his talent has continued to grow. His attention to detail and replication of my thoughts in his words meant next to no editing was required. Thanks for becoming a good friend. I apologise to Karen and David for taking up so much of Douglas' time over the period of the book but I know they must be proud of his skills and I thank them for their patience.

Thanks also to David Luxton for co-ordinating the details regarding the book and smoothing the path, and to Roddy Bloomfield for being so keen to publish the story.

Thanks must also go to Jim Jefferies, Craig Brown, David Moyes and Walter Smith for the time they gave up to help with the book and, more importantly, the platform they have given me throughout my career.

A big thanks also to Dave Lockwood, my agent, who I can always trust to make the right call.

Michael White, Darren Griffiths, Alan Myers and numerous people at my former clubs and current one for their help with facts, and too many family and friends spread over the world to mention for good times and great memories and who have helped me remember details and stories that I had long forgotten. You have helped make the whole experience a rewarding one.

The biggest thank you must however go to my family – my mum, dad and sister, Fiona, as well as my wife, also Fiona, and my children Lucas, Jensen, Kenzie and Ruben. This book is for you, I hope you are as happy as I am with our story so far and will help me with a few more chapters. Without you, it wouldn't have been possible, so I hope you are as proud of it as I am of you.

Douglas Alexander's Acknowledgements

This book would not have been possible without the generosity and knowledge of the following people. I promise to return the books I borrowed and the dinners, lunches or coffees you bought.

David was a pleasure to work with from start to finish. It was a privilege to listen to his story.

Craig Brown, Jim Jefferies, David Moyes and Walter Smith, are all gentleman football managers from the old-school who could not have been more helpful with their time and memories of managing him during his career.

David's family and friends shared their memories with great humour. Particular thanks go to Janet, his mum; Fiona, his wife, and her parents, Guy and Elizabeth Bell; Keith Vonderahe, Ian Eggleston and Paul Nevin. Keith also kindly read through the first chapter for us.

Michael White's meticulous scrapbooks of David's days at Falkirk were generously shared and provided invaluable assistance when it came to composing the Falkirk chapter. Thanks are also due to Michael for his diligent reading of that section.

On the Hearts section, Roddy Mackenzie provided encouragement and advice right from the outset, while Clare Cowan and Paul Kiddie in the club's press office were extremely helpful. David Speed, the Hearts historian, suggested avenues of research and thanks, too, to Ewan Murray who cast the eye of a journalist and Hearts supporter over it when it was completed.

At Everton, Darren Griffiths is simply a prince among the press officers currently operating in the English Premier League. He helped in so many ways, setting up interviews, sharing his own memories, lending books and reading over the completed chapters. Sue Palmer patiently rearranged a meeting with David Moyes when the original one was postponed with Scotland snowbound last Christmas – much to Darren's amusement. Thanks are also due to Andy Hunter and Jonathan Northcroft for their helpful suggestions and observations.

Alan Pattullo was of particular help on the Scotland section, sharing his own research for another book on that fateful trip to the Faroe Islands in 2002 to help jog our memories.

At Rangers, Carol Patton and Stephen Kerr in the club's press office were supportive and helpful throughout; while Robert McElroy was also an excellent source for the facts and figures of David's career at Rangers.

David Luxton provided excellent guidance in the early stages and also negotiated the publishing deal with Hodder & Stoughton on our behalf. At Hodder, Roddy Bloomfield, Sarah Hammond and their colleagues were all patient and professional. Particular thanks go to Mark Handsley, the copy editor, and John Ley, who produced the statistics section.

I have always had great support and advice from my former colleagues at the *Sunday Times* in Scotland. Keith Anderson was a wonderful sports editor whose enthusiasm for his work never dimmed; while Simon Buckland, Mark Palmer, Steven Saunders, Judith Tonner, Neil White and Richard Wilson are all excellent people and journalists, who it was a pleasure to work beside.

Jason Allardyce and Mark Macaskill of the newsdesk in Scotland kept my spirits up, while Nick Greenslade and Alex Butler of the London sportsdesk were helpful with holidays and Alan Campbell kindly covered for me during them.

My parents, Douglas and Christine, provided love and support – as they always have. Above all, thanks to Karen, my wife, and David, my son, for their love and patience which means so much to me.

Photographic Acknowledgements

The author and publisher would like to thank the following for permission to reproduce photographs:

Action Images, AFP/Getty Images, Colorsport, L'Equipe/Offside, Flash Press/Action Images, Getty Images, Livepic/Action Images, Mirrorpix, Offside, Press Association Images, Rangers FC/Press Association Images, Reuters/Action Images, SNS Group.

All other photographs are from private collections.

Foreword
by Walter Smith

BRINGING Davie Weir to Rangers for a six-month period which has lasted four and a half years as I write is one of the best moves I have made in management. I actually tried to sign Davie when I was at Rangers the first time around as manager but the negotiating skills of George Fulston, then Falkirk's chairman, put an end to that.

David was a bit of a late starter. He went to college in America and then to Falkirk, where Jim Jefferies was his manager. I noticed him right away because of how well he was playing against a good Rangers team at that time. His performances on a few occasions when I went to watch Falkirk were also consistently excellent. When signing him at that stage proved a fruitless exercise I was disappointed because I would have liked him to come to Rangers.

When he moved on to Hearts, again with Jim, we kept an eye on him. That remained the case when I left Rangers in 1998 and became manager at Everton. They were going through one of their financial crises of that period and one of my pals phoned me and said, 'I see David Weir has refused to sign a contract with Hearts.' I immediately got in contact with Jefferies, the old bandit, and asked him if they weren't going to reach an agreement what they would do. Eventually, we paid a nominal fee to get him a few months before his contract expired, and having tried to sign him before I was delighted to finally get him.

He was a stalwart in that era at Everton for me. Davie takes everything in his stride but it would have been easy for someone who had signed for Everton to turn round and say, 'That's not what you promised me', as we battled relegation in his first few months at the club, but he didn't, he just got his head down and worked hard. I had to ask him to play in a number of positions, as a wing-back, as a central defender, even in midfield a couple of times, and he did so without complaint. He came through a difficult period for the club and for the people at the club in the way you would expect Davie Weir to do.

Like every other player, you watch them play but you don't really get to know them as people. When he came in at Everton he was a quiet lad who just went about his job. He takes this personality onto the pitch. Although like everybody else he gets a wee bit excited now and again, generally speaking David is an unflustered person and that's how he plays. He's very calm on and off the pitch. The longer you get to know him, the more you see there are other bits to him, however. There's a determination, so that he'll not be swayed by anything. If he has a point to make, he'll make it and make it very strongly. He's got a steely aspect to him that isn't immediately apparent because of the way he handles himself.

I have rarely been involved with a player who is as dedicated to keeping himself fit and playing. When he has knocks, if Davie can possibly play through them he will. For example, he played every minute of every League game for us in 2009–10 as he approached his 40th birthday. It is testimony to him that he has been able to do that, but it is no accident – it is by design on Davie's part. He loves his football. He loves playing. He loves being involved in the game and I think he has given up quite a bit to make sure that continues for as long as possible. He rests between games, he eats the right things and although he'll take a drink, it is very rarely, so it's no coincidence he has been able to play for that amount of time. That's the attitude he has. He goes down as one of the best professionals I have worked with and whatever Davie gets out of the game he deserves.

I think he gains everybody's respect because he's got a common-sense approach to everything. It would be natural that younger players gravitate toward him. He's the type of person you would go to for a bit of advice if you were in a dressing-room and now he is captain of the team, when I ask him about anything specific I get a sensible answer. He has his opinions but with every one of them you can see a strain of common sense running through it. I don't see any difference in him during the time we have worked together. He was exactly the same at Everton as he is now at Rangers. That's a period spanning 12 years and there hasn't been a change in him at all. I suppose you would be disappointed if there was and I don't think he will ever have disappointed a manager he has played for.

Yet it is all very well being a good influence at a club, which David undoubtedly is, but that would not be much use to his managers if he didn't also have excellent ability. His reading of the game and his understanding of it, considering he was a bit later than others to start, are exceptional. His intelligence is a big factor, his game knowledge allied to his ability. A lot of boys have a good level of ability but never really learn anything about the game. David has learned the game inside out. He can read a situation, he sees danger developing. The number of times he's there to head the ball out of the penalty area is no accident. He positions himself where he thinks the ball is going to be and is usually right. That's the cornerstone of what he has been.

I had no hesitation in calling him back into the Scotland squad when I became manager at the start of 2005. To be honest, he has never really told me his reasons for refusing to play under the previous manager, which is typical of Davie. That will become clearer in this book but when I became Scotland manager I thought it was a complete waste of talent for him to be sitting in the house and not playing, so I phoned him and said, 'I have a squad to pick, would you be prepared to come back and play?' He said, 'Aye', and I said, 'Well, that's good then.' There were a couple of generalities about how we were both doing and how our families were doing and that was it. That's how David is. No fuss and straight back into the squad.

Two years later, when I returned to Rangers, I decided I needed him again. It was the middle of January and we'd had a good look at the team on DVDs. While we had one or two decent players at centre-half, none of them possessed an aerial presence and that was a major problem for us. I was looking around and we were having a meeting one day when I think it was Ally McCoist who said, 'Big Davie is not playing at Everton', so I phoned Davie Moyes. He had been disappointed not to be playing in that early part of the season and had stated to Davie he just wanted to play, so they talked and Davie Moyes came back to me and said they would let him come to us. I said, 'Come for six months and we'll see what happens after that', but he played so well for us in that remaining three or four months of the season, we had no hesitation in offering him another year and that's how it has been. We have just operated on a yearly basis since. When we speak to him each summer, it's no fuss, sign another year, turn up and get on with his training and his playing. Taking into consideration David's age and all the things that have been happening round the club, it goes down as one of the best signings I have made without any doubt.

Barry Ferguson had been captain for a number of years and was doing a good job, so there was no reason for me or anyone else to change the captaincy. Then there was that aberration by Barry when he was away with the national team and there was suddenly a void. Davie was the obvious one to fill it. I said, 'Are you happy to take the captaincy?' and he said, 'Absolutely', and again that was it. He has taken to the Rangers captaincy extremely well. Barry Ferguson was a great captain for us but I think considering some aspects of the club when Davie took over – the financial things were starting to bite and we were seeing players leaving – the captain was going to be an important factor in the dressing-room. It's not always easy when you have boys whose contracts are expiring, but I am sure Davie was a big influence in making sure everybody handled that correctly.

I know he has started his coaching badges and he has all the attributes for me to go into coaching and then on into management. The first impression everybody has is 'nice lad, terrific fella', but I can assure you that there is enough steel in him, so that important decisions will be made and carried out. With that wee bit of luck everyone needs, Davie could be a terrific manager.

Walter Smith, May 2011

Doubt

FOOTBALLERS are encouraged to live their lives on fast forward. You know the script. Marry young, mature early, retire early. But what happens after that? How do you fill the void beyond the game? Nobody tells you how to handle that part, but it's always there, always waiting for you. The day you stop playing. Maybe that is why my mid-life crisis arrived early, too. The summer of 2006 to be precise. It started well enough with a wonderful trip to the World Cup in Germany with Lucas, my eldest son, but after the elation of that experience, doubts started to grow in my mind.

I started writing them down, a diary of my darkest fears and worries if you like. The things that were nagging at me. I was worried about how much longer I had left as a footballer, whether I could still cut it at the top level. I was worried about my father's illness, Alzheimer's, and I wasn't sleeping properly. I was worried I would wake to the day every player dreads, the day you simply can't do it any more. Injuries started to magnify in my mind. Fiona, my wife, was pregnant and a test had come back saying there was a high chance of the baby having Down's syndrome. I am sure thousands of other parents have had the same fears, and although subsequent tests showed them to be unfounded and reassured us, it was another significant stress.

One day I wrote how I felt David Moyes, my manager at Everton, and Alan Irvine, his assistant at the time, were looking to see if the time had come to get rid of me, watching me closely every day for any sign I was in decline. I was disappointed when they chose Duncan Ferguson then Alan Stubbs as club captains ahead of me, I wondered if that meant I wasn't considered captain material or wouldn't be around much longer. Every training session became hugely important to me and if I had a bad day there I would self-ishly bring it home with me, being grumpy with Fiona and the kids. With my dad being ill, I felt guilty about being so far away from my mum. Previously, I'd lived within walking distance of them. I was building a new house and that started to get on top of me, too, all the arrangements and whether we could really afford them. My own dad had retired early and I felt that hadn't been good for him, that he needed a focus and struggled to adjust afterwards.

It was a jumble in my mind and it might have finished me as a professional footballer, five summers ago now, if I hadn't made the brief notes on the advice of Danny Donachie, son of the former Scotland international Willie, who worked for Everton at the time. With Danny's considerable help, I started to see through the dark-ness, to realise if I could get my head right then my body would be fine, too. He gave me a brilliant book called *Healing Back Pain* by an American doctor called John Sarno and altered the way I approached things and made me much tougher mentally. I started to break things down into small problems that I could solve rather than letting them build and build into bigger ones.

It is like questioning yourself and writing down your biggest doubts and concerns. Looking back now at my notes they didn't amount to much, but meant a lot to me at the time. They helped me face up to whether I was too old or too slow. They helped me admit that as a Premiership footballer you must accept that there will be usually four players in your position, all of international standard, chasing one or two places in the team. Should I have left,

I wrote, for Birmingham City or West Bromwich Albion, then Championship clubs, when they offered me two-year contracts that summer? Would I see 50 caps for my country? – something that had started to matter to me more than many fans would imagine it might do.

Most of all, though, I wondered what I would do if I was no longer a professional footballer and it frightened me. I analysed my own personality a fair bit and realised I want to be liked and in control of things. Not ideal traits perhaps for football, where your fate lies in being liked by the manager and I wasn't sure I was back then. In short, I was insecure.

Don't worry, I am not going to get all New Age on you in this book. That's not my style. You might think you know me, particularly if you are a supporter of Falkirk, Hearts, Everton and Rangers, the clubs I have played for in my career. You might think I am one of the game's good guys. That I play on for the love of the game. Well, hopefully, you will finish this book still thinking I am one of the good guys, but you should know it is not a love of football that sustains me past my 40th birthday, but a darker motivation. Football is a game played as much in the grey matter inside your head as on the green grass of the pitch. You have to keep winning internal battles with yourself to keep going. Supporters never see them being played, yet will soon notice if you are losing them because then their team will be losing games.

So what keeps me going? What keeps me travelling between Cheshire and Glasgow each week, spending a lot of time away from my wife and my four children and perhaps not being Father of the Year? It's not some altruistic drive and it's not something I am particularly proud of. It's a love of winning, bordering on an addiction, and also that fear of what comes after football. No, I don't need to beat the kids at tiddlywinks, before you ask, or any of that bull that some so-called 'winners' come out with, yet still I need my fix for half an hour after a game. It's a validation for me, proof I still have the same right to be playing the game as guys who are half my age and don't have the grey hairs in their head or the creases in their face.

Winning tells me the managers who tried to replace me with younger models were wrong. It defies the reporters, even the ones who like me, who probably have my obituary to hand whenever they attend a game, in the same way that the Queen Mother's was always ready to roll. When my team wins, it's like me winning. It's a battle for me and it's been like that for three or four years now. Victory is my answer. It chases away, for another week at least, the spectre which hangs over most players in their thirties. That the end is nigh.

I still fear retirement because I know I will never get this buzz again in life. Never. I have close friends who couldn't wait to stop, yet now regret it. They run the kids to school, they play a bit of golf. It sounded idyllic and maybe it was for a while. Then they started to get bored, they started to miss that buzz. It's a nice life for six months and then, I think, it hits you. How many games of golf can you play? How many times do you walk the kids to school? How many times do you read the paper in the morning? Does your wife start to get fed up with you moping around. Does it lead to divorce?

If you have been a professional footballer for 15–20 years, as I have, there's a competitive urge within you that you need to fulfil somehow, and when it's gone there's a huge gap to be filled. When you are sitting in the dressing-room after an Old Firm win, for example, it's the best feeling in the world, with all your teammates walking in the dressing-room, everybody in the same boat regardless of whether they are 21 or 41. It's only half an hour at most and then, as you walk out the dressing-room door, it's finished. Gone. Then you are waiting and working all week to feel that half-hour of euphoria once again.

Would I get this fix if I was back at Falkirk, where my professional career started, now? That's something I often ask myself and I am not sure I know the answer or, rather, like what it implies about me. At Rangers, we win more games than we lose, so most weeks I will get my fix. At Falkirk, we lost more than we won. That would be a real test of my appetite for the game. To come in every Monday knowing I was building toward a probable defeat or draw rather than a probable win. I would most likely start to question myself more if I was losing every week. I would have a lot of bad weekends, going home thinking, 'What am I doing here?' That's why I am no hero for playing on to my age. It's people like John Hughes, my former Falkirk teammate and good friend, who deserve the praise if there is any going. Yogi played into his forties, too, losing more than he won probably, although maybe nobody was brave enough to tell him his time was up.

All older footballers are treated with suspicion, almost as though we are freaks of nature. Arsène Wenger has said complimentary things about me in the past but rarely holds on to players after their 30th birthdays and, if he does, all they get is a year's contract at a time. It's like they could suddenly 'go' at any second in any match. Wenger's an enlightened man who has studied football to a degree few others have but in any other walk of life these days he would be considered ageist. David Moyes perhaps had a similar view and I am sure, given how he leaves no stone unturned to maintain Everton's success, it will be one based on scientific evidence of physical decline.

It will never happen, but if every player was on a year's contract you would get a higher level of performance out of all of them. I don't think there's any doubt about that. I think I was about 33 when I started going on yearly contracts at Everton after David came in as manager. Although I was tempted by those two-year contracts elsewhere back then and the security they offered me, I now see each one-year contract as a fresh challenge. I like the thought of having to earn another one each season and get a buzz when the club make me an offer to stay on each summer. I guess my career has come full circle in a sense, because when you are young and starting out, you are trying to prove yourself, too. So let's start at the beginning . . .

From Shieldhill
to Evansville

I CAME to professional football later than most players do and it is probably not a coincidence I have lasted a little longer at the other end. While my teenage peers back in Scotland were playing 50–60 pressure games per season, I was maturing as a player at a more leisurely pace on a soccer scholarship at the University of Evansville in Indiana. Our season there involved 20-odd fixtures and took much less of a toll on my body. It was the making of me as a footballer but also, more importantly, as a person. It was not about money or gaining a contract in those early days, but about friendship and fun. That, essentially, is what football should be about, yet sometimes in the rush to make it and then to stay in the team pros lose sight of it along the way. My spell in the States has given me a sense of perspective that has stayed with me throughout my career and friendships which remain precious to me to this day.

Before I get to the idyll of Indiana, I should cover a childhood that was dominated by football. I was born in Falkirk on 10 May 1970 and grew up in in Shieldhill, a former mining village on its outskirts. In Shieldhill, we are still referred to as the 'Weirs', a local dynasty almost. Both my grandfather and my father, also David, worked hard and we were perceived as wealthy by local standards. I never met my grandparents on my dad's side, but my father spoke about his dad, Adam Weir, all the time. He idolised him. My dad was also proud he had passed his own 11-plus and gone to the technical school, one of the few who had managed to do it from Shieldhill. I think he got that from his own dad, trying to be a step ahead all of the time.

My mum's parents were still around as I was growing up. Peter Crawford, my papa, died when I was relatively young but Jessie, my nana, is 90 and still alive. My papa was a big football man and a big Falkirk fan, so he would have loved the fact I went on to play for them. He used to take me to a bowling club right in the middle of Falkirk and let me play on the one-arm bandit when I was a wee boy. I was his first grandson and went everywhere with him. He was quite a character.

My dad worked in the Grangemouth Refinery, becoming a foreman there. He was in charge of a lot of people and, as he did with me, I think he ruled with an iron fist. He is an aggressive, argumentative man, on the offensive straight away if he thought someone was taking a liberty. I didn't live in fear of my dad, but I was scared of him. He had that menace about him. I could tell it was the same at his work – he later got me a couple of part-time jobs there – by the way people spoke about him and related stories about him. I had respect for my dad – sometimes he would smack me or my mum would warn me: 'Wait till your dad comes home' if I was misbehaving. I am much the same with my boys now and I don't think that's a bad thing, to be a wee bit scared of your dad.

I remember driving to Stirling one day with my dad and this bus driver pulled out in front of him. He followed him until he stopped and was out of the car and in the bus trying to pull the driver out of his cab. It was road rage before the term became fashionable. Dad certainly had a fiery temperament and a short fuse, but when it came to me and football his patience seemed endless. No matter how hard his working day was at the refinery, he always made time to kick a ball about in our back garden with me when he got home. He would stand in goal until I had finished taking shots at him. He would take me to all kinds of games, too. He took me to Celtic Park to see Manchester United in a testimonial at the start of the season. He took me to an Aberdeen–Dundee United League Cup final and to internationals. I find myself doing the same with my boys now and I am lucky where I live that I can take them to Old Trafford or Anfield. My dad was very good at things like that.

I had a group of friends, there were five or six of us, and we were pretty inventive when it came to keeping ourselves amused in the days before PlayStations and X-Boxes. We created a golf course over the old pit bings near the village. There was a burn which ran through Shieldhill, so we even had holes across the water. It was a proper nine-hole course with lovely flags and everything. There was also a cow field which we turned into a football pitch and set up our own five-a-side league against other teams in the village. We had a wee cricket pitch in the swing park in the middle of Shieldhill and we played there in the summer. When Wimbledon was on we would go along to the primary school playground and mark a court out with chalk. We had running races on an area that was like a 400 metre track or we would be playing on our bikes. We were always out playing in some shape or form and rarely sat in the house.

Football was king, though, and sometimes I would forget to come home for dinner because I was having so much fun playing. Your mum and dad would know you would be in one of three or four places within the village boundaries playing some kind of sport and that you were safe. In those days, my main friends were James and Tommy White, Graham and Iain Scobbie, Craig Hunter, who actually coaches my nephew now at Grahamston Boys Club, and John Ferrie, who was the organiser and leader of our wee gang. He had a hut for us in his back garden. It was properly kitted out with carpets and seats. I think his family kept greyhounds and it was a converted kennel. That was our nerve centre, where we met and laid our plans. Thinking back now, it all ran like clockwork. We would even have golf tournaments with trophy presentations, it was a special time.

There was one night, though, when I didn't need to be called in for my tea or have a search party sent out for me. On Fridays, the old black-and-white Sherlock Holmes films with Basil Rathbone would be on around teatime on BBC2 and I loved them. I would rush home from wherever I was to see them. I have bought them subsequently and now Lucas, my oldest son, sits and watches them as I did at his age. I would eat everything and anything I could get my hands on. Like many boys of my era in Scotland, I probably grew up on tins of Heinz beans and sausages, macaroni cheese and spaghetti.

I started to support Rangers I would guess around 1977 or 1978, when I was seven or eight. Players like Sandy Jardine, Tam Forsyth, Derek Johnstone, Tommy McLean and Alex MacDonald were in the team at that point. My hero was Davie Cooper, and later Graeme Souness as I got older and started to appreciate the game more. I was fascinated by Souness and Kenny Dalglish and the success they had in that era. There was a mystique about them, as you only really got to see them via TV highlights of Liverpool's midweek matches back then.

I clearly remember one birthday when I was still at primary school and got a new Rangers strip. My mum, Janet, told me to keep it clean, but my dad took me out to play and sure enough I fell in the dirt and couldn't wear it to school or take it as PE kit. Most of my battles with mum involved clothes. She had a saying which she still uses to this day: 'David, I don't wish any harm to come to you,' she would tell me, 'but I hope when you are bigger you don't have one wee boy like yourself, I hope you have two.' It turned out I had three boys of my own, so now I know precisely what she meant. She also says that if she'd had me first, rather than Fiona, my older sister, then she would have stopped at one child.

Apparently, I was a good baby, but when I got to three or four I started to get a mind of my own and just wouldn't wear things. Mum used to take me to shops and let me choose clothes but later we would be going out and I simply wouldn't wear them. Mum still tells the story of a family wedding where I refused to get dressed, kept everybody late and then cried so much I feel asleep as soon as we got there. Another time, she bought me a safari jacket for Sunday school but I wasn't too keen on it and soon reappeared at the door with it slung over my shoulder, informing her I wouldn't be wearing it or indeed going to Sunday school.

Looking back now, underlying this apparent disobedience was my shyness, I was never comfortable meeting a lot of people at once as a child. I see similarities now with Lucas, who can be similarly defiant if he doesn't want to do something, but my mum reckons it is Ruben, my youngest, who reminds her most of me as a wee boy. I think I had this comfort zone in Shieldhill that I didn't like being out of and I think my dad was probably much the same.

He had his friends in Shieldhill, too, and it felt like you didn't need to go out of Shieldhill for anything.

The only time Mum had no trouble getting me into a new outfit was when it was a new football strip. My dad didn't fancy flying, so we always holidayed in Britain at places like Scarborough, Southport, Lytham St Anne's and Torquay. We would always get a present during the break and for me it was simply a case of finding the local sports shop and letting me pick something. Apparently, I could also amuse myself for hours by sitting in the bath with my new football boots on to mould the leather.

Fiona was four years older than me and we never got on particularly well as children. I called her a snob and I remember one conversation where I said, 'Fiona, I really don't like you', and she replied, 'David, I really don't like you.' It was almost like a watershed. I meant it and she meant it. Thankfully, our conversations these days are a bit more mature and friendly.

Dad was my coach and sternest critic. Hard but fair. When he praised me, I knew I had done really well because it was so rare. He would always point out what I could have done better. Looking back now, it was good preparation for becoming a professional. I always wanted to be a footballer, but he told me, 'You can be a footballer if you want but you must get your education first.' I had a bit of insight because my mum's brother, my uncle Graham, had been a professional. He played in goal for several clubs. He started at East Stirling, then he went to Sheffield United, York City, Scarborough and Scunthorpe. He would bring me home old balls and keep all his old programmes, stoking my interest further still and answering my endless questions when we went down to York each Easter to visit. I was fascinated by his stories of playing against the likes of Liverpool and Manchester United. He would also organise tickets for me and my dad to go and watch games like Leeds versus Aston Villa when we were down. It all helped light the fuse of my imagination and ambition.

I always arrived back from Shieldhill Primary with my trousers covered in mud and my shoes badly scuffed. One day, when I was around nine, I came in to tell Mum I had lost one of my front teeth in a collision with a metal goalpost in the playground. I was quite proud I had done that playing football. I played in the school team when I was in Primary Five, which was unheard of – it was usually only Primary Six and Seven kids who played and I felt really special getting out of class early for the games. The teacher who looked after the football team was called Bill Allardyce. I was in the same class as his daughter, and he brought me into the team a year earlier than normal and played me in the games and I loved it. We had black and white Newcastle strips, but there was one strip that was a Bukta one, a special one, with their symbol down its sleeves, and the captain got to wear it. I was delighted when I later achieved that distinction and finally got my hands on the special strip.

Dad drove me everywhere for training and games and the whole family used to come to watch me play for Grahamston Boys Club at weekends: Mum, Dad, Fiona and, Dene, the family dog. Anywhere I played, all over Scotland, they were there. The best player there in my time was Stuart Balmer, who went on to have a good career with Celtic, Charlton and several other clubs. Stuart always looked more likely to make it than me back then. Frankly he was bigger and better. My memory is that Dad wasn't too keen on me going on trial with a couple of English clubs who showed interest but I do remember a trial for Rangers in Edinburgh at under-14 or under-15 level. I remember saying to the guy handing out the kit, 'These shorts are too small for me, pal.' He just looked at me, as if to say, 'It is probably not the shorts that are too small, pal.' I was a bit chunkier back then than I am now.

With Grahamston we always had to wear blazers and flannels, which used to rile everybody else up when we played them. If my mum thought I was hanging about with a rough crowd in Shieldhill and moving up to Woodlands High in Falkirk, the nearest second-ary school, would solve this problem, then it backfired as my class there was rougher still. Partly inhibited by my shyness and partly by not wanting to appear a smart-arse to them, I wouldn't raise my hand to answer questions. My parents talked about sending me to Dollar Academy, a famous private school nearby, but I made it clear I didn't want to go.

At primary, I enjoyed school and was always near the top of the class but as I got older, I started to feel it was frowned upon to be clever within my wee social group. There was a pressure not to break ranks and I was always friends with the boys who liked a bit of a carry-on, so it ended up not being the cool thing to do. You have got to have strength within yourself at that age to break out of peer-group pressure and I must admit I didn't have it. I am now conscious with my own kids of trying to get them in an environ-ment where it is encouraged to be bright. It stuck with me that in America it was 'cool' to be bright or good at things. Success was rewarded there, rather than frowned upon as it can sometimes be in Scotland.

My dad would always send me upstairs to swot for any exams that might be coming up and I would instead listen to the radio while half reading whatever it was. When I got to 16 or 17, my parents started to worry about what I was going to do when I left school. They got me to write to Scottish Amicable, the building society, whose headquarters were nearby, and things like that. Mum worked in a bank and I had an interview with the Bank of Scotland. Mum bought me a new, pinstripe suit for the special occasion but I didn't go to the interview. She wasn't too amused to discover this when she asked how I got on. Again, I was stubborn and told my parents, 'I don't want to work in a bank.' My dad was livid that night and said, 'You might not want to work in a bank, but you should still go to the interview.' I did go to another interview, with the Clydesdale Bank in Falkirk, but clearly remember thinking to myself during it, 'What am I doing here?' I am a stubborn so-and-so when I know something isn't for me. I think my mum was desperate to get me pigeon-holed and working, but if something wasn't for me, I simply wouldn't do it. I was very strong-willed and opinionated in that respect, I knew what I did and didn't like. Whatever way you dressed it up, or indeed dressed me up, that wasn't going to be for me.

Just when mum and dad were beginning to despair of me, an opportunity presented itself after I played in a tournament for Scotland under-18 schoolboys at Skegness. We went down and played against various English teams from Greater Manchester, Inner London, Merseyside, all the football hotbeds. Many of those playing were already contracted to professional clubs in Britain, such as John O'Neil at Dundee United, but I wasn't and at the end I was approached by a couple of guys who represented an obscure American college looking for recruits for its 'soccer programme'. Fred Schmalz and Tony Colavecchia were about to change my life for ever. They explained in detail what was involved for over an hour. I didn't say much as they spoke, but inside the feeling grew this was what I had been waiting for and was exactly what I wanted to do with my life.

21

I got the bus back to Edinburgh, where Mum and Dad were patiently waiting to pick me up in the car, I climbed into the back and then poked my head between the front seats to break the big news: 'I am going to America to play football.' They probably thought, 'Yeah, right, David', but when we got home the phone rang and unfortunately my mum's cousin had just died, so it was all forgotten about. It was only when she came home on the Monday night from work to a phone call from Fred that it was back on the family agenda. 'Mrs Weir, did David tell you I had been speaking to him about going to America on a soccer scholarship?', asked Fred. 'He mentioned America, but he didn't exactly say he was going on a soccer scholarship,' replied Mum. Fred informed her he was coming up to see us the next day. Mum got away early from work to find me sitting at the dining-room table filling out all the papers. I had already made my mind up. My bag was almost packed. 'So you are the man that has come to take my son away from me,' Mum said to Fred, although she still let him stay for his dinner.

It all happened very quickly after that. I sat an exam in May to ensure I could handle a degree academically and by August I was driving through to Prestwick Airport with Mum and Dad for my flight to the United States. It was a big deal for a tight-knit family like ours. I remember Dad was crying and it was the first time in my life I had seen him crying about anything. When you are young, you don't think of the ramifications, you just do it, but my parents were both in tears and must have looked as though they'd had a major row when they stopped at the Fenwick hotel on the way back to Falkirk for a meal together.

It was the first time I had been in an aeroplane or abroad. I was supposed to fly to New York, then Detroit and finally St Louis, but when I got to New York I was such a novice I thought I had to get my bags, so there I was waiting for these bags that were never coming and I missed my next flight to Detroit. The girl at the desk said tough luck to me basically, but must have then taken pity on the innocent abroad as she added she would see what she could do. She got me a flight from La Guardia, so I had to get this taxi across New York from JFK to get on this flight for free with another airline to Detroit. I missed my connection to St Louis, but got a later one to meet Geff Schmalz, Fred's son, who is now a high-ranking army officer, and an Irish guy called Ian O'Brien. I had never met either of them before in my life. They were watching for my flight coming in, but I wasn't on it, so they were walking around the airport looking for me. I got in later and was walking round looking for them. OB, as we called him, was an older guy, like the dad of the team. He was nuts, but looked after everybody and eventually he came up to me and said, 'You are David Weir aren't you?' I must have looked Scottish, I guess.

I was knackered after my eventful journey from Scotland but Evansville was still a three-hour drive away. It was real America, off the beaten track for tourists, a small city of around 120,000 people built on a bend in the Ohio River and surrounded by countryside and miles upon miles of cornfields. The University of Evansville was the main thing in the town, with what appeared to me as the whites living on one side of the motorway and the black community on the other side of it. The first thing that struck me was the wall of heat and humidity. I was straight into training in 100 degrees, it was a completely different climate and way of life from the one I had been used to but it was refreshing, too, because nobody knew me or had any preconceptions about me.

The University of Evansville has a good reputation in America for sport and theatre, but is also known nationally for a tragedy in 1977 when 14 members of its basketball team were among 29 people killed in a plane crash in thick fog as they left Evansville on 13 December for a fixture in Tennessee. Keith Vonderahe, a team-mate and good friend of mine at Evansville and to this day, lost his father in the crash and was just six years old at the time. Keith never flew until he joined the soccer team at Evansville and it must have been an incredibly difficult experience for him after what his family had gone through.

It certainly put my own problems settling in the States into perspective. Initially, I would phone home once a week on the Sunday morning and that would make me incredibly homesick at first and sometimes I would start crying, which wasn't great for Mum and Dad to hear, as they weren't to know that most of the time I was feeling fine. I'd probably had a couple of drinks on the Saturday night and then phoned them when I was on a low with a hangover. They were just about ready to tell me to come home when Dad decided to phone Fred. I think it struck a chord with him because he had suffered badly from home-sickness as a young man when he did his national service in Catterick. He told me that he hadn't enjoyed that, but had come through it.

Fred wasn't aware I was so homesick, but he took me under his wing along with Graham Merryweather, an English lad who had also arrived in Evansville. I remember we had these wee mailboxes in Hale Hall, an all-male dormitory where I initially lived with other students and athletes from all sports at the university, and I always checked to see if there was a letter for me, even though I knew there wasn't going to be one most days. Mum would also send over the *Falkirk Herald* and the *Rangers News* to keep me in touch with what was going on back in Scotland. Graham had been picked up at the same trials as me, playing for Nottinghamshire I think, and came over at the same time. He was a competitive, aggressive central midfield player, yet came from a well-to-do family. Roger, his dad, had been Sheriff of Nottingham at one stage and was a real character. I got to know them well and they were nice people. Graham settled quicker than me and we later lived together for three years and became great friends.

My settling-in period was further disrupted by acute appendicitis, which was pretty painful and required an operation pronto. Luckily, I had health insurance at that point because the bills ran to thousands of dollars afterwards. I just handed them on to Fred and he sorted things out for me. Dad took a phone call at 3am one morning to tell him what had happened. Overhearing Dad saying, 'Oh God' and so on, Mum thought I had been killed. She wanted to fly out to look after me but Fred somehow dissuaded her. When she subsequently discovered I returned to my student dormitory after being released from hospital with no one to care for me, she hit the roof. She won't be too happy to read now that my health insurance payments were sacrificed in subsequent years to boost the funding of my social life in the States. It was around $500 for your health insurance and most of us felt that money could be better used on other things.

For my second semester I returned to Britain, at the university's satellite campus in Grantham, Harlaxton College. I was able to come home most weekends then, so that got me through the first year. Then, of course, it was the same trauma when I went back for the second year, until I got a girlfriend called Cathy Harmon and gradually started to settle down. Americans are the most hospitable people in the world in my experience. They want to know you and they want to help you. They will take you for dinner, then drop you off back home. You go into their house and they expect you to just go into their fridge and take a drink. Whereas in Britain we'd consider that rude or at least forward, Americans are genuinely like that and it's not manufactured. That was probably the best thing about my whole experience, the people and the place. Evansville was real America with real American people living in it. I got a proper insight into their life and I liked what I saw. Cathy's parents had this beautiful big house with a tennis court, swimming pool etc. It was absolutely gorgeous. My nana was flabbergasted when she came out to visit in February of my second year with mum and stayed there, she just couldn't believe the place.

It was definitely a bit different from my student accommodation. If you remember the TV series *The Young Ones* with Rik Mayall and Adrian Edmondson, then you will have a rough idea of what the various houses I shared in Evansville were like. When Mum visited she was dismayed to find that six months down the line I was still sleeping on the same – unwashed – bedsheet she had supplied me with the previous August back in Scotland. My bed was simply a mattress on the floor. My wardrobe was a cupboard, with nothing hanging up and everything on the floor. The telly was covered in beer and there would be black bin bags full of empty cans lying around. We used Union Jacks as curtains in another house and there was a big hole in the wall of another one. During one winter we had the electricity, gas, water and phone all cut off at the same time because we hadn't paid any of the bills. We used to go over to the dorms for a shower, a meal and some heat.

There was only one pan, one knife, one fork, one plate. You couldn't cook anything. I existed mainly on foot-long meatball sandwiches from Subway. Every Friday during the season, we would go and buy a keg of beer for that weekend's party and have it chilling for the Saturday night. You couldn't buy alcohol on a Sunday in Indiana, you had to go to neighbouring Illinois. As our house was right on campus, it was the perfect place for parties and sometimes it would be so busy you couldn't move with 60–70 people somehow crammed into it on a Saturday or a Sunday night.

It wasn't too demanding academically, which allowed me to focus mainly on my football and my social life. If my first year had been a huge adjustment from living at home, I had now come out of my shell and really started to enjoy myself. I was growing in confidence and enjoying my life and my football immensely. You had to work a bit obviously – they wouldn't keep you otherwise. You had to meet certain criteria. Graham was clever and I was okay, but Nick, the American lad we lived with, struggled. He ended up leaving after two years because he couldn't get the grades and that was probably because he lived with us in what had quickly developed a reputation as the party house.

Some teachers would make it harder for you because you were in the soccer team and some would cut you some slack. You still had to do the work, but they would maybe give you longer to do it. I always felt the basketball players were at a different level from the footballers. With them, you always felt the academic stuff didn't matter. Our facilities, treatment and food were excellent by British standards but theirs were better still, and yet they were average compared to us in terms of achievement. Their home was a 12,500-seater arena that was packed when they played.

We mostly played in a regional conference and teams from Missouri, like St Louis University, the University of Indiana and the University of Notre Dame in Indiana were our main rivals. Even these games were six-hour round trips or longer, but we also had a few big journeys each year, where we would fly to the west coast or down to the gulf for tournaments. My first was against Indiana University, the University of North Carolina and UCLA, the best teams in the country at that time, and I was so lucky we were ranked as an NCAA Division One college for sport and competed at that elite level. I know lads have subsequently gone to America to junior colleges, in NCAA Division Two, and the standard there has been nowhere good enough to give them a chance of making it professionally. You would play 10 games in your conference, 10 non-conference games and then go on from there if you were good enough. There was a national ranking like the current Fifa ones, published every week by a committee that ranked you on the basis of your results and the toughness of your schedule. At the end of the season, it would pick the top 32 teams – it's more now – to go into this national tournament, the NCAA Division One National Championships, and that was a straight knockout. We made it into that tournament every year.

The season ran from August to December and was so short that you were training every day and playing every two or three days during it. We would practise for two hours a day during the season and miss a lot of classes with all the travelling we were doing. If we went to say Portland or Miami to play we could be gone for four or five days at a time on a road trip. Then the season would suddenly stop and there was next to nothing. My weight fluctuated considerably, as my diet didn't change and sometimes I would come back to Scotland in the summer and struggle to get trousers to fit my thighs. In the spring we would start training again indoors but only on Sunday nights. I guess it could have been viewed as a chance to make up any lost ground academically but we just saw it as the party season – we would even have a couple of beers before training. Sometimes we would organise bounce games on Sunday mornings, thinking nothing of driving the three hours to St Louis required to find opposition of our standard despite the serious hangovers we were usually suffering from.

It was the camaraderie of that team that has stayed with me over the years. Guys like Keith, Graham, Ian Eggleston and Paul Nevin, known as Nev, remain friends to this day and we still meet up regularly. It was a different era in terms of nutrition and sports science and all that. On our road trips we would troop into McDonald's and back onto the bus with a vast array of burgers and it wasn't water or sports drinks that sat in the coolers on it but Cokes and other soft drinks. We were living in each other's pockets, spent our lives together and became like brothers, a family, as a result – developing a team spirit that largely explained our subsequent success. In the summer, we would work together on soccer camps, which was great fun and well-paid. I remember going to Kentucky for one. Another summer Graham and I also worked in a sawmill, which was more like a proper day's work: we got picked up early in the morning and were then dropped off again at night after our labours and paid cash in hand.

I was a country boy and still a bit naive, much to the amusement of my new teammates and friends. The university sports teams were celebrities in Evansville and we were in the local papers every day. I did an early interview with a reporter from the *Evansville Press and Courier*. The girl asked me what was different from Scotland and as everybody waited for me to say something profound about the cultural differences or my personal struggle with homesickness, I came out with, 'Aye, the cars are bigger aren't they?' Not my finest moment with the press, as Nev still reminds me.

At times, it really was like being in *Ferris Bueller's Day Off* or an American teen film of that ilk. I remember Nev was copying me in a test one day, having not bothered to study for it, when our joint effort was spotted by Mrs Dow, who taught our communications class. She liked Nev, who used to butter her up all the time. So she shouted, 'David', and of course Nev acted all disgusted at my 'cheating' and hid his paper away from me. When the papers came back, I had a remark written on mine. 'David, I wish you would stop copying Paul and produce your own work.' I just took it on the chin. I had arrived intending to go into sports science but, ultimately, my degree was in advertising and public relations.

The nickname Nev coined for me, 'Big and Pink', sounds obscene, but was really only a reference to me being big and usually sunburned over there in the heat. There was one particularly bad case after we played at a tournament in Miami and I had to endure the flight back in my tie and suit afterwards with my skin on fire. I was rarely called David or Davie in fact, as the boys had somehow got a hold of my middle name of Gillespie, probably from my passport, and decided they preferred to use it. Gillespie was my grandfather on my dad's side's middle name and remains in the family as my youngest son Ruben's middle name, but it caused great confusion with one lad from Florida, who was convinced I was called Giuseppe and of Italian descent.

It was university, so a big part of the culture was drinking, but at the same time it wasn't legally allowed because we were all under the drinking age in America. Most of us didn't hit 21 until our last year there. We found it particularly difficult to get our heads round this as back in Britain we could all go to the pub and have a pint. They had special police in Evansville called 'excise officers' and their role was to enforce the drinking laws. The head officer was called Ronald McDonald and I had one notable run-in with him.

One night we were drinking and having a bit of fun out the back of Nev's house. I was kicking a ball about with a beer in my hand, which pretty much summed me up, and the excise police screeched up in their car and Ronald McDonald leapt out and summoned me over. I must have been a bit tipsy because instead of meekly handing over my beer and facing the rap, I wiggled it at him and taunted him: 'You are going to have to get it.' Meanwhile, everyone else was making themselves scarce. I remember getting chased round the car, then running round the back of Subway, which was across the road. It was a square building and he was a big, older guy so he was never going to catch me. He came to one corner and I was at the other, ready to get away from him again, when he suddenly shouted: 'Stop, or I'll shoot.' I can remember it registering in my head: 'Did he just say he was going to shoot me?', then thinking: 'He's not going to do that' and I just kept going until I reached the university campus to take stock under a tree before wandering back after the furore died down and opening another beer. He did have a gun, though, and it was certainly a bit more serious than when the police used to come to my mum's door back in Shieldhill to tell her we had been playing football in the farmer's field again.

Fred Schmalz, our coach, was quite a character. We all owe him hugely for giving us the opportunities and the memories but he was a football obsessive, who could talk about the game all day long. He had this free kick which he always made us practise but that never worked in games. We were playing at Indiana, which was the biggest game of the season, our main rivals away from home. The set-up of the free kick was to get Nev smashed by their defenders as the decoy and leave me with a tap-in. It worked once in that game, never before and never after, but we won the game 1-0 and apparently for years afterwards Fred would tell his teams that it worked back in 1989 and would damn well work again. To protect future generations, we tried to persuade the ref not to give it. Nev was the decoy because he was dispensable. Despite my height, I was much too important to be sacrificed. Before that victory over Indiana, a few of us, myself included, got flat-top haircuts. Fred promised he would do the same if we won and proved a man of his word, although we escorted him into and out of the barbershop just to be sure.

If we poked fun at him sometimes and grumbled to each other about his painstaking approach, then we all owe him in respect of the opportunity he gave us. That's always at the back of our minds whenever we meet up and we always end up talking about him without fail. I still meet people now, Americans on coaching courses or whatever, and Fred is always the topic of conversation with them, too. He always kept us occupied and educated us along the way. He showed faith in me despite my initial homesickness and then the appendicitis. We played in a tournament at the air force academy in Colorado Springs that was like walking onto the set of *Top Gun*. We went whitewater rafting there, too, and visited the Smithsonian Museum in Washington. Less impressive, perhaps, was stumbling into a Gay Pride march in San Francisco wearing our Umbro training gear and some silly sailor hats we had bought. Nevertheless, we passionately joined the chants of 'Stop the violence, stop the hate, how do you know your kids are straight?'

Anybody that remembers Evansville's success back then knows Fred. He has retired from the University of Evansville now but still works coaching youth teams in the city. He had something you can't put your finger on but after our generation left the programme its success dwindled. They had a good team before us, then a good team in our generation, then it just kind of fell away. I think they recruited well for a few years and then struggled to maintain their success in that regard.

Fred pulled a tactical masterstroke with me. Turning me into a free-scoring centre-forward in my third year at Evansville, which was our most successful season. We made it to the semi-finals of the NCAA Division One National Championships, called the Final Four, which was at Tampa, and I was named first-team All-American, a selection of the 11 best college players, on the back of scoring 24 goals. Until then, our main striker was Robert Paterson, who had Scottish roots, and was probably the top scorer in the country at the time. Robert later had a short spell at Kilmarnock, but he got injured during this particular season and it was Fred's idea, out of nowhere, to move me up there. I guess I presented a challenge that most centre-halves don't face very often, someone who is big but with a touch good enough to make the ball stick and bring my teammates into play. I loved it. It was refreshing after playing at the back. You got praise for scoring goals, rather than criticism for conceding them.

I was also rattling in the goals at a rate that those who know me only as a defender in Britain will struggle to believe. Despite my own move forward and an injury to another key defender, John

Prow, who broke his arm, we only conceded seven goals in 27 games that season. That was in no small part due to a guy called Scott Cannon, who was from Evansville. He and John Prow were the two Americans in our team I definitely felt could have made it as professionals in Britain. We were a real unit by now, bonded together and all pulling in the same direction. With the season being so short and sharp our run to the prestigious Final Four in Tampa was a bit of whirlwind but our reputation nationally was on the rise and so were the excitement and interest back in Evansville. We had a massive go-away and were treated to dinner at Shula's Steakhouse as guests of Don Shula, the former Miami Dolphins coach, who runs the chain. We also had a send-off dinner with Don Mattingly, the famous New York Yankees batter, who is from Evansville and is now manager of the Los Angeles Dodgers.

Yet after the big build-up, for some reason we didn't do ourselves justice in our semi-final against Rutgers University from New Jersey. I was closely marked by a promising young centre-back called Alexi Lalas. Before the game, Bill Andracki, their goalkeeper, who also went on to play Major League Soccer, was warming up near me and Nev when he suddenly smashed the ball at Nev. It didn't make much of an impression on Nev, or it knocked him out, because he doesn't really recall it, but I can remember it as clear as day. It was definitely an attempt to intimidate us, to get into our heads, a bit of the Wimbledon Crazy Gang stuff perhaps, but we just thought Andracki was a bit mad and shrugged it off. It certainly didn't affect us.

We lost 1-0 and it was a big anti-climax because we'd had such a good run we thought we were going to win. Nev played well that day but most of us didn't. We froze collectively and I missed a chance with a header I would normally have scored from. It was a negative sort of game. I remember the pitch not being that big either. Rutgers scored against the run of play, right before the end of the first half through a guy called Pedro Lopes, who also went on to play in the MLS. Rutgers drew 0-0 with UCLA in the final, it went to penalties and UCLA won. UCLA's semi with North Carolina State University finished 0-0 as well and they also won it on penalties. It was odd that they ended up being National Champions and didn't score a goal at the Final Four but the tight scorelines give you an idea of the standard. Out of that tournament there were probably 10–15 players who went on to play for the US national team in World Cups. UCLA had guys like Cobi Jones, Joe-Max Moore, who was later with me at Everton, and Brad Friedel, who was their goalie. Rutgers had Lalas and there were guys like Kasey Keller at the University of Portland, who we played as well.

The biggest disappointment of that whole tournament was that we had to fly out at 6am the next morning. It was ridiculous. We didn't even get to see the final. In the American system, your season just suddenly ends like that and for some of the lads that's the end of their careers, too. Some of them will never play football seriously again. They will go off to be doctors or lawyers or whatever they become and that's the end of that generation. It can apply to two or three lads or it can be a whole team in some cases. We were certain we were going to be the National Champions, which would have been unheard of for Evansville, a small school. It would have put Evansville on the map for ever.

As it was, we finished the season ranked as No. 3 in the United States, which was still a huge achievement for a college of our size and resources. UCLA, for example, was huge by comparison: a breeding ground for future Olympic, NBA and NFL stars, it invested millions of pounds in sport. We were punching way above our weight. To put it in terms of British football, our run to the Final Four was a bit like Dundee United's to the semi-final of the European Cup under Jim McLean in 1983 or Aberdeen's European success under Alex Ferguson or Nottingham Forest's under Brian Clough. It just happened that a talented group of players came together in that period at Evansville and developed a formidable spirit together. Nowadays, the scouting is much more developed and the bigger colleges would have probably enticed us to them instead. In a sense, we were also victims of our own success because the positions in the team were taken and some promising players probably opted to go elsewhere rather than try to break into it. The highlight of my final senior year was being selected for an indoor tournament in Baltimore. At the end of the week-long tournament, they drafted the best players for an indoor professional league. I never got drafted, indoor football was never going to be my forte.

Yet it was all great fun while it lasted. I never felt pressure playing there, it was just like playing in a team with your pals. I was allowed to develop as a player at my own pace and I grew in confidence as a person. I had stopped playing football in my mid-teens and was going through the motions before I went to Evansville and rediscovered my love for the game. Kids coming through now don't want to be football players, they want to be rich. Money wasn't even a consideration for us in those carefree, happy days in Evansville. We would work on soccer camps in the summer to get enough money to buy our beer, not to get rich. It was all about sharing everything and particularly the experiences we had together, which I will treasure for ever. Mum came over for my graduation and was mortified that I hadn't ironed my gown for the ceremony, but it should really have been a football strip I was wearing. My spell in America had convinced me I wanted to be a professional footballer and also that I was good enough to become one.

2

Learning to defend myself

IF YOU are going to come to professional football late, then it makes sense to take a crash course. In many ways, that is exactly what my four-year stint at Falkirk was. A degree in professional football after the academic one I had completed in America. It taught me how to handle the politics of a dressing-room packed with larger-than-life characters. It taught me how to defend properly, often against the odds, in a team with a confirmed commitment to attacking football under Jim Jefferies. Although we were all in it together, there was sometimes a bit of 'them and us' between the forward-thinking players he packed his selections with, to the delight of neutrals, and those of us who were designated defenders. At times, we felt like an endangered species. Certainly, as a defender in Jim's Falkirk team, you had to learn quickly to fend for yourself and looking back now that was probably not a bad thing for me.

When we were relegated at the end of my breakthrough season as a professional, there were plenty of plaudits for the way we had played from the media but not quite enough points for us to stay in the Premier League. We scored 60 goals, an incredible total for a side at the foot of the table, yet conceded 86. Jim saw entertainment as part of his brief, and I mean that as a compliment. He always felt he could outscore any opponent, an incredibly positive outlook on his part. Yet sometimes when the scoring stopped we had lost another of the classics we would regularly serve up at

Brockville, the dog-eared ground we loved playing at, or on our travels around Scotland. Yet Jim's instinct for taking a gamble also worked in my favour. I owe him and Billy Brown, his assistant, hugely for giving me my chance in professional football and my formative years as a professional under them are ones I will always regard fondly.

They might not have been inclined to take their punt had they seen me standing virtually asleep and covered in dust at a roundabout on the outskirts of the Grangemouth oil refinery waiting for my sister to pick me up one night not too long before I signed for them. Don't get me wrong, I was grateful to my dad for getting me a job in a distribution warehouse in the BP plant there, where he worked, but not as grateful as I was, and forever will be, for the next time he intervened on my behalf. My time in America had made up my mind. I wanted to be a full-time professional footballer. I hadn't been sure in my mid-teens when, in truth, I had become a little disenchanted with the game, but now I had matured and knew what I wanted. Easier said than done, though. From all the letters I had fired off to clubs in England only one offer, of a trial with Leeds United, had come back. Little did I know that Dad had also contacted Falkirk, our local club, on my behalf.

Now this was quite something in itself because my father was far from being a Falkirk fan. Although we lived in the town, he never liked them much. In fact, I remember him saying to me a few times they had 'the worst fans in the world' and 'you'll not be playing for them', but, typically, he put my future ahead of his own feelings. Or maybe he was just sick of seeing his son moping around the house not doing a great deal with his life. It did the trick because something in it stoked the interest of Jim, a manager who was to become such a significant influence on my career. Jim had a hunch about me and also got a favourable reply when he checked with Bill Parker, a Falkirk scout who had watched me in my teens and said I was worth another look.

When my dad got the reply he basically ordered me down to the ground. Not that I was arguing too much. In America, the Holy Grail for us all had been a professional contract back in Britain or Europe. When I reported to the away dressing-room, full of young hopefuls three or four years younger than me, I was determined to repay my father's faith and also do myself justice. It took a while before I saw a ball, though. Jim is old school when it comes to pre-season. He likes you to run. And run. And then run some more. I don't think the sports science backs it up now, much to the relief of his current players probably. Running wasn't a problem for me: I was naturally fit at the time, desperate to do well and actually quite enjoyed it.

I played in some trial matches before being quickly offered a contract. Jim says now he and Billy were worried someone else would notice me. The negotiations didn't take very long. They brought me into the office and offered me a one-year contract on £175 a week. I would have signed for £75 a week and that's not an exaggeration. I think my squad number was 35 and I thought it was brilliant I had a number at a professional club. It was just a chance for me, an opportunity. In America, I'd made my mind up. Up until then, I'd said I wanted to be a professional footballer, but I didn't really know what it entailed. Coming back from America, I knew that's what I wanted to do, to give it a shot. I didn't know what else to do to be honest, I really enjoyed my football and I believed I could be a success, so it was a good feeling and I thought it was the start.

As a boy, I had played for Grahamston and then it was Dunipace. I fell out of love with football when I was about 15 or 16, I think, and then I went back and played for Dunipace's under-18s team. That was when Celtic saw me. Davie Provan was the coach. He writes about that now and again in his column for the *News of the World* because he released me. He said I wasn't good enough. I never played with Celtic really. The full-time boys and the better ones from the boys' club would play in the youth team. I never got a chance with them. I remember going to Motherwell for the quarter-finals of the Youth Cup and thinking I had a chance of playing, but I was the 14th man.

It didn't bother me that I was a bit older than the lads I was changing with back then at Falkirk, just as it doesn't now at Rangers. We seem to put age restrictions on people at both ends of the spectrum. If you have not done it by 16 or 17, then it's too late for some people, but I had definitely improved in America. It gave me a sense of perspective. I had grown up, I was an adult and I knew what I wanted to do. I appreciated it more when I came back. You get an idea of how fortunate you are to be in the position I found myself in. I don't want to be holier than thou, but you really do. I used to come back every summer or at Christmas and have to find part-time jobs. Besides that one in the distribution warehouse, I tried various others including being a postman – which I enjoyed a lot. All of this gave me a grounding in the world outside football before I entered the game properly and perhaps that has served me well over the years. Some players who come through the traditional system, particularly at leading clubs, never get that sort of experience of life and then it hits them suddenly when they are released or, if they are successful, when their careers are over. It's not that they take it for granted, they just don't know anything else. It is hard for them to get perspective.

I started in the reserves and I was delighted with that. The lists would be put up on a Friday, the reserves and the first team. If the first team were playing Aberdeen at home, the reserves would play Aberdeen away. It was brilliant. That was me, living the dream. I had never been to Aberdeen in my life, so going to places like that was a big adventure for me. It was the old Premier Reserve League, a good standard, and a league where you had to win your games. I loved it, although it didn't last for long because after six reserve games I got my chance in the first team against Dundee United on 24 October 1992.

The list went up on the Friday as usual but I was on the first-team one rather than the reserves. Even when I saw my name in the squad list, I just thought, 'I'll not be playing.' I found out I was at half past one – you just turned up and Billy or the gaffer would read the team out. I wouldn't have been expecting to play, I guarantee you that, and I wasn't aware of who I was playing directly against really. Although I later got to know Duncan Ferguson very well.

In that game, Klaus Augenthaler was there with a view to signing him for Bayern Munich. I will never forget that. So that was the sort of level he was playing at at the time, but at that age, when you are 21 or 22, you aren't particularly interested in that. You are caught up in yourself, in making sure you are right. I wouldn't have seen it as a test particularly. If he had given me a going over, fair enough, but I wouldn't have let it affect me. I would have learned from it, but it wouldn't have knocked me back. As it turned out, I was praised for how I handled Duncan.

My dad was there. He used to come to all my games. He loved it.

He used to love going through to Tynecastle and Ibrox and all these places because he went to them when he was young and now he was going to watch his son play there. He would go and watch football all the time. He was a Rangers supporter but I think he had an affinity for Hearts as well, as his dad had taken him there in the Dave Mackay era. I didn't know it then, but I would go on to play for both the clubs he had followed.

The Falkirk team I broke into was packed full of contrasting and lively personalities. Ian McCall, John Hughes, Eddie May, Brian Rice, Tony Parks, Richard Cadette, Neil Duffy, Tommy McQueen, Neil Oliver, Stevie Fulton, then there were the younger boys like myself, Gary Lennox, Scott MacKenzie, Jamie McGowan, Nicky Henderson and Billy Lamont, the reserve goalie, who was my pal. It was a great dressing-room, full of characters, but I was coming from university where it was exactly the same. I was living with three guys in a house in America, so this was just like living in a bigger house. I loved it. I was still at home for the first wee bit, but quickly got a flat and I was living the life, quite often at Rosie O'Grady's, a nightclub in Falkirk that was then run by Paul Hughes, a mate of mine. The manager knew our movements, of course, and phoned me one morning and said, 'You better get yourself in here for 10am, or you are fined.' This was at 9.35, so I had to get up and get there for 10, which I just about managed due to living so close to the ground then. He was winding me up, but I had slept in, which is something I don't often do, so obviously I had enjoyed the night before.

Our games were rarely dull. I had only been in a couple of weeks when we beat Airdrie 5-1 at Brockville to the delight of our fans. A fortnight later, we lost 3-2 at Celtic after being 2-0 up in a snow-storm. On Boxing Day, we drew 3-3 at home to Hibs and before that we had lost 3-1 controversially at Motherwell when Tony Parks, the former Spurs keeper, who had come into the side at the same time as me, was sent off. Tony was a great character, who loved a bit of banter with the fans behind his goal. It was through him I first met Fiona. Fiona was hairdresser to Tony's wife Simone. 'You should meet David Weir, he's a really nice guy, you would like him,' said Simone. 'I'm not interested in footballers, my friend is going out with one of them, one of the goalkeepers,' replied Fiona. 'My husband is the goalkeeper,' said Simone. Fiona said it must be the other one (Billy Lamont) and she said, 'He's married as well, it can't be him.' What's the chance of that happening? It was Parksy who was seeing the girl, of course, and Fiona was now backtracking rapidly.

Simone introduced me to Fiona all the same, and they still speak, but Parksy was just a Jack the Lad, probably the one with the highest profile as a player. He'd played in the 1984 Uefa Cup final for Spurs, which they won on penalties, so I was looking at him, thinking, 'I have watched this guy on the telly.' That was a big thing for me at the time, because I was coming from nowhere and suddenly sitting next to these lads. Tony was crazy but a nice guy basically. He's now working for Tottenham Hotspur as goalkeeping coach and he had good opinions and good ideas. He always believed in what he said but every so often he would just go off the rails and do something completely daft. Then he would come in and he would be the same again. It was just a moment of madness every so often.

Yet Tony wasn't the only nutter at the club, far from it. I loved John Hughes, or Yogi, as he is known to everybody, in particular. He was an inspiration to me as a young guy starting out. He is still the best captain I have played under. He has a genuine will to win, to do well. He's got pride in his team and he would look after his teammates. People like Yogi made Falkirk a great place to be at that time. It almost became normal at the time but looking back now, Yogi was constantly taking his clothes off. He would be in the gym doing bench presses with no clothes on. That was his hobby.

He famously walked past starkers when Martin Geissler, now with ITN, was interviewing Mo Johnston once and another time he challenged George Miller, the commercial manager, to a race around a deserted Brockville as it was getting dark. All the wives and girlfriends were watching from the directors' box as Yogi started stripping off as he ran, and then, literally, streaked past George as he turned to see what all the commotion was. Yogi was the leader of the pack, daft, would do anything for the team. I think that's what I liked about him. He had seen the other side of life, had had quite a hard upbringing, and you could tell it meant something to him and he wasn't going to throw his chance away. He inspired you. He was one of these people who made you think, 'He's on my side and will look after me.' He definitely created a good atmosphere within the team. Tony was in a clique with Jamie McGowan. Yogi and Eddie May were best friends back then, but I think they are best of enemies now. After Eddie succeeded John as manager at Falkirk in the summer of 2009, he made a few critical comments about John's approach but struggled to match him as a manager and was sacked the following February.

Brian Rice, or Chipper, was everybody's pal and really funny with his one-liners. He always used to say to me before every game, 'Remember, Horse, we're in blue.' It made me laugh and relax. Horse was an abbreviation of 'Dark Horse', my nickname, because I was always coming in quite quiet and smart and they thought I was really the man about town. It was Scott MacKenzie who gave me it. In pre-season, you would come in and Brian would be sitting there saying, 'Three hundred days to Magaluf.' He would genuinely know the figure and count it down every day. If you were sitting in a dressing-room after a bad result, you would say, 'How many days, Chipper?' and he would say, 'Two hundred and forty-six' as quick as a flash. He was a good player, a great passer with great technique. Not really athletic in any way, shape or form, but give him the ball and he could put it anywhere. He would always be on at us constantly: 'Keep it, keep it.' He was a great storyteller, particularly about his time playing for Nottingham Forest under Brian Clough. He was very close to him because a lot of the time Chipper would be the odd man out when the team was picked and Clough would take him under his wing. He used to go and get Clough's drinks for him and stuff like that, but I think he learned a lot from him.

Tommy McQueen was very sensible, a good player, who had played at Aberdeen then West Ham. He had excellent technique, too. I always remember him saying things to me like 'When you get your new contract, make sure you get an inflation-based raise every year'. He lived like he played to an extent, very particular and careful about what he did. He was just an all-round good player, who had played at a high level down in England and that, for me, was impressive. I think, even then, I knew that's what I wanted to do, perhaps because I had already travelled. Although I was also desperate to play for Rangers. When I later heard Rangers were interested in me, I had tunnel vision about going there.

Neil Oliver was another great guy to play with, a lad who would get you out of trouble if you made a mistake. He always bore the brunt of Yogi's antics and you always felt with the gaffer and Billy if something went wrong it was Olly's fault too. I think they brought him from Berwick with them, so he was the one who would get the blame. It was like Laurel and Hardy. He was the one that would be sitting here, scratching his head, saying, 'Not me again.' He was a funny lad with a dry sense of humour but really tight with money. He played on that and he and Yogi were good friends as well. Neil Duffy was another of the unsung heroes in the team. A quiet guy who would put his body on the line for the team. He played everywhere, right-back, left-back, centre-back, midfield, and scored a lot of goals, a lot of headers where he would take a chance to get into the box and put his head in bravely. There was also the late Forbes Johnston, another quiet lad, who had trained to be a lawyer. He was one of my peers and was in the Scotland under-21 squad. At the end of my first season for Falkirk, we both went off to play for the British Students team in Buffalo, Canada. It was a great trip.

That jaunt helped me get over our relegation, which had hit me hard. As it was my first season, I felt responsible somehow and wondered whether I had blown my chance of making it as a professional because the club made it clear there would have to be cutbacks in consequence. Things had looked bright at the start of February, when we knocked Celtic out of the Scottish Cup, increasing the pressure on Liam Brady, who was then their manager and hastening Fergus McCann's takeover. I was named man of the match and Ibrox welcomed us warmly when we went there in our next Premier League match. The cheers were still ringing out at the end, too, but because Rangers had thrashed us 5-0. At that point they were approaching their peak in Walter's first period in charge and almost made it to the final of the inaugural Champions League after eliminating Leeds United.

That was the start of a slide for us. We lost 3-1 at Tynecastle the following week and then 3-1 at Motherwell when I scored an own goal. There was a boardroom battle going on in the background for control of the club but that was no excuse. Celtic exacted revenge for the Cup defeat by coming to Brockville and winning 3-0 and we went out of the Scottish Cup in the quarter-final the following week, after another defeat at Hearts. We gave ourselves a lifeline at the start of May by thumping Hearts 6-0 at home. I scored, with a header, and it was a day on which Chris Robinson, who ran Hearts at the time, made a mental note of Jim as their potential future manager. Yet a 2-1 defeat at Motherwell the following week to a Dougie Arnott goal nine minutes from the end confirmed we were going down. We had plenty of admirers for our attacking approach, but that wasn't much of a consolation as we faced up to life in the First Division and those budget cuts.

Jim's tactic was, if in doubt, get another forward on, that was always his way. He was never defensive. He always wanted you to attack, but he was also very, very critical of his defenders as well. Very demanding of them. Besides the gaffer and Billy Brown, we were coached by John Blackley, the former Scotland defender, a nice man but another hard one, from the old school. He would soon be telling you if you made a mistake. That was our style, to try and score more than the opposition basically. That was the motto, but you were exposed a bit as a result. It was a hard grounding for me, purely because of the level I was coming from to the level I was now at. I really enjoyed it but it was a real learning curve and we were losing the majority of games, so it was difficult. When you are losing more games than you are winning it is brutal, you get down on yourself, you start questioning yourself. At the time, I thought that relegation was partly my responsibility, no doubt about it. My contract didn't even enter my head. I would have signed anything the club put in front of me to stay on and try and help them back into the Premier League. I wanted to put it right.

Things might have been worse if we had not sold Kevin McAllister to Hibs for £235,000 before the new season started. He was an extremely popular player with the fans and they protested against Hamish and George Deans, who controlled the club at the time. I could understand their feelings. I had watched Kevin from the terraces at Brockville before he went away to Chelsea and he was amazing. He was still a fans' favourite when he returned, but perhaps he typified the 'them and us' split between the attacking and defensive parts of the team. He would always be one of the ones pointing back at us when we lost a goal. Sometimes with good reason, sometimes not. For our part, we knew Kevin had all the skill in the world and could go on a dribble and beat four people, but if he lost the ball or we didn't score then we were vulnerable on the break and would have the finger pointed in our direction as defenders. It was a constant debate on the pitch and in our dressing-room.

Despite losing Kevin, we started the season well. A 3-2 win over Dunfermline, who our fans detested, went down well and proved the first shot in a battle between us and them for the title, which would go to the final day of the season. We won 5-1 at Morton next, with Tony Parks being called 'Stavros', due to his resemblance to Harry Enfield's famous Greek character, by their fans. We knocked Hearts out of the League Cup thanks to a late winner from Eddie May and were then eliminated on penalties in the quarter-final on penalties at Tannadice after a 3-3 draw. All our goals in that match were scored by Richard Cadette, a very talented striker Jim had signed. With his back to goal, Richard was one of the best players I have seen. He wouldn't move at times, he was lazy, but if you gave him the ball, he held on to it. It stuck all the time. He had good touch and movement that could lose defenders. Richard scored another hat-trick as we beat Dunfermline 4-1 in the quarter-final of the B&Q Cup, a competition for clubs outside the Premier League, that we would go on to win by beating St Mirren in the final. Richard's goals and ability didn't always go down well with the opposition fans, who shamefully subjected him to racist abuse, a scourge which I am glad to say has largely been eradicated from the game during the course of my career.

We beat Dunfermline at Brockville again in January to keep our promotion momentum going, but the manager was furious when we followed it at the end of the month with a Scottish Cup exit at Stranraer. Jim was a manager who didn't hesitate to give his team a kickstart via the transfer market in the days before transfer windows and we all knew from his anger and comments, both private and public, that changes were on their way. Sure enough, Dragutin Ristic and Jamie McGowan soon arrived while others left. Our form had probably picked up before they arrived, although they both made good contributions in the run-in. Jim was a master of chasing away any complacency by making changes.

Our next meeting with Dunfermline came on 26 March at East End Park, where we came from a goal down to draw 1-1, a key result in our season as it turned out. The crowd was over 13,000, the largest of the season in the First Division, and underlined what was at stake. We had now lost just once in 22 League games, and although a couple of draws at Airdrie and Clyde checked our momentum slightly, we were still on course. The penultimate

Saturday of the season was a sweet one for us. We beat Hamilton at home, while Dunfermline were losing at Airdrie. George Fulston, Hamilton's chairman, announced straight after losing to us that he was going to take over at Falkirk, ending a troubled period in the boardroom, or so we hoped.

It was on-field matters which had most of our attention, though. All we required on the final day at Clydebank was a draw to secure our return to the Premier League. We took the lead through Nicky Henderson after six minutes and, although John Henry pulled one back, it was a match we were never going to lose. It was a great feeling sitting in the dressing-room afterwards, being praised by the manager for the part I had played in getting us back to the Premier League and being told by him that if a transfer to Liverpool or Rangers, both of whom were said to be interested in me, came about, then I would go with his blessing.

When we returned to the Premier League, we showed we had learned the lessons of our relegation. We were still good to watch but less likely to lose games now. We started the season strongly and the characters just kept coming. Jim liked rescuing damaged goods and getting them for a bargain. Taking all the waifs and strays and turning them into a team. Like Brian Rice, Steve Fulton was a proper passer of the ball and became a good friend of mine. He was famously described as the 'new Roberto Baggio' as a young-ster at Celtic and it sort of hung over him afterwards. Other players would have recovered from that, but it probably weighed heavier on Steve because of his nature. Contrary to popular belief, he was mobile, one of the quickest players in the team, even when we were together later at Hearts, in a sprint. People assumed he wasn't because he was heavier but he definitely was. Anybody who played with or against him would tell you that.

I got on well with most of them most of the time but not always. Ian McCall was the man about town. Callie thought he was a student. He got the train through to Falkirk because he didn't drive and would be late or wouldn't turn up at all now and again. He was a talented footballer, but I always got the feeling he could have done more and we fell out over it. One day in the programme, when asked about my dislikes, I said something about not making the most of your attributes or not having any regrets. I always remember Callie having a go at me for that. I don't know if it rang a bell with him, although it wasn't specifically directed at him. He made it into a big issue.

Joe McLaughlin was another guy in the team. He'd had a good career at Chelsea and was quite straight. He was the one that would let you know he had been captain of Chelsea, but in a funny way. You had to be funny and have a wee edge to you in that dressing-room, you wouldn't have lasted otherwise. Those were the lessons I was learning. You had to stand up for yourself. That was all part of the grounding for me. These players had been around at big clubs, so it was like a minefield and I was learning all the time. I probably wouldn't have dealt with that when I was younger but I was more confident when I came back from the States. I had matured. I'd lived away from home for four years in another country and found I could handle myself in that environment. I needed this in the early days at Falkirk. Dressing-rooms can be fierce places, especially when results are going against you. You would lose a goal and they would be pointing the finger at you. It was probably the cruellest dressing-room I have been in to be honest, maybe because it was the least successful.

Later in my career, Walter Smith and David Moyes could go off the rails of course, but with Jimmy and Billy it was every second week they would be losing the plot at somebody. I don't know if that was due to our results being up and down or whether that was them as people, but it just seemed someone would be constantly getting an in-your-face hairdryer. That's what it was like. When they weren't happy with our performances, new signings would suddenly turn up the next day,. They would arrive on the morning of the game and would be playing in the afternoon or that night. They would leave in the same way, with a wee tap on the shoulder. The manager would always be walking about at training on his huge mobile phone, wheeling and dealing, that was his image, as though he had just walked off the set of *Wall Street*.

Yet we started 1994–95 strongly, unbeaten in our first six matches, a run which included Falkirk's first win at Ibrox in 67 years in a memorable League Cup tie. Richard Cadette was superb that night and scored both our goals in a 2-1 win. We were in a yellow strip and on £1000 each to win the game, which is a lot of money now, but at the time, being four or five times my weekly wage, felt like a lottery win. I was pleased with my own performance against a front three of Mark Hateley, Brian Laudrup and Gordon Durie. Particularly Durie, as he was a player who often gave me real problems, something underlined when I was sent off for pulling him back a few weeks later in a League game. I later got to know Gordon in the Scotland squad and still see him around Ibrox. If he thinks I am giving him a funny look sometimes, it is probably because I am still suffering from flashbacks.

Despite the bonuses, there must have been some money left over because the manager was soon out signing some more colourful types for a dressing-room hardly short of such figures. Frank

McAvennie arrived on a short-term deal while John Clark came in for £100,000. With McAvennie, my recollection was of him sitting in the dressing-room naked, laughing with his big teeth on display. He was a very good footballer but obviously past his best when he came to us. He still had a go, but wasn't as fit as he had been. He was another big character in the dressing-room and it was great for me to mix with people like that at that stage in my career. John Clark was a big lad, who still managed to be larger than life, a good footballer who could have achieved more if he had got a grip of himself. Keeping himself in the nick he should have done wasn't John's strong point, but he could score with powerfully accurate free kicks and play centre-half, midfield or up front. He could play anywhere. In that dressing-room, Frank and John fitted in right from the start.

One of John's searing free kicks helped us to a win over Celtic at Hampden, this being the season they used the national stadium for League games while renovating Parkhead. Then we came from a goal down to grab a point at Ibrox. It was just the nature of that team that we felt we could beat anyone. Even against Celtic and Rangers you always felt you had a chance. On their day, they were all very good players.

Off the pitch, we were a handful, too, as a hotel in Marbella discovered when we went there for a mid-season break during a spell of cold weather before Christmas. 'Boozy Bairns Trash Hotel' ran the headline after we ran amok, to the chagrin of our manager and the chairman. Jim liked taking us away. There was always the trip to Magaluf at the end of the season. He encouraged that, but this one ended up as a shambles. We got there and I think we were drinking straight away. He always used to say, 'Do what you want, have a good time but don't disrupt the hotel or cause any damage', but we abused his trust in us and the next morning we were called into a meeting where George Fulston read the riot act, banging the table and, I always remember, shouting, 'We bring you to paradise and this is how you treat us.' I think a couple of the lads got sent home and others came back missing eyebrows etc. I remember the cameras being there waiting to welcome us back – it was big news. Looking back now it was just a recipe for disaster, taking players away and telling them they could have a free rein. It was just a matter of time before it kicked off.

Maybe our next trip was a punishment: a February friendly away to Ipswich as both sides had been knocked out of their respective cups. We drove down there on the day, which was a long, long drive, five or six hours, played the game, stayed overnight, had a night out again in Ipswich and then came back up the next day. It was sold to me as a chance for them to have a look at me as they were interested in signing me. I remember it being a good game and George Burley was their manager. George had trained with Falkirk briefly the previous season and played one game while I was out with a hamstring tear.

The spring brought some more firepower, with Jim losing patience at a lack of goals. First Paul McGrillen and Steve Kirk arrived from Motherwell in an exchange deal which saw Eddie May move in the other direction. It worked. They gave us a bit of impetus. Stevie Kirk was good for a goal a game at the time. He just seemed to pop up at all the right times and get on the end of things. Paul McGrillen was a cheeky wee guy, always getting himself into fights he couldn't win.

Like Forbes Johnston, Paul later committed suicide after his career ended. You would have thought Forbes was as well-equipped as anybody to cope with life after football as he was a qualified lawyer. Yet he obviously enjoyed the football more because that's what he chose to do. Football was his priority and he was in the under-21s and had great hopes. He was a really nice guy and I used to go through to Edinburgh with him and his girlfriend at the time, who was lovely as well. He was clever, a wee bit different, but he fitted in. Just another character in that dressing-room. His subsequent death and Paul's make me wonder if footballers are given enough support once their playing careers end and they head off alone into the real world.

Jim's next signing for Falkirk topped the lot. Mo Johnston was like a breath of fresh air. He was probably the highest-profile player we'd had. Maurice was at Hearts at the time and still in the news, as he always was. He was fantastic, he just fitted straight in. He had no airs or graces, no superiority complex. He just got his hands dirty and got stuck in. He was really well liked. We used to come in and train and then go home. He said, 'Have we not got any food or anything here, we'll sort out some food. We'll just get a big pot, boil some pasta and some sauce.' A couple of the girls who worked there would cook us a big bowl of pasta. We'd get some sauce and go into the boardroom and just sit and eat on a Friday, just for chat and to get some decent food.

Maurice started up front and did all right but then ended up going back into midfield, giving 100 per cent and being one of the team. He was also really good socially. I remember him saying, 'I am going into Glasgow tonight, do you want to come?' I didn't have any ties at the time and was up for it. He got this limousine to come and pick us up. Maurice had to be careful when he was in Glasgow, obviously, having played for both of the Old Firm, but I think he had a share in a pub or something so we went through there. It was an experience for me, getting my eyes opened in a good way. I had probably never tasted champagne before. He lived through in Edinburgh and would invite you there for something to eat, too. He didn't have any delusions of grandeur.

Helped by these new arrivals, we pulled out of our mid-season dip to finish fifth. We felt like we were an established Premier League club, on our way to more success. Little did we know what awaited when we came back from our summer break. Jim was pursued by Hearts, who he had supported as a boy and then played for. They had sacked Tommy McLean and wanted him as their new manager. It was only going to end one way, although our hopes rose when Fulston said he would give Jim a seven-year contract to stay and Jim told the press he would. That was on the Saturday morning but by the Monday afternoon he was gone, he simply couldn't resist Hearts. Around the same time, we lost Yogi to Celtic and it felt like things were falling apart.

Jim and Billy had built the club up. Nobody blamed them for going because everybody knew Hearts was Jim's club and it was an opportunity after what he had done for Falkirk, but I think everybody realised it was the end of what had been a fantastic era, probably the best one in a lot of the lads' careers. I think Falkirk fans still regard it fondly and I know Jim goes back and still gets a good reception. I bet there are not many can say that. They were halcyon days for the club. He brought the characters I have mentioned plus people before me, like Simon Stainrod, who were big favourites, too.

Yogi's departure was a big blow for me personally and for the club. You are losing your manager and then your captain and the writing is on the wall. The next appointment was so important in regard to where the club was going to go in future. Was the chairman going to take the next step and have a right go or was he going to stand still? I think the appointment of John Lambie suggested the latter. It felt like the chairman had brought in his pal rather than the best candidate. He'd come from Hamilton and Lambie from Partick and we always thought Falkirk were a bigger club than those sides. It was probably seen by the fans as a big step backwards when that was his chance to get them onside.

Between Jim's departure and Lambie's arrival I was involved in a car crash before our pre-season friendly against Portsmouth. I was injured at the time and had gone to the gym with Andy Seaton, one of the young lads. I had a cast on my foot so I couldn't drive. The streets around Brockville were kind of like an American grid system, so you would drive and there would be cars coming over crossroads and Andy seemed to think it was funny to speed up and drive straight through. A car coming the other way hit us and we rolled over. I remember lying upside down in the car thinking, 'What the hell has he done?' It was just him being stupid. He had probably done it and got away with it before, but I was in the car with him the time it goes wrong. I remember getting the seat belt off and getting out the car. We were both all right, but the lad that had crashed into us was a Falkirk supporter who was going to a wedding. He couldn't believe he had hit Falkirk players. I don't think I would have been as good about it as he was. We were very lucky – it could have been a disaster.

Our form was and we didn't get our first point until our fourth League match. It seemed all my friends at the club were on their way out. Billy Lamont was released and then later called back when we had a goalkeeping emergency. Brian Rice knew his time was up as soon as Lambie got the job – he told me as much.

I like to think I give everybody a chance, but it just seemed to me Lambie had no enthusiasm for the game. He never really loved the game. It was you are all on your last warning, it was all about fear and intimidation. Don't get me wrong, there had been elements of that in Jefferies' approach, too, but at least there was a feelgood factor about it as well. With Lambie, it just seemed everything was doom and gloom, everything was negative. He was bringing in players who weren't necessarily improving us and his whole demeanour was wrong. Gerry Collins, his assistant, tried to be funny and was all right, but there was no rhyme or reason to the training. I remember going to training and being told, 'Go and warm up and I'll think about what we are going to do.' I remember that quote as clear as day. It just wouldn't have happened previously. Billy would have had everything marked out. You would know exactly what you were doing and you would feel like you were a professional. It felt like you were going back in time and that it was making it harder for you to succeed.

It was like the break-up of a team. Gradually, it just drifted further and further away from what it had been like. When Steve Fulton left for Hearts I wished it was me. There wasn't any empathy with Lambie from the supporters either, right from the start, and it quickly became obvious we would be fighting a relegation battle rather than chasing a European place as we had the previous season. When we lost 4-0 at Kilmarnock in December, the travelling support chanted for him to leave. I was from Falkirk, so I knew the local feeling. He brought in Albert Craig, who was a good enough player, but the feeling around the club was that he was a pal of the manager and Gerry. Andy Gray also arrived and was a good player, a London boy, a bit of a wide boy but not a bad one. He fitted in, worked hard and was good for the club. He was more like a Jefferies signing but Albert Craig was very much a lambie one.

At the end of January, we lost at home to Stenhousemuir in the Scottish Cup third round. It was a disaster. The fans stayed behind to demonstrate and Lambie needed a police escort out of Brockville. We came in for training the next day and were told we were going to Peebles Hydro. It was quite a long drive and my recollection is we had a few beers before we had a meeting, which quickly degenerated into a farce. It became us against them. I remember saying my piece, which was unlike me, but by that stage I'd had enough and knew it was only going to end one way. It was just a piss-up down there to get away from it. I don't think anything was achieved or put right.

We signed Tony Finnigan and Dominic Iorfa but it didn't seem there was any method in the way the team was going. It just felt like they brought players in, hoping they would do something, but nothing seemed to be working. Next there was a story that a Falkirk fan tried to run Lambie off the road when he was with his wife in the car. It was obvious he wasn't enjoying it either. You could tell he was having a few drinks from the state he was in some mornings and that he wasn't handling the pressure very well. It seemed the job was too big for him, in terms of keeping a lid on things. It wasn't working for either party. In March, after we lost at home to Partick, he resigned. Collins took over from Lambie but nothing really changed and you just got the feeling it wasn't going to last a long time. Falkirk appointed Eamonn Bannon as the new manager before the following season started, but I never played for him.

We were officially relegated after a 4-0 defeat at Celtic and Collins came out afterwards and said we had been laughing and joking about it in the dressing-room. I think that was him trying to get his retaliation in first, saying, 'It's not my fault' to people on the outside looking in. We finished the season playing to small crowds and bottom by six points. It was not how I wanted my Falkirk career to end, not after so many good memories, but the truth is I was now desperate to leave and had been from the middle of that season. It was probably the season I have enjoyed least in my football career. It was a really frustrating time, after all the highs we'd had. I started to question where my career was going. I needed a change, a new challenge, and my former Falkirk manager was about to provide it.

3

Hearts surgery

THERE were three clubs interested in ending my nightmare at Falkirk. Aberdeen never followed through on their initial interest, so on the same day in the summer of 1996 I met the other two with Bill McMurdo, my agent at the time. It was an Edinburgh derby, Hearts versus Hibs, and as it would often turn out when I played for them in these games, Hearts emerged victorious.

I met Hibs first and I went with an open mind. Alex Miller, their manager, told me he wanted me to play wide right in a five-man defence. He said that was my best position and then went round the houses telling me what I wasn't good at, informing me I wasn't a particularly great player basically, but also telling me how he would improve me. These days when a player goes to meet a manager, they are told how wonderful they are. I came out thinking the opposite, but that was just Alex being honest with me. He was a good coach and when I later got to know him better in the Scotland set-up I liked him. He was a good football man and certainly knew his stuff. He told me I would be getting £650-a-week in my first year, then £750, then £850.

Then I went to Hearts and spoke to Jim. I knew what he was like, so it wasn't a difficult meeting and I got a good feeling from it. He told me what I guess I wanted to hear: 'You'll love it here, we'll get you back playing and enjoying your football.' His contract was £750-a-week, then £850, then £950, but even though those terms were slightly superior to Hibs' that wasn't part of my decision. I wasn't listening really by that stage and I never negotiated. I never even thought about that. Lads now will know what they want before they go in but I hadn't a clue what a Hearts or Hibs player would earn then and what I should be looking for. I was earning maybe £500 a week at Falkirk at the time, but money genuinely wasn't a factor for me. I just wanted to get back to enjoying my football and feeling that my career was going somewhere again.

Jim and Hearts quickly made good on their promise to me. The first thing I noticed was I came back to an enjoyable atmosphere at a football club. That was my abiding memory, that it all felt fresh again. I had become stale, I had been at Falkirk too long and I wasn't enjoying it any more. I felt like my decision had been vindicated straight away. Although there wasn't a training ground or a base as such, Tynecastle had a bit of history about it. Falkirk had history as well, but you were now in a big city and it felt like it meant more to more people. Hearts fans are very passionate about their club and people on the outside don't appreciate how important it is to them. Often, it is only when you go to a club you find that out. It felt like a step up. Rightly or wrongly, it felt like I had gone to a bigger club.

It also felt like something was happening at Hearts. Jefferies had an affinity for the club and you felt he was going to be there for a while building something. This was his club and it wasn't just a stepping stone for him, he was trying to put something in place. He was always outraged when we got beaten at Falkirk or Hearts – I don't think that ever changed – but you could just tell it was his club, that he was comfortable in that environment and it was where he wanted to be long term. Not that you didn't feel that at Falkirk under him, but everybody has got their own club, haven't they?

Training was very much the same as Falkirk, which was comforting for me. I knew what I was going back to. I knew I would be going into training and enjoying it every day. That makes such a difference, going into your work and enjoying it. It was always competitive as well, there was always an edge to it. It always involved a game of some sort. It would be old versus young or east coast versus west coast. When I went through, I was always on the young team, and in east versus west I would be the one who would make the numbers up if they were short so I kind of floated. Historically, the old team had always beaten the young team at Hearts but we were beating the old boys – guys like John Robertson, Dave McPherson, Neil Pointon, Gary Mackay and Gilles Rousset. At Falkirk, it had always been Hearts versus Hibs in these games, and because Yogi is a Hibs man he was always desperate for Hearts to get beaten in them. Jim was the opposite obviously, so there was always a real edge.

Just as he had at Falkirk, Billy took almost all the training. Jim would come in on the Friday and do his shooting drills and so on but the rest of time he would be there watching everything with his phone glued to his ear. From what I hear from Gary Locke, Billy and Jim still work much the same way and are making progress again at Hearts with their approach. Billy is the tracksuit guy, on the training pitch and in the dressing-room, getting into people all the time. He probably knew the players better and had a wee affinity with them. He's very human, Billy, very down to earth and on the shop-floor. He would nail you in a minute if you stepped out of line, but you always got the feeling he was an ex-player. Although he was that wee bit older, you felt he could still see your point of view. Billy could feed the gaffer ideas as well – you often got the impression Billy had a big influence on the gaffer but the gaffer didn't realise it. They have known each other since secondary school and are still hilarious on the touchline together. Cursing and gesturing in disgust to each other and so on. They'll never change.

Hearts as a club had this thing about fitness. They had Bert Logan, the sprint coach, and other people like George McNeill affiliated with them. Up in the wee gym among the nooks and crannies of the main stand, there were competitions on the speed ball plus things like pull-ups and dips which I had never done and was never any good at. A lot of the young boys were fit and strong beyond their years. Craig Levein was injured at the time but he was the king of all that. He was the champion at the speed ball. There were echoes of Jock Wallace's Rangers about it, a real pride in being fitter and stronger than other sides. Walter Kidd was a big part of this ethos. Alex MacDonald and Sandy Jardine, who both played for Wallace at Rangers, were probably the instigators of it at Hearts in their impressive period in charge in the 1980s. Craig had obviously played under them and I would imagine had followed it through. You would be up there in the afternoons and even all the young boys would just be like beasts at it, like boxers a lot of them, with big shoulders and chests and all the rest of it.

There were four distinct groups in the dressing-room. There was an old group of Hearts players Jefferies had inherited, then there was a young group with real potential and then he brought in a few from abroad and a few younger lads on the way up from other Scottish clubs. Not what he had done at Falkirk, where they had been up and were on their way back down and he was trying to drag them up again. He had gone for lads who were on their way up, maybe because his budget let him do that now. He could actually spend money on players, whereas he probably hadn't had the opportunity before. When I went to Hearts, Brian Hamilton and Craig Nelson went the other way. I don't think Neil Berry was included in my deal but he went to Falkirk for free straight after it, so Jim was clearing the place out. He was always ruthless in that respect. You could tell there was something happening and he had his ideas of how he was going to do it. It was a really quick turnover.

Despite there being these distinct groups they all mingled well, there wasn't a 'them and us' culture at the club. Jim just made you mix, you didn't have a choice. There were no superstars, he hated that. He probably thought that a lot of the lads there prior to his arrival were on bigger money than he had been used to paying lads and Hearts weren't getting performances out of them. I am only guessing, but that would be my feeling. He would be trying to get some new blood in, hungry guys on less money, who were going to produce for him. You had to perform. Neither Jim nor Billy would suffer people who weren't putting it in.

We would have nights out regularly. Robbo and Neil Pointon would organise our trips away. I am sure we said we were going to watch Liverpool against Celtic in the Uefa Cup in 1997. We stayed in Southport and never even watched the game on the telly. It was just an excuse for all the married lads to tell their wives. I was at the age where it was easy for me to go out and some of the younger lads at Hearts would go through to Falkirk regularly with me. Guys like Gary Naysmith, Paul Ritchie, Allan McManus, Gary Locke would come through and have a great time with us.

Gary Locke was a big part of the spirit we had. He was suffering injury-wise but was still such a good influence in the dressing-room. He knitted all the young lads together and made the new lads feel welcome. He would always be organising some event to bring us all together. It created an empathy and team spirit that served us well. I took to Gary immediately and we remain good friends. We would go to the supporters' clubs everywhere, learning all the Hearts songs in the process, all over the east of Scotland and down in the borders as well. Every Saturday night, we would be going to a supporters' club somewhere. We would just play it by ear after games. A pal or two of mine would come through from Falkirk and Lockie would have his friends and we would just go for it.

Nowadays, players couldn't think of anything worse than going to a supporters' club on a Saturday night, but we absolutely loved it. We would go for a few drinks beforehand and then go along later. You were treated like a king. Phone cameras hadn't been invented, so things like a story getting out of you speaking to the wrong girl or having one too many wouldn't even enter your head. It wasn't an issue. The fans there were delighted to see you enjoy yourself. There was never a bad word said to you. They were all the same sort of places. Miners' Welfare clubs in places like Musselburgh, Wallyford, Loanhead. We'd go all the way down to Galashiels and they would put us up for the night. It would be great, it really would. Each supporters' club was dafter than the next about Hearts. It gave you a real sense of so many people caring so much about the club you played for. It gave you a perspective on that, made you feel like you were part of the club and also how much it meant to them. Lockie would know somebody in every supporters' club. He was a massive Hearts fan. His dad and his brothers still sit behind the dugouts at Tynecastle and he would be there with them every week if he didn't work for the club.

The foreign boys would just laugh at us when we told them our stories afterwards, although they were quite a laugh at times themselves. We played Red Star Belgrade early in my first season in a Cup Winners' Cup tie and Jim decided he wanted Pasquale Bruno, the experienced Italian centre-back he had signed from Torino, to man-mark Dejan Stankovic, Red Star's playmaker. Apparently, Pasquale just smiled and said, 'I understand, Jimmy, you want your best player to mark their best player.'

Pasquale took his instructions literally. I have never seen anything like it in my life. He actually marked the guy in the warm-up. This was the next big thing to come out of the former Yugoslavia and I saw Pasquale going up and speaking to him in the warm-up and jogging along next to him and stuff. He was quite an intimidating lad, if you didn't know him. If you knew him, you couldn't meet a less intimidating one. I really had my eyes opened. It was 10 against 10, he was marking this lad and he never left him from the warm-up to the end. For the whole game, he Velcroed himself to him.

He was very Italian off the pitch, too. He lived in the Caledonian Hotel, which for me, coming from Falkirk, was the grandest hotel in Edinburgh, and he used to eat across the road in Bar Roma. We would have lunch with him now and again and that was also the nicest restaurant in Edinburgh, I thought. It was like you go in there once and you have done really well, but he was in there having his lunch and dinner every day. He was a senior statesman – he'd had a great career in Serie A with clubs like Juventus and Torino and earned the nickname 'the Animal'. You could just tell from the way he carried himself, he had been there and done that, but you could have a laugh and joke with him. That was my overriding memory of him, that day against Red Star Belgrade when he just terrorised that young Serbian starlet.

Pasquale was sent off as we lost 3-0 at Ibrox in September, along with yours truly for yet another confrontation with Gordon Durie. Neil Pointon and Paul Ritchie followed shortly afterwards, leaving us to finish the game with seven players and face an SFA inquiry. Nevertheless, it was an early indication that we were ready to challenge the Old Firm's traditional dominance of Scottish football.

Gilles Rousset was another foreign father-figure to us. Nothing was a problem for him. He was very calm and nobody could dislike him. He was a very good goalkeeper as well but he'd had a bad game in the Scottish Cup final just before I arrived, where Hearts had lost 5-1 to Rangers. We started the new season well, though. Our League form was decent and we also went on a run to the League Cup final after a shaky start when we needed penalties to get past Stenhousemuir. We won at St Johnstone, beat Celtic in extra time at Tynecastle, then got a break when our semi-final against Dundee was played at Easter Road, which I felt gave us an advantage as an Edinburgh side. So it proved, as we won 3-1. Waiting for us in the final? Rangers of course.

Jim was delighted to get another bite at the cherry so quickly. The Scottish Cup final had been in May and now this was the League Cup final in November coming along. Hearts hadn't won a trophy since 1962 but you just got a feeling that something was happening, that there were opportunities there. The final itself was at Celtic Park because Hampden was being renovated and the game was in doubt right up to kick-off due to heavy snow. I can remember being in the dressing-room beforehand and we all thought the game was going to be off. Instead, it became something of a classic. A game people still talk about now.

Rangers quickly went 2-0 up, Ally McCoist scoring both of them in the first half-hour. McCoist's movement was such you would never actually see him during a game. He was always on your shoulder and you always knew he could score. He wasn't a fantastic footballer that would kill you with a brilliant touch or score from 30 yards, but was just so clever in the penalty box with his movement, knowing where he was and making sure he reached the second balls before defenders. A master of his art.

Yet Hearts didn't fold this time as they had previously in the Scottish Cup final, instead we came back like a steam train. Steve Fulton put us back in it with a goal just before half-time and then we equalised on the hour through John Robertson. We had come out believing we could get back into it. Neil McCann played brilliantly that day, yet was to be upstaged by Paul Gascoigne.

We later heard that there had been a fight between Gazza and McCoist at half-time and also that Gazza went and had a drink in a lounge near the tunnel before coming out again. The story was he walked in and had a brandy before coming back out to play. Whether it was the fight, the drink or our equaliser, something suddenly put Gazza into that extra gear that made him such a special footballer. For 10–15 minutes he was unplayable and scored two fine goals. He went into overdrive and nobody could get near him. There was absolutely nothing you could do about it. It was the same when England beat Scotland at Euro 96 the previous summer or a few weeks before that tournament when he scored an amazing hat-trick for Rangers against Aberdeen at Ibrox to clinch the title – it was like another gear he had that no one else did and there wasn't any rhyme or reason to when he found it. He just decided it was time.

Yet we were still well in the game and that was the nature of

Hearts at the time, the Jefferies philosophy from Falkirk had been successfully transplanted into the club. If they score one, we'll score another one. You never felt you were out of the game, even at 2-0 down or 4-2. I scored a late goal to make it 4-3 and although it proved only a consolation, at least Hearts had given a better account of themselves this time.

It was also revealing for me to get a close look at the Rangers team that would go on to win its ninth consecutive title that season. You could see a desire to win had been ingrained into the likes of Richard Gough and Ally McCoist, hence his dressing-room disagreement with Gazza. You learn that very quickly at Rangers – you've got to win. Looking back now, I can see they helped each other develop that. It became a self-fulfilling thing in the sense that it is passed down the line when you become a Rangers player. However good a player you are, if you have not got that, then you have not got a chance at Ibrox. Graeme Souness was probably the man who started it, I know the gaffer talks about how he learned so much from him in how he approached things and his mentality toward the game. At that time, Rangers were the team. You never got that impression with Celtic. You always felt you had a chance against Celtic, or I did. I always felt Rangers had a wee bit better calibre of player. I don't know if that was because I was a Rangers supporter and held them in higher esteem or whatever, but that was my genuine feeling. I always remember Goughie coming in after they won and being magnanimous. We were probably thinking, 'Oh piss off', he was probably the last person we wanted to see. Yet when we beat them later in the Scottish Cup final, he did exactly the same thing, and I remember saying to myself, 'Fair play to him.' It was a lesson in how to conduct yourself the same in defeat or victory and it increased my respect for him and for Rangers.

Although that Scottish Cup final victory was still 18 months away, we sensed we were getting closer to both Old Firm clubs as we progressed. The feeling we could beat them gradually grew among us. In my first season, the manager was still shaping it and getting things into place, getting it exactly the way he wanted it. That takes a bit of time but over the course of the season he started to get his players. We got to the League Cup final and then finished fourth in the League. We were still a bit hit and miss at this stage in terms of consistency. It was a sickener to lose the final, but we got a lot of credit for the way Hearts had played, Neil McCann in particular. It was if the team was still on the up. That was quite an important step that we had to take, a cup final where we acquitted ourselves well and had a go. The last Hearts team froze in the final because of circumstances so it was almost like a step forward, a progression. It was my first final, so it was almost as if you had to have a wee taste of the other side of it before you got the real thing. That was how I felt. We had run them close. We really had a good go at it and we now knew exactly what it would take to beat them next time.

Tynecastle was a great place to play. I have been really lucky in respect of stadiums in my career. Goodison and Ibrox are great as well. I couldn't have picked four better in fact because Brockville was like a cup tie for every game. They were all tight, proper football stadiums, not artificial or manufactured as some are these days. When I first played at Tynecastle, the school end was like the old Jungle at Celtic Park – a real football ground. A lot of times when you change a stadium, you lose that. Hearts never did. If anything the new stands added to it, they just enclosed the atmosphere. At Tynecastle with the floodlights on, you could almost feel like the players from 50 years ago were there with you. In the tight tunnel and dressing-rooms you could smell the aroma from the brewery nearby as soon as you arrived. It just had a particular ambience all of its own which I loved.

My dad did, too. He had gone through to Tynecastle as a boy to watch Dave Mackay, one of his heroes, so used to love seeing me there. He would get the train through from Falkirk, which he enjoyed. He wasn't great with driving – he was a bit prone to road rage, as I said. He would get the train then go and have a few pints. He would go with Fiona a lot of the time or my uncle Douglas. They would always end up sitting next to Paul Ritchie's dad and invariably end up fighting with him. I think they were similar fiery characters. That was my dad, he would get in a fight in an empty house. I used to tell myself I am not going to be like that when I am older but I definitely inherited some of his fiery nature. I just hide it well and try to be the nice guy. They always say look at the mother-in-law to see how your wife will turn out later in life, but if the same rule applies to men then I am surprised Fiona is now my wife given what she used to go through on Saturday afternoons.

'I don't know who is worse, your dad or his [Paul's] dad,' Fiona would say afterwards. She was in the middle of it and they'd both probably had a few beers. My dad just couldn't shut his mouth and they were most likely both passing comments on our play. Paul and I got on fine – we would probably laugh about it. That's a wee idea of how my dad was, and I knew he was like that. He would be a nervous wreck at games, kicking the people in front of him, hitting whoever was beside him and all the rest. Fiona probably needed a few drinks inside her, too, to sit and suffer it.

Drink also featured heavily in my first Christmas night out at Hearts. We always used to plan our Christmas nights out meticulously but invariably we would get beaten on the Saturday and the manager would cancel them. We'd still go, rightly or wrongly. We were supposed to be going to Newcastle but Jim informed us: 'You are not going, how can you go after a performance like that?' Oblivious to this, Craig Levein turned up, as agreed, in full fancy dress. He had come as Rod Hull and Emu and made quite an effort. We were saying, 'We are not allowed to go', and he was saying, 'Shaddup, we're going', because he was old school and they would always go anyway. We were all a wee bit intimidated by Jefferies, but the older players weren't. Craig said he would go and sort it out, maybe he let Emu stick his head round the manager's door to ask on our behalf. Although the knee injury which prematurely ended his career stopped him from playing, Craig was still the club captain and really good with me. He held the dressing-room's attention and had an aura about him. You could tell people took him seriously, apart from when he was walking about with Emu on his arm that is.

We ended up going on the Christmas night out, but we went into Edinburgh, to Rose Street, which thinking about it now was absolute madness on our part. We got a lock-in in a pub, one of Neil Pointon or Robbo's friends, I think. This would be about two weeks before Christmas. We were in the pub drinking and milling about outside of it as well. I remember, at one stage someone spotted Alan Rae, the physio, and we were all diving into the pub and pulling the curtains in case he saw us.

All the new boys had to sing a song on the Christmas night out – you had to get up in the middle of everyone, stand on a stool and sing. That kind of thing is my worst nightmare. I had been shitting myself for weeks about it, even practising my song by putting a CD on in the car on the way through to training and singing along to 'Wonderwall' by Oasis.

There were maybe four or five of us to sing and Craig Levein was holding court, the master of ceremonies, the Simon Cowell of this particular *X-Factor*. He would drink tequila with fresh orange right from the off, no messing about with pints or anything like that. I remember thinking, 'This guy must be mad, how can he drink like that?'

Craig was pulling the names out of a hat until eventually only Colin Cameron and I were left, the last two to go up to sing. It was horrible. Of course, Colin got picked before me. 'Right, what are you going to sing?' booms Craig. '"Wonderwall" by Oasis,' replied Colin. My face must have been a picture at this point. 'You are fucking joking, that's my song!' I was sitting there drinking my pint of lager, thinking what am I going to do? I had no back-up plan, it never entered my head that somebody would steal my song. It was my first Christmas night out. I remember getting up and singing a pub song that didn't make any sense. As I stepped down after this woeful effort, Craig just said, 'Fucking shit singer, but not a bad player.' He had a cutting comment about everybody's performance but was brilliant with me. He used to say, 'You can play by the way', which gave me a lot of confidence, as, to a certain degree, I was filling his shoes because he'd had such a lot of bad luck with injuries.

There was a picture of Craig in his Scotland strip on the wall at Tynecastle and he had the captain's armband on. I used to stare at it thinking, 'How good would that be, to play for and captain your country?' It inspired me. I definitely remember thinking, 'I want that to be me.' You go to Hearts and you see internationals, having the band on, whether it is for one game or two games or whatever, and you start to think, 'This is the kind of club where these things can happen to me.'

The subject came up when I was renegotiating my contract. It's not like now, where you meet with the chief executive. Back then you would go and negotiate directly with Billy and Jim. You can imagine what that was like. Billy would say at the end, 'Are you happy with your contract, son?' I'd say, 'Yeah, I am happy, but I would quite like something if I play for Scotland.' 'Play for Scotland, son, do you honestly think you'll play for Scotland?' snorted Billy, batting me down straight away. Making me feel like that was the least likely thing that was going to happen to me. That's typical Billy. He probably thought I could play for Scotland but the last person he would tell is me. He wanted to make sure I kept my feet firmly on the ground.

The nights out were part of the process of bonding together the team that would go on to lift the Scottish Cup. As he had shown at Falkirk, Jim had a knack for team building and you could feel one coming together at Tynecastle. Colin Cameron was what I would call a typical Jefferies player. Not a silky footballer but a hard-running one, who would throw himself in for anything to get a goal despite his size. He would work back and forward and would come off the pitch having given his lot. A really good team player. He would just keep coming and coming. He'd already had success with Raith Rovers, so Colin, probably more than most of us, had a wee inkling of what it was all about and was extremely influential.

All the new boys were hungry to succeed. Neil McCann was a hungry, hungry guy. Colin was hungry. I would like to think I was quite like that at the time. We all wanted to do well, maybe using Hearts as a stepping stone to move on, and the younger lads from the club's youth system were probably the same. Paul Ritchie, Gary Locke, Gary Naysmith, all these lads. We were all probably thinking to ourselves we are in a good place here. Steve Fulton was another big part of that team. The fulcrum of it. He was the one that could make passes, the Brian Rice of this team, and he had the respect of all the boys for his abilities. He was just as mad as he had been at Falkirk. People would wind him up and he would maybe take the bait now and again and stuff like that. He was that kind of player. The fans were always on at him. He was an easy target Stevie, but the boys loved him.

I give a lot of credit to the older guys, too, though. They could have resented us as their replacements and ruined the atmosphere at the club but instead they made us welcome. Although their places were threatened, the likes of Neil Pointon, John Colquhoun and John Robertson were friendly and good sounding boards for the team, acting as its elder statesmen. Neil was always helpful with advice and was good fun, too. You felt like he was part of the team, not separate from the younger, dafter boys. He'd had a proper career with Man City and Everton, so he got a bit of respect for that, and was a very good player, a very good athlete. Gary Naysmith was coming through and pushing him hard for his place, yet Neil never complained.

I always got the impression that Jim felt Robbo represented the old school, so there was a wee bit of friction there. Robbo was Mr Hearts and Jefferies was the new Mr Hearts if you like. Robbo would talk about football with anybody. He and Tracy, his ex-wife, were like Mr and Mrs Hearts. They were very accommodating and like the centre of the club. They had been there for a long time. Robbo was always liable to get a goal whether he was a sub or started. He never used to go and get warmed up before games – instead he'd be in a warm bath relaxing and reading the paper or the programme. Robbo was a good player, but you always felt he was trying to prove something to Jefferies. It was so apparent.

Gary Mackay was a proper old pro, a genuine Hearts supporter, dyed in the wool. He'd had a great career and took the club seriously and set good standards. He would say his piece to the younger boys and would always let his boot boy – I think it was Gary Naysmith – know he had to have his towels perfect and his boots clean. I really liked him but he was a bit more serious.

We would go for a drink with the older players to these posh bars where Dave McPherson, Robbo and Neil Pointon had obviously been going for years. Dave was from a different generation and had been at a higher level than a lot of us, winning trophies with Rangers, and probably took it a bit more seriously than we did, too.

Don't get me wrong, they had no airs and graces about them, they were out for a drink like the rest of us, but it was like we were mixing in different circles, like we were the upstarts going to these places in Morningside and those kinds of areas. Edinburgh is a great city for pubs. Montpellier's was one of their regular haunts – Monty's they used to call it – and we'd often go there after games for a drink. There was a really good atmosphere between the older boys and the younger boys, a coming together. I didn't feel there were any barriers between us.

The foreign boys were more up for a bit of lunch and a glass of wine. They did mix but weren't as wholehearted about it as the Scottish boys, as you can imagine. I think if results are going well that helps and the manager condoned the socialising to a certain extent. He didn't actively encourage it, but, at the right time, he and Billy loved the fact that all the boys would go out together. A lot of people ask how does that make you win on a Saturday? It doesn't necessarily make you successful, but you do get to know each other, have a laugh together and get a bit of empathy for the people around you.

Stéphane Adam was the team's heartthrob, very French and always well-dressed. A wee bit temperamental perhaps. When he was on it, he was very good, but sometimes, if he wasn't on it, he didn't contribute a lot. He and Gilles were quite close. That was the running joke we had, that everybody who signed got to bring a pal with them. Pasquale got Stefano Salvatori, another Italian, Gilles got Stéphane, another Frenchman, Stevie Fulton got me from Falkirk and Neil McCann got Jim Hamilton from Dundee. It was bring a friend.

In my second season at Hearts we improved our consistency and were in contention for the title until the final month of the season. We were full steam ahead, first or second in the league – at the minimum we thought we were going to split the Old Firm. When we drew 0-0 at Celtic Park at the end of March and then beat Falkirk 3-1 in the Scottish Cup semi-final at Ibrox the following week, we were still very much in contention on both fronts.

The Falkirk semi-final was a bit awkward for me as I was still living there. It was weird. The year before Falkirk had reached the final at Ibrox and I went on the supporters' club bus from my pal Tommy McMillan's pub. The whole town went and we had a great day, a proper fans' day. So to play against them the next year when I had been there supporting them, wanting them to win, was weird. Now I was back at Ibrox playing against them in a semi-final. I remember Kevin McAllister ran riot and Jim had Gary Naysmith, who was playing directly against him, pinned up against the wall at half-time in the dressing-room. Kevin was on fire and scored a great equaliser. It was a strange, strange feeling. I had played for Falkirk, had relatives who were fans and was out and about in the town every day being a part of the place, but you can have no loyalties in that situation. My recollection is that we stole it through late goals from Stéphane Adam and Neil McCann. Falkirk were the better team and particularly Kevin, but I was delighted to be in another final again so soon.

Unfortunately, our League challenge fell away at the end to leave the Old Firm fighting it out, with Celtic preventing Rangers from claiming 10 in a row on a tense final day of the season. Our problems started with a 1-1 draw at home to Motherwell at Tynecastle straight after the semi-final, when Tommy Coyne scored a late goal to equalise. Colin Cameron had a problem with his pelvis and was playing through the pain and he was a big part of our team at the time. That goal knocked the wind out of us. In the next game we played Hibs and they beat us 2-1 at Easter Road. Hibs never beat us, we had their number regularly whoever the manager was. Then we drew 1-1 with St Johnstone and lost 3-0 at home to Rangers. That was five games where we picked up two points. In the end we lost the League by seven points, but dropped 13 in that five-game spell in the last month of the season. It was a massive disappointment.

Hearts had this reputation as chokers from the final week of the 1985–86 season when they lost the League to Celtic on the final day of the season and then lost the Scottish Cup final to Aberdeen a week later. Our team had made two cup finals against Rangers, but lost both of them, and our third shot at them was now looming in the 1998 Scottish Cup final at Celtic Park. There was that feeling in the air that Hearts had had a good season but wouldn't win anything again. Robbo, Craig Levein and all those people had played in that 85–86 side as youngsters. They were part of a generation who had tasted that bitterness. For us younger ones, it was irrelevant really, but the club definitely had that feeling hanging over it. It did not help that in our eight League meetings with Celtic and Rangers that season we had not managed to win once.

Yet we knew they rated us. I certainly did, because they had already tried to persuade me to sign for them. I had spoken to David Murray, Rangers' chairman, during that season and I knew Neil McCann had gone and spoken to him as well. We both knew we had been, yet we never spoke about it. It was almost like it was an open secret between us. I went through to Murray's offices on the outskirts of Edinburgh. He had a flip-chart up with his team for the next year and told me Dick Advocaat was coming in as manager. Stefan Klos was on it, and others too.

I wanted to go to Rangers. He gave me a contract on the money I wanted and said, 'We will put it in a drawer and we will try and buy you, but if we don't then you will come next year.' I had another year left, but I insisted: 'I need to speak with the new manager before I sign a contract.' Thinking about it now, I can't believe I did that. I can't believe I didn't just sign it. I can't remember exactly what he said, but it was along the lines of 'No problem, I'll get him to ring you.' The call never came and there would be a reason for that. Neil McCann and I have never spoken about it to this day, but I would imagine he had the same meeting and signed the contract and Rangers eventually agreed a fee with Hearts for him. Whether they didn't think I was a priority or they couldn't agree a fee, they never did that with me. I remember thinking at the time, 'I want

£10,000 a week.' It was the first time in my career I had a figure in mind as I negotiated a contract.

We prepared down at Stratford-upon-Avon for the final. We trained at the agricultural college and it was stunning setting, surrounded by beautiful countryside. There was a cricket pitch and we agreed to have a game to keep Neil Pointon, our token Englishman, happy. We had no pads on and I couldn't believe the speed the ball was coming at. Looking back, one of us could have been injured on the eve of the cup final but lads being lads we were just trying to leather the ball as hard as we could. I remember getting hit a couple of times and thinking this is tougher than it looks on the television. It was nice to get completely away from football – there was no atmosphere of an approaching cup final, which can be a long build-up. There were no distractions at all.

We started the game like a dream. Steve Fulton was brought down for a penalty and Colin Cameron converted it nervelessly despite having required a cortisone injection to play through his pelvic injury. We scored a second just after half-time through Stéphane Adam and started to believe we had a chance. Then Ally McCoist came on and scored with about 10 minutes to go. After that, it was just about holding out.

Right on the full-time whistle, Ally broke through and I brought him down on the line of the area, literally the edge of the box. Willie Young was the referee and when he blew his whistle it was one of those moments, a career-defining one. I just didn't know what he would give. I thought I was outside the box, or I wouldn't have done it, but I didn't know for sure. Honestly, it couldn't have been any closer. I remember him giving a free kick, being relieved, then thinking they have still got a free kick and I was sure it was

y sister Fiona and I in the back garden in
ieldhill.

The Weir family on holiday, invariably
somewhere that didn't involve an aeroplane.

ona and I with Mum. I'm wearing my favourite jumper.

At Woodlands High School, just before I departed for America.

Celebrating a goal in the States in 1991 during my successful spell as a striker.

Scoring for Falkirk against Motherwell, with Mo Johnston and Kenny Clark (referee). Brian Martin and Rab McKinnon try to stop me.

Jim Jefferies is the manager whose methods moulded me into a professional at Falkirk.

Billy Brown always made training enjoyable, except when leasing us out on the pre-season slog – in this case at Hearts.

In action for Hearts against Dunfermline, a few months after I joined them from Falkirk.

Gary Locke was a great influence in the dressing room at Hearts, and remains one of my best friends in football.

National service – Gary Naysmith, Robbie Horn, Paul Ritchie, Colin Cameron, myself, Neil McCann and Steve Fulton celebrate various Scotland call-ups.

After our 1998 Scottish Cup win, we parade the trophy on a open-top bus on the Royal Mile in Edinburgh.

Craig Brown and his experienced staff created superb atmosphere in the Scotland squad, here during our 1-0 win in Germany in 1999.

ona and I on our wedding day.

Newly born Lucas, just before I went in for my Achilles op.

um and Dad, with Lucas, on one of their frequent visits to Cheshire.

At Everton, Duncan Ferguson was good on the pitch and a good laugh off it.

Newcastle United's Alan Shearer didn't do banter but he did enjoy a battle.

Liverpool's Michael Owen catches me with his studs as a Merseyside derby comes to the boil in September 1999.

eing the funny side – Gazza gets a laugh om Alec Cleland during a pre-season endly.

Role reversal – I didn't score many for Everton but Kevin Campbell, a fine centre-forward, seems to approve of this one against Charlton in 2001.

only goal for my country came against Latvia in 2001, Craig Brown's final match in arge of Scotland.

Myself, Paul Dickov, Gareth Williams, Scott Severin and Lee Wilkie on the ferry in The Faroe Islands in 2002.

David Moyes transformed Everton, although I initially thought he wanted r of me as part of his revolution.

Theatre of dreams – Bill Kenwright, the chairman, applauds after we beat Fulham in David Moyes' first match in charge of Everton.

They shall not pass! I formed the best centre-back partnership of my career with Alan Stubbs at Everton.

Brian Laudrup taking the free kick. Coisty was furious, slamming the ground and everything. He still is. Speaking to him since, and I now know exactly what he means, despite all the trophies Rangers have won and he's won, he remembers the ones they have lost more, because it is rarer and the hurt is there. He will bring that up quite a lot with me, especially whenever we bump into Willie Young.

Goughie came in to congratulate us, which was impressive as I said earlier. I would love to say he saw a dignified scene when he arrived in our dressing-room but it was quite the opposite. We had bottles of champagne and were jumping in the bath like idiots. It remains one of the best experiences of my life. We went upstairs to the lounge at Celtic Park to have some drinks up there. A few of the Rangers players came up, like Coisty and Ian Durrant, and were being brilliant with us, too. Then we went down to the bus but waited for what seemed absolute ages while Steve Fulton did a drug test. There was no shortage of drink on the bus and it was rocking.

Eventually, Steve came out and we just started driving back along the M8 to Edinburgh. We cut up the bypass and onto the Western Approach Road and further along toward Gorgie Road it was just absolute madness. People were hanging off bridges, the streets were swamped and the bus was crawling along. Eventually we got out onto the roof through the skylights. We were driving along Gorgie Road and it was surreal. They wouldn't let you do it now but we did.

We eventually came into Tynecastle and I can remember coming off the bus, worse the wear for drink, and Hazel Irvine of the BBC grabbing me for an interview. I was not at my best, but somehow slurred my way through it. Then we went straight into the Gorgie

Suite and had a massive party in there. They told us the Caledonian Hotel had rooms for us all. Fiona and I were walking along Gorgie Road toward the centre of Edinburgh from the stadium as night turned to morning when this police car flew up behind us and stopped suddenly. A guy got out and said, 'Mr Weir, can't have you walking tonight, son.' They put us in the back of the police car and dropped us at the Caledonian. It was one of those nights you wanted to last for ever.

Next day, it was back to the stadium and a lot of the boys were still half-cut. I didn't even have a drink the next day. I wasn't interested by that stage. We went up to the City Chambers on the Royal Mile and met Eric Milligan, who was a big Hearts fan and the Provost back then. He had a civic reception for us, then we went on an open-topped bus that came down the Royal Mile, down the bridges and then along Princes Street. They said there were 250,000 people to see us. There were certainly Hearts scarves everywhere and you just don't get the opportunity in Glasgow to do that. That's why it was such a special occasion. At Hearts, we got the benefit of that. It was a great thing to do and even when we got back to the stadium it was full of fans as well and we took the Cup out into the stadium and showed it to all the fans inside Tynecastle.

Yet in a sense this party was also a farewell one to the club for many of us. Several of the lads, if they are being honest, had made up their minds to leave Hearts. Myself, Neil McCann and Colin Cameron, people like that. It felt like we had the confidence in ourselves to move again, probably to England or to Rangers and Celtic, as it was then, and probably still is now. Winning the cup was the confirmation to ourselves we could go on again, but it was also our reward to the Hearts fans. It was our last chance to thank them by winning something in a sense. The following season, the atmosphere at the club would sour and the Cup-winning team started to scatter. More immediately, though, I had a World Cup finals to look forward to.

4

France 98

AS A child I lay on the carpet of our living room floor listening intently to the radio commentaries of Scotland games, dreaming of one day playing for my country. In those days, midweek matches were rarely televised and you had to wait for the Scottish Cup final or the Scotland–England game to see a game live on TV. When my dad later took me to internationals at Hampden it was a major day out for us. As his only son, I was always close to my father, but on those days our bond always seemed extra special. The train from Falkirk into Glasgow, then another train out to Mount Florida before the short walk to the stadium. It was a big adventure we were setting out on together, special days that will stay with me for the rest of my life.

My dad would tell me to watch guys like Terry Butcher, Willie Miller and Alex McLeish and learn from them, but inevitably I would become engrossed in the game and forget his sound advice. We were there together in 1985 for the Rous Cup match, when Richard Gough's header gave us a win over England. If you had told me then that I would go on to play beside Richard at Everton and win 69 caps for Scotland I would have suspected you had taken too much of the laughing juice.

When the call came from my country in May 1997, it was in slightly surreal circumstances. I was on a bus full of Hearts players bound for the airport and our end-of-season jaunt to Magaluf, a Falkirk tradition that Jim Jefferies had taken to Tynecastle with him. We were full of the joys as we had just beaten Rangers in the final game of the season, securing a hefty bonus in the process, and were ready for some fun with our newly acquired spending money. I suspected the high jinks had already started when Bert Logan, the sprint coach, came up the bus to tell me that Craig Brown was on the phone at the front for me. Yes, younger readers, it was so long ago that we didn't have mobiles.

Wary of a wind-up, I expected to hear somebody trying to impersonate Craig Brown. I'd probably already had a couple of beers by that point and my response was along the lines of 'whatever'. Yet when I picked up the phone, it really was Craig calling me into his squad for friendlies against Wales and Malta followed by a key World Cup qualifier in Belarus. I was so taken aback I offered to get off the bus there and then to join up, but he just told me to go and enjoy the break and report in when I could make it back. I'd love to tell you that I lived like a monk in Magaluf, preparing for my national service, but at that age you think you are bulletproof. At least I made it back on time, unlike some of our boys who were called up to the under-21 squad. Although I took plenty of stick as I came back up the bus and throughout our trip to Majorca, I think it was also seen as a bit of a breakthrough for us all by the boys I played with. The likes of Neil McCann, Colin Cameron, Steve Fulton and Paul Ritchie would all win caps later on, but at that time there were no Hearts players in the Scotland squad.

As a naturally shy person, I would have preferred to have had a teammate to talk me through it. I was apprehensive that I wouldn't fit in or do myself justice, ruining things for the rest of the boys. In retrospect, though, it was probably a good thing that I didn't have someone to hold my hand. It forced me to come out of my shell and mix immediately with my new international colleagues. It helped, of course, that the man who had called me up was such a gem of a human being.

Craig made me feel comfortable immediately. He had that knack, it was part of what made him such a great manager to play for. He made you feel special from the start, like you had done him a favour rather than the other way round. That he appreciated you could be somewhere else doing something else and had instead come along and shown commitment to him. It wasn't rose-tinted spectacles with Craig, he lived in the real world. He was expert at creating an environment players wanted to be part of.

His attention to detail was often astonishing and also extremely comforting. Newcomers like myself were told where to get their suit, what time training would be and so on. He was approachable, so if there was anything you weren't sure of you only had to ask. He was so organised and attentive he immediately made you feel like an international player. Everything was sorted out, nothing was vague. We were still paid to play for Scotland back then and the appearance fees and bonuses were clearly laid out and significant sums, certainly to me then, which again made you feel that you were part of a professional approach to it all. I am still mindful of how well Craig looked after me when I see new players coming into the Scotland squad these days and try to help put them at ease. Now, further on in your career, you sometimes forget that all these lads are coming into the squad for the first time and how big a thing it is for them and their families. You take it for granted they know everything, but they don't. It's all new to them and exciting. It is interesting to see how people take it.

I tried not to get too carried away by my call-up against Wales, but looking back now it was a big deal. It was in front of 8000 fans at Rugby Park rather than in front of a packed Hampden, yet it was significant because it represented another step up for me only five years after I had belatedly come into the professional game. My family were out in force, my parents, my godmother and my Uncle Graeme. My dad was never a demonstrative sort, but I knew it meant a lot to him and mum. In the starting team, Neil Sullivan, Christian Dailly and Brian McAllister were all making their debuts, too, as Craig was looking for new contenders at centre-back. The trio of Tom Boyd, Colin Calderwood and Colin Hendry had been superb together for Scotland, but the two Colins were injured. I remember it was a proper game of football, not a friendly, but we lost it to a John Hartson goal.

We stayed down at Troon at the Marine Highland hotel, which was a great place. You were away from it all and you were getting the best of food and so on. It was an old-school hotel. We would go for a walk around the golf course to relax and it was kind of idyllic looking back now. What I'd always imagined being away with your international team would be. We'd train in the morning and Craig used to have lots of meetings so you would know the other team inside out.

My second game was against Malta in Valletta five days later. I came on at half-time for Brian McAllister but didn't do myself justice at all. I simply wasn't used to being a substitute and wasn't properly prepared. I made a mental note to be ready the next time, if there was one. I wasn't up to speed with the game. We ended up winning 3-2 but Craig wouldn't have been pleased at conceding two goals to Malta, as I discovered when he picked his team to play Belarus in the qualifier a week later.

Just going to Belarus was a shock to the system. It was so basic. You would be scared to sleep on the sheets and you just felt so sorry for some of the poor people you saw there. They just had nothing, really nothing. It was sad. We took our own chef over and he prepared all the food for us, but even then he struggled to make it look good because it was so basic. I spent most of my time playing cards with Billy Dodds and Darren Jackson, who were looking after the new boy.

I still thought I had a chance of playing. I remember hearing the team and it was a hammer blow to discover Craig hadn't picked me. I thought, 'What have I done wrong?' When you are that age, you just expect to play. I was used to playing. It was probably the first time I had been dropped or not been picked. It was one of the biggest disappointments I'd had. 'He's not picked me, he doesn't think I am good enough,' I thought to myself, 'playing Craig Burley at centre-half, he's playing somebody out of position because he doesn't trust me to play.' Of course, it was logical based on what I know now about Craig. In fact, I probably got an early start. Some lads had been in squad after squad without getting a start, so I was playing relatively quickly compared to other people. He made you serve your time. There was an acknowledgement of that within the squad. It worked as we kept a clean sheet in what was a pressure game and won 1-0 through Gary McAllister's penalty.

It was an important result on the road to qualifying for the following summer's World Cup finals in France and it was not lost on me that I had come into the squad at an opportune moment. I didn't play in the home win over Belarus at Pittodrie, a match postponed for 24 hours after the death of Princess Diana, or the subsequent victory against Latvia at Celtic Park which clinched our qualification. I was going to the World Cup on the back of it, but I didn't feel like I deserved it or had earned it. Like a lot of other people in the country back then, I was probably complacent to a degree about what had been achieved. I had grown up in an era when Scotland had qualified for five consecutive World Cup finals and here we were off to France 98 immediately after Euro 96 in England. Back then, there seemed no reason to suspect that we couldn't maintain that pattern.

I hadn't been involved in the campaign from the start to the finish, so I didn't have the experience or the input into games. I knew what was going on, but I wasn't at the hub of it. I probably didn't realise the significance of the game. To beat Latvia at home to qualify for the World Cup, you think I would take that all day, but it was a tense one for those involved in it. Goals from Kevin Gallacher and Gordon Durie eased the strain and it was only afterwards, looking at the faces of our experienced players, that I started to realise the significance. The likes of Gary McAllister, Colin Hendry, Tom Boyd and Jim Leighton weren't people who showed their emotions, but I could tell it meant a lot to them and for the right reasons because it was a big achievement. We hadn't qualified for USA 94, so it was Scotland's first World Cup finals for eight years.

I was having a good season with Hearts and was involved in Craig's squads for the friendlies which followed so I knew I had a decent chance of going to France, although the feeling I hadn't really earned that honour persisted. I remember going along to the launch of Craig's autobiography in Edinburgh and feeling I shouldn't really be there. He was thanking me for coming along and I was feeling it should be the other way round. I was given three more caps against France, Denmark and Finland in our warm-up matches and began to settle into life with the Scotland squad.

It was all new to me. Jim Jefferies would have a meeting to name the team at half-past one on a Saturday afternoon and that was the only meeting he'd have, unless we were in trouble. Then, we would all have a meeting and would be throwing punches at each other by the end of it. With Scotland, there was much more analysis of the opposition. Craig's feeling was that knowledge was power. That the more you knew about the opposition, the better chance you had against them. Yet at the same time, he had this wonderful way of belittling the side you were about to face so you weren't in awe of them. He was brilliant at it. How many times were we told an opposition striker was 'a wee Dougie Arnott' – the former Motherwell striker – 'but not as good'. He had these sayings which he always came out with. 'He could walk under that table with a top hat on,' he would say of a small striker, or 'He couldn't keep the ball in a telephone box', of someone with a poor touch. Craig's manner demystified these players for us, made them seem like the guys we faced every week for our clubs. He was the least likely person in the world to be rude to anybody or disrespect anybody, it wasn't that. He was simply trying to relax his team and give them a chance. He was such a cute psychologist.

Craig's team was more structured than the club ones I had played in to that point, everybody knew what everybody else was doing. Jim and Billy's teams were more off the cuff. Craig would detail what teams did from free kicks and corners, then say this is how we are going to play against them. There were to be no excuses that you didn't know your role in any given situation that might come up. It was like a game of chess almost. It felt like moving up a level in terms of preparation and there was a bigger build-up to games as well. It meant more, it was more important, because you had put all this preparation into it. You were performing a role rather than just doing your best, so you had to concentrate more and there was more pressure on you. Craig was probably ahead of his time in terms of the level of detail he went into and the sort of background and information you would get. He was top-class on that, he really was.

Craig liked a joke and a laugh but he wouldn't have us being disrespectful to other people around the hotel or elsewhere. Anything like that, he wouldn't have at all. He treated you like men and expected you to act accordingly. If there was a sweetie paper lying around, he would pick it up. He was from a different generation, a stickler for things like pulling your socks up. He was almost paranoid about everybody looking the same, everybody wearing the same stuff. He thought little details made a difference. He wanted to see and hear that his players treated people properly and his antennae twitched at any reports of bad manners or loutish behaviour. He was like a schoolteacher but one you respected and liked, a moral guardian almost.

His backroom staff were from much the same mould. Gentlemen with a twinkle in their eye and a few stories to tell. They all made their own contributions, had all been there for a long time and seen it all. The likes of Hugh Allan, the trainer, Professor Stewart Hillis, the team doctor known simply as 'the Prof', John MacLean, his assistant and now successor, Eric Ferguson from Dundee, another veteran trainer, whose catchphrase was 'I'll just gie you that wee rub', Stewart MacMillan, who looked after the players and who we all called 'Omar' because he looked a bit like Omar Sharif.

Brian Hendry did the video analysis and also organised afternoon matinees, which helped pass the time and created a sense of camaraderie that served us so well. Almost all of the squad would be there and you felt like a social outcast if you didn't make it along. Omar and Brian would be handing out sweets, blankets and pillows. Brian would always be cracking jokes or telling people the wrong plot details if they came in late. 'He's shagged her, she shot him . . .' Ian Durrant would moan it was crap and Brian would say, 'Shut up, Durranty, if nobody is dead in the first 10 minutes you're not happy, it always has to be car crashes or car chases.' His company would get access to movies that we had never seen, but now anybody can get them. It was like you went away and ate chocolate and drank a can of Irn Bru, sitting in the afternoon in the hotel watching films, and got a wee game of football at the end. The food was unbelievable. You would go down to the Marine and you would be having fish and chips for your lunch and ice cream. All the things you would probably never do now, that was the norm. It was a wee bit special.

You would be lying sleeping and Omar would be banging on your door with his big Scotland kitbag crammed full of chocolate, shaking it, saying, 'What do you want, what do you want.' It was like when kids pour all their Christmas selection boxes into one big bag. 'Do you want any ginger?' Omar would add, as he made himself comfortable on the end of your bed and assured you: 'I've looked after the boys for years, they were always stumbling in but there was never any controversy, I have seen it all, I have seen the birds in the room, I have seen the bottles of wine, but nothing has ever got out, never a story.'

There were plenty of strong characters among the players, too. Gary McAllister, Colin Hendry, Jim Leighton, Tom Boyd and John Collins were the senior players at the core of the squad. They formed a committee who would discuss things with Craig and address any issues before they became a problem. Nobody made it hard for you, nobody made you feel unwelcome or put barriers up.

Darren Jackson was really good fun, one of the boys who kept things going. He used to get the piss taken out of him a lot but would take it really well. He always used to try really hard with his clothes. Too hard. You could just tell Darren thought he was a Premiership player in the making, but, importantly, he could laugh at himself. Billy Dodds was just dead normal. Bubbly, sociable and approachable. The sort of person you would want about your squad if you were a manager. Billy involved everybody and was up for a laugh, but wouldn't take any shit either. He said what he felt. Like me, he was relatively new to the squad but it felt like he had been there for 10 years. Billy wouldn't wait for somebody to speak to him, he would be right in there. He and Craig Burley were quite tight as they both came from the Cumnock area. I always remember thinking during training that Craig was a good player, one of the best in the squad and a bit underrated.

John Collins looked after you. I never had a a problem with John. When I went down to Everton, he took me to his house for dinner and tried to help me out. He was really accommodating and a genuine guy. I know when he was manager of Hibs he got a reputation of being a bit 'holier than thou' and 'my way or the highway', but that wasn't my experience of him at all. Mud sticks, especially up in Scotland, and one instance of falling out can tar you. I think when you look at the turnover of Hibs' managers of different personalities then it would seem there is a deeper problem there than any one individual.

Colin Calderwood is the current boss at Easter Road and played in my position for Scotland when I joined the squad. You could see how there would be a wee bit of threat there for some people, but he was never like that with me, always very straightforward. There was no edge to him. Tom Boyd was the same. Mr Consistent. He just did the same things well in every game. Good with his right foot, good with his left, good in the air and quite quick. Good at everything, without being really special at anything, but always in the team and capable of playing anywhere you asked him to across the back.

Craig was loyal to these players, the ones who had done it for him, and newcomers were made to feel they had been selected to join an elite, but not because these guys acted like they were anything special. The likes of myself, Christian Dailly, Jackie McNamara and Simon Donnelly were the new generation, I guess, but were introduced gradually, and one or two at a time. You had to become part of the group rather than having your own group or clique of new boys, which was a good thing.

Gary was the highest-profile player in many ways and the leader of the group. It was a disaster for him personally and for the team when a serious knee injury ruled him out of the finals. We lost another senior player as we prepared beforehand in the United States. Andy Goram handed Craig a letter informing him he wanted to return home. Perhaps he suspected that Craig would stay loyal to Jim Leighton in the finals or maybe he had his own personal reasons.

The two goalkeepers could not have been more different in character. Jim was always very quiet and intense, all business, but decent with it. Andy was more rough and ready, yet likeable – a guy you would meet in the pub who also just happened to be a world-class goalie. He just disappeared one day. We were just like, 'Where's he gone?' Craig handled it with his usual calmness. There never seems to me to be an open conflict between keepers, although there might well be. It is the same with Allan McGregor and Craig Gordon now. They are never pally, never close, but there's always a respect. You seem to get that between all goalkeepers because it's so obvious only one of you is going to play, whereas in any other position they could maybe accommodate you both by finding a role somewhere else, so it is quite ruthless. It is quite a funny dynamic really and the dynamics of a squad are extremely important.

My recollection of Andy is there was no badness in him at all but he liked a glass of wine, liked to eat the wrong things and liked the ladies, although he always trained really hard. That was what he had been like all his life and he wasn't going to keep it under wraps for five or six weeks, which you need to do at a World Cup. Probably that was part of Craig's decision, getting people in the group who would handle being away. The players who are playing aren't the problem because that's their focus, it is the players who aren't playing. He probably knew if Andy Goram wasn't playing, he would be a time bomb just waiting to go off. It is probably the players who aren't playing who make you have to think, 'Will they get bored and get up to something?' I expected to be one of those players but myself Jackie, Simon, Jonathan Gould, Scot Gemmill, Scott Booth and so on were probably just happy to be there. I roomed with Scott. We had the worst room in the hotel and we'd always end up in someone else's room playing cards to pass the time. They would have balconies, while we seemed to be stuck in a corner in a cupboard!

Nobody wanted Andy to go of course, but people forget now that Neil Sullivan had come into the frame, too, and was approaching the peak of his own career, which is still going strong now. He and Matt Elliott, another converted Englishman, were really good friends and they both settled in quickly.

The players had picked where they wanted to prepare. Craig asked us and we wanted to go to the US. It was exciting for me going back to America because people I knew that only six years previously I had been playing with at college were coming to watch the games. That was a big plus for me. We got a bit of time to look around New York. We were in a great hotel in New Jersey and there was a shopping mall right across from the hotel. Little details like that are so important when you are taking a group of players away for a lengthy period. It can be the nicest hotel in the world, but if there is nothing to do then they are soon bored. We drew 2-2 with Colombia in the Giants Stadium and then went to Washington for a few days, where we drew 0-0 with the USA. The heat in that game against the US was ridiculous. I remember thinking to myself, 'We shouldn't be playing in this', and I had played in America. Alexi Lalas, an old adversary from my college days, played for the USA, as did Joe-Max Moore, who would later become a teammate at Everton.

Our World Cup base was at Saint-Rémy in Provence. We had the run of a beautiful big house with a pool. It was almost like a big family. We got to know the staff and our omnipresent security guards. You could walk down into the town and there would be next to nobody there. It would be like a normal French village. It was very relaxed, with restaurants and coffee shops. We'd go down to eat in a restaurant in the village now and again to break it up and you wouldn't really know there was a World Cup on. In many ways, the teams involved in a major tournament are in a cocoon away from the expectation and excitement that is gradually building. It is a slightly surreal experience. At least we didn't have to wait long to make our entrance. The draw had dictated that we would play in the opening match against Brazil, the holders, in the Stade de France.

We left Saint-Rémy behind and transferred to this big chateau in the middle of nowhere outside Paris. It felt like a cup final. I remember this helicopter landing and Tony Blair came to meet us at the hotel. He was wandering about and John McBeth, a member of the SFA hierarchy, was following him everywhere he went. It was blatantly obvious. Tony Blair was like, 'Who is this guy, get him to —' and they were almost grabbing him and trying to drag him towards the officials. All Blair was interested in was talking to the players, the Hendrys and McAllisters. We all shook hands with him and he was very good, very natural. I know people said later he was manufactured, but he wasn't like that with us. He had made a big effort. He had flown in a helicopter specially to see us prior to the game and I think with things like that you start to realise the significance of it. I remember the transfer from the hotel to the stadium was breathtaking. I have had plenty of police escorts going to games, but this felt like the bus was doing 150mph through Paris, like something out of a movie, through red lights, through everything. It felt like it really was something special. It was then I started to feel the butterflies in my stomach.

It was strange experience for all of us who were not in the starting line-up for that game. You are so near, yet so far from playing in the biggest tournament in football. You are part of it, but also not a part of it. You are there, but you are not really making an impression or getting your opportunity. At my age then, and as it was my first tournament, I probably thought there would be more to come. So you are patient and try and be ready if you do get a chance. If I had been unprepared in Malta a year previously, now I was telling myself, 'I could go on here and I better be ready if I do.'

Craig raised a laugh and relaxed us all by returning to the dressing-room to inform us that the Brazilians were 'shitting themselves'. As the camera panned along Scotland's line-up, John Collins gave a cheeky wink and Darren gave one of those big grins of his. That was typical of Darren, who would have felt he belonged on that stage beside Roberto Carlos, Taffarel, Aldair, Junior Baiano, Dunga and the front three of Rivaldo, Bebeto, Ronaldo.

Rivaldo, Bebeto, Ronaldo . . . I had seen this side on its way to winning the World Cup in the United States four years earlier during a holiday there to catch up with some of my old college pals. I went to see Brazil and Sweden draw in Detroit. We were there for a while. It was a great experience, a proper carnival. We couldn't have picked a better game to be involved in with the Brazilians being what the Brazilians are and the Swedes being what the Swedes are. You are going from being a spectator at one and four years later you are playing in it. Quite a jump.

They scored after four minutes through César Sampaio but we were well in the game and equalised with a penalty from John Collins before the break. At half-time, the subs stayed outside and the atmosphere was just incredible. It was a lovely feeling. There was a wee pocket of Scotland fans in the corner jumping up and down to the World Cup theme, 'Carnival de Paris'. Bouncing, like nothing I have ever seen. It sounds strange, given what was to follow, but it was one of the highlights of the World Cup for me. You realised how many fans were there and how much it meant to them. As a player, you didn't really get a sense of that sometimes. I knew my family and friends were there and it was fantastic. You didn't feel like you were in the World Cup a lot of the time because you were so far away from it, but just being there and seeing that at half-time gave me a connection. If you are not playing, that's probably the next best thing for feeling part of it, feeling involved in it.

Having since been to the World Cup in Germany and the Euros in Switzerland with my boys it was the same. I think they have all been really good atmospheres. As a player, you really do miss that. I don't know if there's an argument for giving them a wee taste of it. Footballers get a lot of good things, but they kind of get so close but so far. We get the travelling but we don't really get to see places. Some managers try to tackle this. On the European run we went on with Walter Smith at Rangers in 2008, he gave us the opportunity to see places. We used to go on the morning of the game for a walk. He would take us around the Acropolis in Greece or round a park in Germany. You got a wee feeling of where you were and that was like going back to my college days, when we went whitewater rafting in Colorado Springs and things like that around games. We went to Israel with Walter and I remember walking along the beach on the morning of the game. I was thinking, 'What are we doing here?' In Scotland, it was winter and we stopped at this café and everybody sat down and had a laugh and a coffee. I remember thinking, 'This is brilliant.' It was so simple but before a big game, a European game, why does it all have to be pressure? With David Moyes it would be 'We are having a meeting and watching a video.' I am not saying that's wrong. It is just interesting how different people do things differently and yet the outcome is probably the same.

We lost to an unfortunate goal, when the ball bounced off Jim Leighton and into our net off Tom Boyd after Cafu got in behind us onto a pass from Dunga. You are always disappointed when you don't win, you've got to be like that. There's always a worry you are going to get embarrassed against Brazil, but Scotland gave a good account of themselves and were well in the game. I remember my mum saying she was on the train going to the game with my dad and the Brazilians were saying, 'Four-one to Brazil' and the Scottish guys were replying, 'That will do for us because then we've scored.'

That was the Scottish mentality. My mum has great memories of that day and my dad was there and his memory was fine then, too. That still means a lot to us all.

We couldn't feel sorry for ourselves as the next match against Norway was quickly upon us. We needed to take something from it, too, but fell behind to a goal from Havard Flo right at the start of the second half. It was the same team that had started against Brazil, but when Colin Calderwood hurt his hand shortly after the Norwegians had taken the lead a change was required. Craig told myself and Matt Elliott to get warmed up. One of us was about to play in a World Cup, but which one? I got on well with Matt, but I guarantee he would have been thinking the same as me – 'It is either me or him.' I might never have played in a World Cup if Craig had made a different decision that day because Matt never did. Scot Gemmill, who was my friend, never did, and Scot had served his time more than anybody in the squad. I hadn't really done that to the degree he had, so he probably deserved it more than me, that is just the luck involved in football and how quickly it can change. I remember Craig shouting for me, so I ran along the touchline and suddenly I was on.

I came on after an hour and within six minutes we equalised. Craig always had this thing about aiming passes between a left-sided centre-back and the left-back, trying to catch at least one of them on their wrong foot. Maybe it stuck in my mind because that's where I put a long pass and Craig Burley was onto it in a flash and finished with a cool lob over Frode Grodas. It remains the last goal Scotland have scored at the World Cup finals and I guess it finally made me feel as though I was part of it all. The atmosphere within the game changed as well and we should have gone on to win it. We were right back in it. I came on as centre-half, the right one of three with Colin Hendry and Tom Boyd. Craig had been playing right-back, but Jackie came on for Darren and Craig went into centre midfield and the changes worked well for us.

There was no euphoria afterwards. I was just grateful I had contributed. Grateful that I played. You never got too high or too low with Craig. You never got that feeling that things were great or you had done really well, it wasn't like that. It was always about the team and what we were doing next and how we would handle it. It was very low key. He was conscious of how everything was perceived and how we were going to play it. He was clever, astute at keeping things in perspective and not getting carried away and saying or doing the wrong things. You would never be in a situation where you would think I am a bit special here. It was probably only later that you realised you were involved in something that doesn't happen very often.

If we had won, we might only have needed a draw from our final game against Morocco to qualify. Instead it was last-chance saloon and we needed a win. Now I was starting in a big game. Again we fell behind, this time to a goal from Salaheddine Bassir. We rowed at half-time when Kevin Gallacher moaned about the lack of service to the strikers and a few of us turned on him. I was annoyed with myself when Abdel Hadda basically ran away from me for the second goal two minutes into the second half. Jim Leighton should have saved it, too – he touched it but the ball still went in. It was a great disappointment because that was the game over for us. Craig Burley was sent off for a tackle on Bassir, who then added a third goal to our humiliation. It didn't suit us going to try and win a game – it wasn't really Scotland's way of playing – but Morocco had some good players, Noureddine Naybet, Youssef Chippo, Hadda and Bassir among them.

After Paris and Bordeaux, when my family and friends had attended, I don't think anybody was in Saint-Étienne to see our exit in the same stadium where we had narrowly lost to France in a warm-up friendly the previous November. It was very low key. It wasn't a particularly nice hotel and downstairs, as we were going to the game, Rod Stewart and all the Scottish showbiz set were in the bar drinking. We were looking at them enjoying themselves, but it just felt such a different avenue we were going down.

We flew back to the base at Saint-Rémy afterwards, then on to Glasgow the next day downhearted. Norway beat Brazil in the other game and ended up going through, which was hard on Morocco. Norway were probably the worst team we had played and the players were deeply disappointed. If you win you are happy, if you don't win you are not going to be happy. It's great the fans are staying there clapping, as many did in Saint-Étienne, but if they hadn't been there clapping it wouldn't have changed anything. Your over-riding feeling is disappointment, whether they are clapping you or not. All that matters is the result. Whether you are getting booed or cheered, it doesn't change. It dictates everything. Everything else is just a secondary issue. All this stuff that you play for the fans and you play for the jersey is rubbish, you play to win. Scotland fans are fantastic wherever they go – some of the places we have seen them and some of the receptions we have had. The support you get is amazing, but I am afraid it doesn't change the game or the result or how you feel afterwards.

Being part of a World Cup is an incredible thing, especially given what's happened since – we've not been near it. Scotland had been to Euro 96 and then World Cup 98, so why would you not think that would continue? Even the ease of getting there, from the Euros in England to the World Cup in France, was great for us and our fans. You think, 'How easy is this?' Now it has all changed. The last World Cup was in South Africa, the next Euros are in Poland and Ukraine. Then the World Cup is in Brazil, then Russia and then Qatar. That was like a golden time for Scotland, for the ease of getting there and for actually being part of the party.

Like a lot of people in Scotland, I had grown up with the World Cup as something I could count on. I was four when the 1974 finals were played and too young to remember them, but I have memories of 1978 and, definitely, of 1982. Scotland in Argentina, the Holland game, and the disappointments beforehand. Spain, and the games against New Zealand, Brazil, Russia. I was 12 by then and you are probably at the peak of your interest and the time difference would be right to watch the games before bedtime. That is always quite a big thing as well for kids.

Now, I have a laugh and a joke with the Scottish boys at Rangers sometimes because I can say, 'Have you played in a World Cup?' to them. You just throw it in because you need ammunition now and again at my age. You've got to be able to stand up for yourself. You have got to have something to throw back. I appreciate how lucky I was to have that opportunity and there's not many people do get that chance. The majority of the foreign lads have played in a World Cup or been part of one so it has not really got the same impact, but the Scottish lads take it in the right manner. I think.

I have been there and I have done it, but, ultimately, it was a disappointment. We weren't successful. It was a failure and I didn't do particularly well. Okay, I helped at one of the goals, but I could have done things better. I wish it had gone better. We could have qualified. My abiding memory of the World Cup is of that disappointment, if I am honest. Whereas with things like qualifying for the Champions League with Everton, winning the Scottish Cup with Hearts, winning the League and getting to the Uefa Cup final with Rangers, there's a lot of positives involved. I never really contributed to qualifying and, to tell the truth, I wouldn't say it is one of the highlights of my career. It's one of the headlines, but not a great memory.

5

Heading south

WHEN I was at Falkirk and Hearts, there were two clubs I was constantly linked with. One of them played in blue and the other was based on Merseyside, yet neither was Everton. Liverpool and Rangers had followed my professional career with interest almost from the start. After Falkirk won promotion back to the Premier League at the end of my second full season, Jim Jefferies came into the dressing-room at Clydebank's Kilbowie Park and told me how well I had done for him and that I deserved all that lay ahead of me. It was so unlike Jim, it almost felt like he was saying goodbye, particularly as I was about to go on trial to Liverpool, where Ron Yeats, the chief scout and former Scotland centre-back, was championing me.

I drove down for the trial, and they really looked after me while I was there. Roy Evans was the manager at the time and I stayed in a hotel near Melwood, the training ground. It was a really friendly club – John Barnes and Jamie Redknapp took me out for lunch, for example. I just trained, played and felt I did all right in the few days I was there. Jim was keen for me to get back to Falkirk for a civic reception that had been organised for us. I remember Neil Ruddock running about with a bin liner on to lose weight, Steve McManaman flying with the ball at his feet, and playing in these five-a-sides, where the goals were made of a solid bit of wood. Robbie Fowler would just get the ball and from any angle, anywhere, it was 'bang, goal'. He was a phenomenon, a natural.

Ron took me round the flats, saying, 'This is probably where you will live.' I think he took me to Southport and told me I would be earning £1100 or £1200 a week. That sounded like a lottery win compared to my wages at Falkirk back then, but the figures meant nothing. They could have said £500 a week and I would have still been delighted. I don't mean to sound flippant but at that time money genuinely didn't play a part in my decisions. I was young and had no family responsibilities. It was all a big adventure to me and money was the last thing on my mind. Sammy Lee gave me a pair of boots because my old ones were so battered – a pair of Adidas Predators, which were in fashion at the time. I felt at home, thought it almost a done deal as I left to come back to Scotland, but Liverpool decided to look elsewhere and when, later that same summer, they went out and signed Phil Babb and John Scales for a combined outlay of more than £7m I guess I had my answer.

Bruce Rioch, Bolton's manager, was said to be interested. They had a strong side at that point with a strong Scottish influence and good players like Alan Stubbs, Jason McAteer and John McGinlay. A meeting was also arranged with Mark McGhee, who was managing Reading, but I am afraid I am still waiting for Mark to turn up for it. Rangers were also very much in the running and probably my personal preference. Jim Jefferies and Walter Smith had all but done a deal for me to move from Falkirk to Rangers after meeting manager-to-manager, when George Fulston, Falkirk's chairman, asked David Murray for a bigger fee than the one they had already agreed and another chance had gone for me.

I must have stayed on Rangers' radar afterwards, though, because, as I have already discussed, Murray invited me through to a meeting at his office in Edinburgh during the 1997–98 season when Hearts were vying for the title and said they wanted me to join the following season. Ron Yeats stayed in touch, too, and kept mentioning me to Liverpool managers, even after I moved to Hearts and Gérard Houllier took over from Roy Evans. I remember Ron called me once to tell me that he, Houllier and Phil Thompson were driving up to Scotland to watch me play on the midweek after Christmas 1998. Ron was desperate for me to do well and even briefed me on things that would go down well with the Frenchman, telling me to make sure I returned to my position quickly after going up for corners as that was one of the things Houllier liked to see from centre-backs. We were playing Dundee at Tynecastle and I was sent off after 17 minutes. The ball went over my head, I tried to get to it and I caught the guy I was marking as last man. I was absolutely devastated. I thought that was it for me and that I would never get another chance like that. Their scouting trip was reported in the Merseyside press, on the back page of the *Liverpool Echo*, I think.

I'd definitely decided to leave Hearts by this point. The atmosphere at the club had soured after our Scottish Cup win. Steven Pressley and Gary McSwegan had come in from Dundee United on more money than many of the existing players were on and that created resentment. Pressley, in particular, was unpopular. The culture we had created, the one that had taken us to our Scottish Cup win, became more 'them and us'.

I had also probably got myself in a position where I thought, 'I need to start earning now.' If money hadn't mattered to me previously, it did now because Fiona and I were about to get married and thinking of starting a family. If you go away and start mixing with the Scotland squad as I had, you hear stories of what people are on and people tell you directly what they are on at their clubs, the sort of money you can earn. It does turn your head a bit. I was earning a decent wage at the time, but probably thought to myself, 'I want to be part of that, I am as good as these boys.' At that stage, I was 28 going on 29, and it dawned on me that this could all be over in four or five years and that I had to make them count to be comfortable when my career was finished.

I was in such a rush to move, I was stopped for speeding as I was leaving Edinburgh to go back to Falkirk after hearing of Everton's interest. It was on Valentine's Day 1999, I think, and I couldn't wait to get away, my mind was made up. I still had a wee doubt about Rangers – I even considered phoning Murray to let him know Everton had come in for me – but my recollection is that by then a big part of me wanted to go to England, too, and that I was excited by the prospect of playing in a new league against new players and at new grounds.

I met Walter Smith in the house of Bill McMurdo, my agent back then. Afterwards, I jumped in the car with the gaffer to drive down to England, but we stopped at Hamilton services because Jim Jefferies had phoned him. He asked to speak to me and said, 'What's going on?' I replied, 'I am in the car driving down to Liverpool and I am going to sign for Everton.' Jim wasn't too happy to hear that. 'We've not agreed to let you go to Everton,' he said. 'Your chairman has,' I responded.

My mind was made up. I hold Jim in the highest regard and have great respect for him, but I wasn't turning that car around for anybody. It was very much 'I'm off, you better speak to him about that.' I was ready to go. I passed the phone back to Walter and Jim spoke with him and that was that. Hearts got somewhere in the region of £250,000 for me. I never moved for much money.

I remember being really excited driving down and just gibbering away to the gaffer. I am usually a quiet person, but my memory is of me talking the whole way down because I was genuinely excited about what lay ahead. I'd never had a conversation with him before, but I instantly found I could talk to him. He was a proper, Scottish football man with a nice way about him. Because of who he was and what he had done at Rangers, you had an impression about him, but he never overpowered you with that. It was just me and him in the car and he was telling me I would have to find somewhere to stay, which hadn't even entered my head. He told me about the area of Cheshire he lived in and which he thought I should have a look at. I did and have been there since. Walter lived probably less than a mile from where we live now. The rest of the time, he was just talking away about his sons and what they were doing. It wasn't football chat.

During the journey the feeling the move was perfect for me grew, particularly knowing there was a strong Scottish influence there. Everton might have had financial problems at the time, but that wasn't really an issue for me. In my experience footballers don't think of the financial position of the club they are joining. I only ever thought about it for football reasons, the league I was going to, the players I was playing with and against. It is very rare for a player to decide on a move based on the background at the club. I think the profile of the club and the history of the club are always more important. Even now, for me, if I got the chance to sign for a club like a Leeds or a Blackpool, it would be Leeds because it is the bigger football club and Everton was like that for me. It ticked all the boxes.

I had never been to Goodison before, but got a good feeling for it straight away, too. It wasn't dissimilar to Brockville and Tynecastle, although they were older and tighter. It was a wee step up the ladder, but along the same lines. My first game was at home to Middlesbrough, a night game under the lights. We won 5-0 but I can't claim much credit as it was 4-0 when I came on as a sub at right wing-back. Nick Barmby scored a couple – he was playing really well at the time. I remember having a free header from six yards out, which I should have scored with, and thinking, 'Thank God, it wasn't 0-0.' I was straight into the impressive Marriott hotel in the city centre, the same one Liverpool had put me up in during my trial, and you just got a feeling immediately that you were in a real football city.

I signed at the same time as a lad called Peter Degn, a Danish under-21 international. He stayed in the hotel with me, so we were quite close in the first couple of weeks. Peter was a lovely lad but a bit of loose cannon. He loved the casinos and would come into the changing-room with cheques for £15,000 and things like that. He never played much but he lived the rock star lifestyle all right.

I would get picked up and taken to training by Bill Ellaby, a Liverpudlian lad who was Walter's friend. He still works for Everton and was the player liaison back then. It was really exciting going up to the training ground for my first day. I had never had a training ground before at my previous clubs and Bellefield, Everton's old one, was full of character and, indeed, characters. It had a real homely feeling to it and a sense of history. It was built for the World Cup in 1966 and Brazil trained there, then Everton commandeered it. It was a great place, small enough but big enough, too, with a wee house sitting in the middle of all the pitches. You would go upstairs to eat and there was a gym. It was perfect. We would come in from training and a lady called Mary would throw our dinner down at us and tell us about the latest antics of her tearaway sons.

Walter had only become manager of Everton the previous summer, yet that didn't really register with me when I arrived. If I had been there before he came in it would have been different but that wasn't the case. I just knew him as the manager of that club right from the start. John Collins was very good with me, took me to his house for dinner with him and his young family and made an effort to keep in touch and make sure everything was all right. I like to think I did the same later with people like Gary Naysmith and James McFadden when they joined our Scots colony in exile.

Alec Cleland was another Scot at Everton who really helped me settle in. He'd left Rangers and was probably buzzing at moving to Everton, when a couple of months later the gaffer got the job. I don't think Alec and Archie Knox saw eye to eye, so it turned into a bit of a nightmare for him. Alec stayed a few miles from me and our kids ended up going to the same nursery. He would come and drop his wee boy, Alexander, off and come and pick me up and we would drive into training together, so we had a year of travelling in together and I got to know him well and Fiona got on well with his wife, Debbie. We used to go out for lunch and dinner with them and the kids were similar ages and went to similar places. To his great credit, Alec was never bitter. He was always out of the team or injured, but never negative. He never wanted the team to get beaten.

I soon realised I had been parachuted into a relegation battle. In those days, there were no transfer windows as such but there was a signing deadline in March and it was clear we needed further reinforcements. Scot Gemmill and Kevin Campbell came in right on the deadline and, to be frank, we were really in the mire at that point. We had to start getting a few results. We were in the relegation places with six games to go. In one of my first games, at

Blackburn, myself and David Unsworth, two defenders, were the central midfielders. We battled to a win with Ibrahima Bakayoko, who the club had paid £4.5m to sign from Montpellier the previous summer, scoring twice. It was a big, big pressure game for us at the time. When Everton go to Blackburn they fill the stand behind one of the goals and there is always a really good atmosphere. Playing in that game, I remember thinking to myself, I like this, I could really get used to playing in this and going to all these new stadiums and just being excited by something different. I was trying to take it all in and be part of it but still realising we were in real trouble with regards to the club's immediate future. Everton had never been relegated, so that was constantly getting churned out and I am sure the manager was more aware of it than we were.

If Bakayoko didn't work out for him or Everton, his purchase of Kevin Campbell for £3m from Trabzonspor proved inspired. Kevin scored nine goals in eight games as we lifted ourselves up the league with four wins. This run included a 6-0 victory over West Ham, who we always used to smash, at Goodison in which Kevin got a hat-trick. He just came in, hit the ground running and made a big difference for us because up until then we had been struggling for goals. It was during this run-in that I established myself in the side as a right wing-back, following my time on the bench and then in midfield after arriving at the club.

Scot became a good pal of mine and he made an impact, too, albeit in a less obvious way than Kevin. Scot lived in Knutsford and we often travelled in together to training. He had come from a football background with his dad being a famous Scotland international, then playing for Brian Clough and beside Roy Keane at Nottingham Forest and he just knew the game inside out. I loved sitting talking to him about football, we had similar ideas and I could have listened to him for hours. He was a very underrated player. He had a great career, but never got the praise he deserved. He was playing for Nottingham Forest in a right good era for them, then playing for Everton. He was a selfless player for his clubs and Scotland, but he was always on the fringes and never got a sustained run in the national team. He was unlucky to play in an era when we had playmakers like John Collins and Gary McAllister. He had a different angle on things from everybody else. Not that there is a typical footballer, but Scot was definitely not one. He was very thoughtful but could mix and was liked by everyone. He's articulate and he's still my friend now, we still speak regularly. Probably, like me, he saw his dad being aggressive and decided to be different. His dad was feisty, but Scot had a gentler nature. He wasn't married back then, although he has a son now, and loved his music and his travel.

The main difference I noticed compared to Scotland was that everybody seemed to be bigger and stronger right across the board. That was my first impression, rather than the football itself being out of this world. There were obviously special players and good players, but it didn't seem like a big jump. The players were bigger, stronger, fitter, more professional, though. When English teams came up to Scotland in pre-season, they just seemed like giants when we played against them for Falkirk and Hearts. I was big and could handle myself in that way, of course, but that was definitely the obvious thing. We never had a fitness coach at Everton although most of the other clubs seemed to. My view was why do you need a fitness coach if you are a professional football player and Walter was obviously of a similar mind. Archie Knox was his fitness coach.

Initially, I was buzzing with just going to all the new grounds. I went to Elland Road very early on in my Everton career, away to

Newcastle for a heavy defeat in the FA Cup and that was a great stadium, away at Man United and away at Liverpool. My first trip to Anfield in April 1999 was when Robbie Fowler famously snorted the touchline after scoring twice in the derby. The Everton fans used to absolutely hammer Fowler about being a smackhead, so I didn't see anything wrong with what he did in response. If I was a football fan it is the last thing I would be doing, especially with someone as good as him. He was just laughing it off, but instead got in trouble for it.

Fiona had been to a lot of games in Scotland to watch me but she was in the Anfield Road end for that one with Billy Lamont and said she would never go back, after seeing the stuff that was being thrown, objects and abuse. It wasn't like her, as she is not easily shocked. Buzz on the other hand, said he really enjoyed it. After it, we all went out in Heswall over the water for something to eat. Jamie Redknapp came into the same restaurant and again made a point of coming over to talk to us about the game.

I remember going to Sheffield Wednesday and thinking what a proper big club that was with 35,000 people there. If anything, I was a wee bit disappointed with Stamford Bridge, but White Hart Lane was the best of the lot for me, my favourite ground. It is a proper football stadium, close, enclosed, symmetrical, everything you would want one to be. As a player, when you drive into a stadium you always look at the cars in the car park with interest and Tottenham always had the best cars. It always had that feeling of money about it, a proper Premiership palace. After the game, we would always watch the opposition coming out with their wives. It is almost like we were judging them on their cars and their wives rather than their ability. Although when we went there, we always got a bit of a chasing. They always seemed to be a good side with really good forwards like Les Ferdinand, Robbie Keane and Fredi Kanouté. Spurs were our polar opposites in that period – great up front, but not so strong at the back. They were a good side, especially at White Hart Lane, and you would always go there and think this is going to be hard today, this will be a test. To be fair that was true at most grounds in the Premier League at that time.

That first season was all about survival and when you have just come into a club I don't think you buy into that as much as the players who have been there longer and lived through the struggle. You realise you have to stay up, but you don't have the same pressure as everybody else. You haven't been through the long haul with everybody else and sometimes that can be a good thing. With Kevin scoring and Scot creating, we won the final three matches in April and ultimately finished 14th. We finished seven points above the relegation places so it was quite a gap but it never felt like that and it was a stressful time for a lot of people at the club.

Nevertheless, it was seen as an improvement on the previous season, when the club had only survived on goal difference after a nail-biting final day, when a draw with Coventry City was just enough to keep Everton up. I think I can remember watching that game on the television, not realising the significance, that I was going to be involved in it soon myself.

Howard Kendall was sacked four weeks later by Peter Johnson, the then owner, although this experienced manager, who had done so much for the club in the 1980s, discovered his fate via the press rather than as he should have. Before Johnson appointed him, after Joe Royle resigned, he needed a caretaker and the story goes that he was sitting in the car park at Bellefield trying to decide between Neville Southall and Dave Watson, the two most experienced players at the club, when Neville arrived in his car and spotted Alan Myers, the club's press officer at the time, and shouted, 'All right Myers, you fat —.' For some reason, this seemed to narrow it down for Johnson.

Dave stayed on as part of the staff after Walter arrived. He was Mr Everton. He was the first-team coach, so he would do all the warm-ups, and was more on the coaching side than the playing side by that stage. He was a good guy, very funny, very dry, and I still see him as Fiona is friendly with his wife. He was a proper Scouser, born in Scotland Road, or Scotty Road as they call it, which is where all the Scallys are supposed to come from. Dave had done well for himself in football but still had that bit in him where you could tell he hadn't forgotten where he came from and was always full of fun. As a player, Dave was a typical English centre-half for me. Very aggressive and good in the air, someone who didn't take any chances and was a proper captain. The only person who could wind Waggy up was wee Danny Cadamarteri. Danny was hyper, full of beans, and couldn't shut up. He and Dave used to always be at loggerheads. Dave could banter with anyone, but Danny just got to him. He would have his shorts pulled up for the warm-up and Danny would imitate him and Waggy hated it.

We certainly had plenty of centre-backs, hence my posting to right-back. Craig Short was another of them and had been round the block. Like Dave, Craig would head it away, kick it long and keep it simple. He was a straight-talking Yorkshireman, who would always say what needed to be said. In a derby before my time, when Howard Kendall was still the manager, they were walking in at half-time and Craig said, 'Gaffer, you have got to change it out here, we are getting murdered.' 'You're right son,' replied Howard. 'You come off.'

I also got on well with Nick Barmby, who was from Hull, and the same, very straightforward. Nick had a high-profile career. I think he lived in Warrington during the week but his family still lived in Hull and he would commute back to see them at weekends and on his days off. That was another difference from Scotland, where you were never that far away from the club you played. In England, you got this impression people were coming from all over and not putting roots down anywhere. It was more transient.

David Unsworth was from Preston, not a million miles away from Merseyside, yet always portrayed himself as a big Everton fan and an adopted Scouser. Now he's working for Preston, I notice he has managed to reinvent himself as extremely proud of his roots there. David's not daft. Some of the young lads at that time at Everton were definitely daft, though. Lads like Michael Ball, Richard Dunne, Franny Jeffers and Danny Cadamarteri were all breaking through during Walter's time. I was going on 29 but in much the same mindset as them at that time. I was down there on my own and would just laugh at them. I certainly wouldn't be taking them too seriously or trying to lay the law down.

That was Archie's job and Walter's assistant was just what I expected he would be. What I'd had all my days with Jim and Billy at Falkirk and Hearts. He was very similar to them. There were no grey areas with Archie, it was either black or white. He nailed you if something needed said and, whoever you were, you got it if you messed up. Archie just laid his cards on the table. He wasn't complicated, but I liked him. He was a funny, funny man. Very good with the one-liners. He had all the staff on their toes, winding them up constantly, and was really good round the place.

Marco Materazzi was another character, although not necessarily a particularly good one and I wasn't too surprised when Zinédine

Zidane headbutted him in the 2006 World Cup final. Materazzi was high maintenance, stereotypical of what you would imagine an Italian footballer to be. He was quite immature back then but a good player, there was no getting away from that. Materazzi and Olivier Dacourt had been two of Walter's first signings for the club yet he had to sell them a year later as the club's financial position deteriorated and Johnson stepped down as chairman. Olivier was a loss, as he was really good midfield player from the Patrick Vieira mould, had good English and mixed more than many French players do. A lot of them are quite stand-offish, but Olivier was a wee bit more hands-on and aggressive, sometimes too aggressive actually. He was always getting booked and suspended for his tackling. Their sales brought in more than £10m and Bakayoko, Short and John Oster also left, with only Mark Pembridge and Richard Gough arriving. The club was cost-cutting, there was no getting away from that.

I held Gough in high esteem for what he had done at Rangers, being a Rangers fan, and, as I mentioned earlier, I had been impressed with his dignity in defeat when Hearts won the Scottish Cup. Yet closer up he wasn't exactly what I expected. I expected this Braveheart type who goes round everybody before games, rallying the troops, but he wasn't at all like that. If anything it was about making sure he was right. Richard had to be 100 per cent, with massage every day, sleep every afternoon. He was quite temperamental that way, more like a foreign player to an extent and not what I expected at all. Yet he did well on the pitch for Everton and was always good with me.

In the dressing-room at the time there was definitely a feeling that there were a lot of players who weren't playing and were just in the treatment room or were injured or had fallen out of favour for one reason or another. Malcontents is maybe not the right word, but they were certainly discontented and that dragged the atmosphere down generally. This group included Gareth Farrelly, who had scored the goal which had kept Everton up before Walter arrived, Mitch Ward, Terry Phelan and Danny Williamson.

You just felt they all needed a move and a fresh start somewhere. I was used to smaller squads, where everybody was either playing or close to playing, and there just seemed to be this group of players who weren't anywhere near it. I am sure I would have moaned, too, in their position, but, as I would later discover, there comes a time when you are not playing when you just have to accept it and move to a club where you will start games. Others like Joe Parkinson, who had been a very good player for the club, and Slaven Bilić were out of the picture with injuries.

Walter also changed our first-choice goalkeeper as I prepared for my first full season in English football. Thomas Myhre gave way to Paul Gerrard. Paul was a funny lad and a good keeper who had played for England under-21s, but everything seemed to go against him. He was one of those players who just never seemed to get their fair share of good luck. I played in the game where Paul was down injured and Paolo Di Canio caught the ball and refused to score. Nowadays, I guarantee Di Canio would get a yellow card for deliberate handball, but the referee let it go then. It was a different era. He was congratulated afterwards by Fifa, which was right. I know he's not an angel by any means, but that was such a decent thing to do he deserved praise.

Our start to my first full season in English football was tough with Manchester United at home followed by visits to Aston Villa and Spurs. We took only one point, courtesy of a draw on the opening day at Goodison, from our first nine but after that we started to settle down and pick up points. A 1-0 win at Anfield in a televised Merseyside derby on a Monday night at the end of September 1999 was the highlight of this period. It remains Everton's last League win there. We needed a result to say sorry to our supporters after being knocked out of the League Cup by Oxford. Kevin Campbell scored after just four minutes, steering the ball under Sander Westerveld at the end of a flowing move from us. Then it turned tasty as we held out for the remainder of the match. Westerveld and Franny Jeffers were sent off for an altercation, Steven Gerrard went for a high tackle on Kevin Campbell and Michael Owen might have as well for a bad challenge that nearly broke my leg. That wasn't his track record at all I must say, but he did me in that game all right. It was a great game and a great result for us. Dave Watson told us the next day he had gone into the manager's office and Gérard Houllier and Phil Thompson were there. 'Are you all right Davie?' they asked. 'Yeah I am okay,' Dave replied. 'Apart from I have to go into hospital tomorrow.' 'What for?' they said, concerned. 'Oh, just to get this smile off my face.'

Another great game in this spell was a 4-4 draw at home to Leeds, in which I scored my first Everton goal in dramatic fashion. It was a good Leeds team at the time and they arrived seeking an 11th consecutive win. I played right-back and Richard and Dave were the centre-halves. They were both getting on and it probably planted the seed in my own head that I could extend my career, too. It was a proper end-to-end game of football. Kevin Campbell put us ahead, again after four minutes, but Michael Bridges quickly equalised. Kevin scored again, only to see Harry Kewell cancel it out with a curving shot. Don Hutchison gave us a 3-2 lead at half-time but Bridges and Jonathan Woodgate put them 4-3 ahead before I equalised right at the death with a header. Nigel Martyn, who was later to join us at Everton, was Leeds' goalkeeper and I have a great picture of me scoring against him somewhere. It was a great feeling and the perfect end to a great game. I can still remember it all like it was yesterday.

An equally clear, if less fond, memory is of a 5-1 defeat at Old Trafford in December 1999. It felt like I was responsible for every goal and that Paul Scholes had almost singled me out for punishment. He was dropping balls over my head, just where I couldn't get them. It was the kind of day where you start to think, 'Is he deliberately taking the piss of out me here.' Everything he touched was working and Ole Gunnar Solskjaer was finishing everything off and scored four that day. Scholes could do a lot of damage. He was the best I played against in all my time in England.

When you were playing Arsenal or Man United you knew that, collectively, you could get a doing. Like it used to be at Rangers and Celtic for the other teams in Scotland although I don't know if it still is. You used to go there and think, 'We need to play well today or we could be on the receiving end of a cricket score.' Losing four or five goals definitely wasn't out of the equation. You knew when you stepped on the pitch that they were capable of doing that to you. You never felt that with Chelsea, who weren't the power they would later become, Tottenham or Man City at the time. You never felt it against Liverpool. It was always going to be about a goal here and there in those games. Yet with Man United and Arsenal, I always felt before away games, not at home, a wee bit of fear if I am being honest. I knew what they were capable of.

Yet that defeat proved the start of a great run in which we lost just once in 12 games, moving from 12th to seventh in the Premier League and beating Exeter City, after a replay, Birmingham and

Preston to reach the quarter-finals of the FA Cup. Unfortunately, we then lost 2-1 to Aston Villa at Goodison. Joe-Max Moore got our goal in that game and proved a good addition to our squad. His was a name that I remembered from my college football days and he was what I would call a proper, 'God dammit' American. He was hard-working, wanted to hone his finishing all the time, could score a goal and was aggressive.

Abel Xavier was another newcomer and a really good guy, even though he looked a bit strange with his bleached beard and quiff. He was another worker and he was up for it, proof that appearances can be deceptive. He may have looked a bit like Poseidon, the Greek god of the sea, but he could play and was good about the place although he did take a bit of stick, particularly when Gazza later arrived at the club. They hit it off and used to have a laugh with each other and keep the place going.

Mark Hughes, in contrast, was very quiet. He just came in, did his work and got off home again. Mark would sit in the corner of the dressing-room and never interacted much. The boys used to have a laugh at the way he trained because he was really poor. His career was fantastic, but he was rubbish in training. He'd played for Barcelona, Bayern Munich, Manchester United, three of the biggest clubs in the world, so you could not question his pedigree, but maybe he was one of these guys who needed it to be competitive to get going properly. By that stage he was a bit older, playing in midfield and doing a job for the team. With all these players I had images of what they would be like and discovered they were just normal people. Just like the dressing-room at Falkirk, but they had been at bigger clubs and were bigger names. That's why I always say to young lads in Scotland now not to be in awe of them because they are just people. They will have media profiles and you will have an impression of them, but they are just the same as you. It's not as different as some people would have you believe.

Our season in the League petered out after our FA Cup defeat to Villa and we even dropped out of the top half of the table when we lost at home to Middlesbrough on the final day of the season. That was a sour note to end on but at least we had been safe all season long, establishing ourselves in mid-table. It might not have sounded much, but after the relegation battles of the previous three years, it represented progress.

Yet there was more upheaval in the summer. Don Hutchison had fallen out with the manager over a new contract and left for Sunderland, while John Collins headed to Fulham, but the biggest blow to our morale was probably Nick Barmby refusing a new contract and moving across Stanley Park to Liverpool for £6m. It was a big deal because Nick was back in the England squad and Everton were proud of helping him get him back to that level, as he had been a prodigy when he was younger. He was the poster boy at Everton at the time. Crossing the park to play for 'them' was not quite Rangers–Celtic, but not far away. To do it direct, as blatantly as that, was a big, big thing. Nick was a brave lad, that was the way he played and the way he was. I am sure he would have had the pick of a few clubs and could have gone elsewhere with less hassle. He was top-class at the time.

The manager used the money to bring an interesting bunch of new signings to the club before the 2000–01 season started. Alessandro Pistone, Steve Watson, Thomas Gravesen, Niclas Alexandersson, Alex Nyarko, Paul Gascoigne and Duncan Ferguson. The dressing-room certainly promised to be lively with that lot bouncing around inside it.

Thomas Gravesen's arrival for his first training session sticks in my mind. He wasn't late but he must just have got a flight over to meet up with the rest of us. We were training as far away from the gates at Bellefield as you could go and I just saw this lad jogging over with his shirts pulled up, a wee tight T-shirt on and completely bald. It was like a character out of a comic. Yet again, though, appearances were deceptive. Thomas may have looked like a hard man but was actually a ball player and the famous story that Real Madrid later signed him when they actually meant to get Lee Carsley as a midfield enforcer is believable. In training, Thomas was the best I have seen at keeping possession, at finding an angle, making a pass – he never gave the ball away. We used to joke that Tommy had never been in the middle all year when we played possession games. Once, when he did lose possession, he refused to go in the middle. 'It's not me, I am not going in the middle,' he said and that was that. He was also the best I saw at head tennis. We used to play it in the gym at Bellefield in a corner with a wall side and an open side. Tommy could play either side and was unbeatable when he played. One of the best technical players I have played with. He had what people call 'soft feet', meaning he had good control, and could see a pass and play it over any range.

He was car daft and at one stage I think he had a Porsche Turbo, a Mercedes SL63 and a Range Rover, three 100-grand cars basically. He just rotated them and had them parked underneath his apartment in Liverpool. Then, as soon as the winter came, he sold all of them and came in a Nissan Micra that was worth five or ten grand and drove it for the next six months. That was Tommy for you. Different. The boys would be like, 'Tommy, how the hell can you go from a Porsche to a Micra.' He would just say, 'It is raining, cheap insurance, why would I drive these cars in the wet?' Thomas was completely mental, but likeable with it. He was really strong-willed and would argue to the end of the world if he believed something was right. There was no backing down, he just couldn't see another person's opinion. Now, he changes his home like he used to change his cars. Living in Liverpool for three months, Miami three months, Las Vegas for three months and Denmark for three months of each year.

Gazza obviously came with a bit of baggage and a big reputation, but as a person he was great. He was always first into training. He virtually lived in Bellefield. By that time he didn't have his family with him. He was on his own living in a hotel and he was in for training at 8am when they were opening the place up, having his breakfast and playing head tennis all day. He was full of fun, I really liked him and got on well with him. Gazza held Walter in high regard. You always got the impression he respected Walter and wanted to please him. He thought he kind of looked after him and gave him some of his better football years, so you always had the idea he just wanted Walter to be happy with him. Archie was the one who managed him from day to day, who would be on his case all the time. Gazza would moan about Archie, but he secretly liked that somebody was as interested in him as that and cared enough about him. He wanted to be loved, basically. He would go through phases where he would be in the gym doing sit-up after sit-up. He would be doing a thousand sit-ups and his body would be like a body builder's with the muscle definition but he wouldn't be able to play on a Saturday because he wasn't fit. He was addicted to the gym and to exercise.

He always talked about his book, the excellent autobiography he later produced with Hunter Davies. He was fixated with money, always worried about having enough to survive, and said to me,

'When I write my book, I'll be okay.' I liked him and tried to reassure him about it. I said I knew I would like to read it and was sure other people would, too. *Who Wants to be a Millionaire?* was the big TV show at the time and when the computer game came out we all played it on the bus on our laptops on the way to games, it was good fun. Gazza got into it to the point of an obsession and he must have thought I was clever because I received 'Phone a Friend' calls, as Fiona will testify, all night from him and first thing in the morning. He would give me the question, I'd say, 'Go D, Gazza' or whatever and he would just hang up, then phone you back an hour later. That summed him up, but you couldn't help but like him.

Duncan had been sold to Newcastle without the manager's consent by Peter Johnson and now returned as captain under Walter. The supporters adored him. He was aggressive and with the right service you just couldn't handle him. Of current-day players, Andy Carroll is very similar to Duncan. I made my debut against him for Falkirk and played against him for Everton when he was at Newcastle. If he was up for it, he got the whole dressing-room up for it. He was a leader in that respect. There's not been many of them in my career, but, when the occasion took him, he could definitely be like that. On his game he was fantastic, but he wasn't fit for a lot of the games.

He would get sent off a lot of the time because he just got frustrated. I don't know if it was because his body wouldn't let him do what he wanted to do. He just had this aggression he couldn't get out, for whatever reason, but he was a top, top player even in training. He didn't train all the time, but when he did he loved it. We used to do finishing after training, just having a bit of fun, but he was very serious about it and took pride in his work and always wanted to be the best. He used to buzz if one of the boys said, 'You were good today, big man.' Gary, Faddy and I used to love saying that to him. He would say, 'Thanks, I thought I was, I was brilliant today.' Or if you went the other way and said, 'You weren't the best today', he would say, 'Aye, but I wasn't the worst.' He would be in the gym doing weights and wouldn't lift big weights but if some of the boys did use big weights, showing off a wee bit, Duncan would just go in and do 10 with the big weights to show he was streets ahead of them. He liked to let you know without you thinking he was letting you know.

If his kids were being christened, he would invite everybody. If you turned up, he was genuinely pleased and appreciated it. If people didn't turn up, then he held it against them. He would be devastated by people not turning up, and rightly so. James Beattie got into bother for something – I think he was carrying a case of beer and was in the paper with a girl. Something that was nothing, but he was in the papers down there which was unusual. Duncan had a christening the next day for one of his kids and a few lads never turned up, leaving just empty seats in a marquee in his beautiful garden, yet Beatts turned up even though it would have been easy for him to make an excuse that day and Duncan appreciated that. He loved kids. Later on my boys would come into training with me sometimes and he was brilliant with them. He would make a fuss of them and would really buzz off the kids, even the fans who were kids. Young children especially, he was really good with them.

I really liked Duncan and still do. He kept himself to himself, he wasn't overpowering or someone who dominated the conversation or anything like that, but he always had an input and was held in high regard, almost feared a wee bit. He was very quiet but menacing, yet on the other side of it you could laugh at him. He hated Jim McLean, his former manager at Dundee United, with a passion.

Gary or Faddy would bring in the *Daily Record*, which Jim had a column in, and he would occasionally mention Duncan. The big man would be furious at this. 'Is he still making a living off of me? I built that stadium and painted it for him,' he would say. When the YTS or the young pros got into trouble at Tannadice, McLean would send them to labour with the workmen to teach them a lesson. Apparently, Duncan was the only YTS who had a hard hat with his name on it.

We used to get some laughs out of him. You could tell his wife dressed him in the morning. He was always immaculate. He always had smart trousers on while the rest of the boys wore jeans. Trousers, shoes, jacket, shirt, he would really look the part. He took his role as captain seriously, too. It was just an old-fashioned dressing-room at Bellefield, but the captain had this steel locker, like a seat with a big padlock on it, and gave the key to the kitman and he would just have a wedge of money in there. Whatever happened through the year, we would just keep it for Christmas. Duncan would always be unlocking it, looking at the money, counting it and putting it back in for the Christmas night out but his plans for our bash in December 2000 fell flat, much to his chagrin. Duncan had organised this bar which printed tickets for you and you gave them out to who you wanted to have them, girls basically for the younger lads. We were going fancy dress into Liverpool and had organised this nightclub with tickets again for that. Everything was organised down to the final detail and everybody had paid for everything. It would cost a small fortune and had been talked about for weeks but, as is always the case, the game before the Christmas night out turned into a disaster. We lost 5-0 to Manchester City at Maine Road. Gary Naysmith scored an own goal and it was one of those days when everything that could go wrong went wrong. I was staying in Cheshire at the time and was surrounded by City fans. It was like my worst nightmare. After the game, Archie said, 'You are not having a Christmas night out, you can't possibly have one now, so don't even think about it.' So Christmas was cancelled and we were in the next day. I think we ended up going out for a few drinks anyway, but it was an absolute disaster and Duncan was gutted.

That defeat was our worst of an awful campaign. We were in the bottom half of the table all season long and finished 16th. We were knocked out of the League Cup on penalties by Bristol Rovers. I missed our 3-0 home defeat by Tranmere in the fourth round of the FA Cup at Goodison, but cringed as I sat watching Paul Rideout tear us apart. Things were going from bad to worse and the fans were getting increasingly unhappy. In April, we lost 3-2 at home in the derby as Gary McAllister bent a late free kick into our net from what seemed miles out. Walking off, I was absolutely gutted, and Phil Thompson was walking ahead of me saying, 'We deserved that.' I got a drink bottle from the masseur, wee Jimmy Comer, turned round, threw it and it hit him on the back of the shoulder. He turned round and wee Jimmy was standing there with all the water bottles looking as guilty as sin. Thompson later said in his book that he liked to see a bit of fire like that in a player and that he thought Liverpool should have signed me when he scouted me with Houllier.

When we lost 4-1 at Arsenal in April, one of the punters came onto the pitch and offered his shirt to Alex Nyarko, our midfielder, which shattered him. Walter and Archie couldn't believe it. Fair enough, it hadn't really happened for Alex. You could tell the talent he had by some of the things he did and he could have become a top player but he just couldn't put all the pieces together. I don't know whether he didn't have long enough or it wasn't the right kind of football for him, but he was a very genuine, humble guy and that just destroyed him. He couldn't get his head round what had happened. In his eyes, he was giving his best and this punter had come on and basically said to him, 'I could do a better job than you.' That was the end of him and we all knew we could be next if things didn't improve at the club in the following season.

6

Your country doesn't need you any more

PEOPLE sometimes laugh at footballers for their short-term view of life. The cliché, of course, is that we are only focused on the next game. In reality, we do look a bit further ahead than that, but we tend not to peer too far into the future. The reason is that you soon come to accept in football that nothing lasts for ever. Players come and go around you, as do managers – just when you are getting used to having them around. I have had a relatively stable career in those terms, yet there is always a demand for change, which threatens the status quo.

The squad which had taken Scotland to the World Cup in France broke up quickly in the years which followed, perhaps too quickly with hindsight. Players were either chased into retirement by the criticism of fans and the press or chose to go on their own terms. Between 1998 and 2002, Scotland lost some pretty serious players and perhaps that left a seed in my own mind that you don't always get to choose when your international career ends. Your country needs you, until it doesn't need you any more.

I saw it happen to guys like Jim Leighton and Gary McAllister in our bid to reach the finals of Euro 2000 in Belgium and Holland. I remember sitting talking with John Collins right at the end of that campaign, in the posh hotel in London we were staying in before heading back to Everton together, and him telling me he planned to stop playing for Scotland despite the 1-0 win at Wembley we had just been part of. I couldn't get my head round it. John and Barry Ferguson had just passed England off the park on their own pitch and we had almost salvaged qualification after losing 2-0 to them at Hampden. It looked like they could play together for years to come, setting a measured tone to our play in midfield. I thought John was mad to stop when it seemed he still had so much to offer. I couldn't imagine making the same decision as him back then, but I have since come to understand exactly what went through his head.

He saw a chance to go out on a high, with a good memory. He was sensible enough to realise that. He had watched several other Scotland players go out ingloriously, with the fine service they had given their country largely forgotten at the end. All the lads we lost in that campaign had been successful, established players and it never really came to a glorious end for any of them, did it? Your abiding memory of Gary, Jim Leighton and Andy Goram, and all these guys who served their country so well, isn't what it should be really. It was tarnished to an extent by how it ended for them all.

When you are at the age I was back then, 27, and just breaking into the team, you see this happening to these lads and you just take for granted that it's a natural progression. Then, suddenly, you become one of the older lads yourself and realise how significant it was for them. As a young person coming into the squad you don't see it with the same eyes, whereas older players will watch the young lads coming in and it will remind them, I suppose, of how quickly they have gone from being a novice to being considered a veteran. Your life in football flies past and it can all be over before you know it.

All this stuff was probably in my psyche later on, when the

Faroes row happened, which I will discuss later in detail. How had I gone from being a newcomer in 1997 to one of the senior players by 2002? It was just five years, yet that transition for me showed the turnover Scotland had seen in personnel during that period. You start to get pretty cynical about it when you see the same thing happen to so many senior players. You think it goes with the territory, you get it in your mind that this is how it is all going to end for pretty much everybody. Players strive to get to that magical 50th cap which gets them into the Hall of Fame or Roll of Honour or whatever it is called now. I saw them do it and it was always in my own mind, too, every time I turned up, but there is a counter-argument that you can overstay your welcome and that instead of being able to choose the manner and timing of your departure you have it forced upon you.

Some people saw our heavy defeat by Morocco at the World Cup as a natural end for Craig and many of his players. Jim Leighton, for example, was blamed for at least one of the goals and maybe a few people were waiting to pounce on him after that. He had turned 40 that summer and people were starting to refer to his age when he made mistakes, just as they will do now with me. Yet when younger players make the same mistakes their age isn't an issue, is it? When Jim made those mistakes for Manchester United in the 1990 FA Cup final against Crystal Palace and was famously dropped for the replay by Alex Ferguson, his age wasn't mentioned as a factor.

I missed our opening Euro 2000 qualifier in Lithuania but he kept a clean sheet there, although it was soon forgotten when we laboured to a 3-2 win over Estonia at Tynecastle in our next match. That proved to be Jim's 91st and last cap for his country. He became the scapegoat for a poor performance by all of us. It was a sunny day at Tynecastle and Estonia were really up for the game. We were twice behind and required three goals in the last 20 minutes, two of them from the effervescent Billy Dodds. I was really disappointed afterwards – it was my home stadium and though we had won it felt more like a defeat, like we had got out of jail with the late goals.

Estonia were far from the worst team in the world, but we had scraped a win when we were expected to roll them over. Craig was angry afterwards – he didn't like losing soft goals to anybody and we weren't used to losing goals like that under him. Scotland had qualified for two successive tournaments on the basis of not conceding goals and being hard to beat.

Billy also scored in our next game, a 2-1 win over the Faroes at Pittodrie. We were 2-0 up at half-time but got sloppy in the second half and conceded one from a late penalty. It came straight off the back of the Estonia game, the following midweek, and you could definitely feel the anxiety surrounding it. Hampden was being renovated at the time and the games were being taken round the country and that special feeling, that certain electricity, the Glasgow international games have got was missing. It was definitely different. Maybe for friendlies it works, but for qualifiers it definitely removed some of the edge for me. It became more like playing these countries at a neutral venue. I think it's also a fact we are not comfortable when we are the favourites and expected to take the initiative. I don't think it suits us to go and force a game and open up a bit and be expansive. I think we are better sitting tight, being quite dogged and taking our chance when it comes along. As soon as we take too many chances, we suffer for it. It has been a pattern in our football for quite some time now.

The next casualty was Gary McAllister. He had scored that vital penalty in Belarus to take us to the World Cup finals but had missed out on them with a knee injury. Yet as we lost 2-1 at home to a strong Czech Republic side at Celtic Park, our first home defeat in a qualifier since 1987, all that counted for nothing with some supporters, who booed him in the second half after he misplaced a pass. That was really sad. I remember driving back down to Liverpool right after it and thinking to myself how harsh an end it had been for Gary. He had just missed the World Cup with a bad injury after playing a big, big part in helping the team qualify, so there was no personal satisfaction from that for him, no involvement. He had just come back from that and now his international career, after 57 caps and being captain of Scotland, ended with him being treated like that.

People failed to appreciate that the Czechs were a very good side, having added new talents to the team which had reached the final of Euro 96 in England. They had creative players like Vladimír Šmicer, Patrik Berger and Pavel Nedvěd at the peak of their careers. They killed us with two goals inside eight minutes in the first half and I was annoyed I allowed Šmicer to get in behind me for the second of them. We pulled one back in the second half through Eoin Jess and came close to an equaliser a couple of times but it ended as a damaging defeat.

Gary announced his international retirement in the aftermath and we all understood his reasons. It was a transitional time and the player who had come on to replace Gary against the Czechs was one who would make an immediate impact, albeit a short-lived one. Don Hutchison was a really good footballer and a lad who took to the international stage and thought to himself, 'I belong here.' He was with me at Everton at the time but you just never felt with Don that he was in it for the long term. He was a bit of a chancer and had a few ups and downs in his career, but I liked him.

He was funny and could also make cutting comments that bordered on cruel. He was ruthless in that respect. He could destroy opposition players on the pitch with his remarks. For example, I remember him giving Chris Sutton terrible stick one day in the season when Sutton was struggling at Chelsea after his £10m transfer there from Blackburn Rovers. Don was a bit of maverick character who saw this as sledging and thought it could help his team win games. It was all a bluff in my opinion, but with some people it worked. Don just thought, 'I'll have a bit of this and see where it takes me.' He could play all right, though, he could find a pass, was good in the air and could play up front or in midfield. He had been round the block a wee bit, as high as Liverpool and as low as Hartlepool, so he had seen all sides of the game and was determined to enjoy his 15 minutes of fame to the full.

Don scored the winner in our next match, a 1-0 win over Germany in Bremen that got the critics off Craig's back to an extent. I was playing right wing-back, which I did a lot at that point for Everton and Scotland. It didn't bother me one bit. I was athletic enough for it and I wasn't one of these people, rightly or wrongly, who would say, 'This is my best position' or 'That's where I want to play', I just wanted to be in the team. It gave me more strings to my bow in terms of getting a game and it worked for me.

That night I was marking a lad called Horst Heldt, who was in their team alongside more famous names like Lothar Matthäus, Didi Hamann, Jens Lehmann and Oliver Bierhoff. It was a really good performance in our new salmon pink away strip. It was certainly a proper game because the Germans wouldn't like getting beaten, especially at home. They were under a bit of pressure themselves at the time. It was typical Craig to pick what looked like a tough game, but one where he thought he could get a result. He was clever that way, picking Germany when he knew they were perhaps not at their best. He maybe pinpointed them and thought to himself that might be a game to get us back on track because he wouldn't take a game on if he thought there wasn't going to be something in it.

Colin Cameron and Paul Ritchie, two of my former Hearts teammates, came on for their first caps that night, too. I had just joined Everton and I really looked forward to coming up to the Scotland games and meeting up. It's amazing how quickly you drift out of what's happening in the Scottish scene living down in England, so it was good to get back in among all the gossip. Yet sometimes the distance of playing and living in England was good for me after a Scotland game. You are in a car, you go down south and it's like you shut that door and open another one. You were going back to sanity almost. If you are an Old Firm and Scotland player, you might have to live with the ramifications of the game or your own performance in it for weeks afterwards.

The majority of the time, I would just jump in my car and drive down that night and if Gary Naysmith was there he would come with me. Different people did different things. The London lads would stay overnight and fly down in the morning. I could have flown down, but rarely did, I just drove. Players can't sleep after games, you see. We are knackered physically, but mentally we are stimulated. I always remember hearing the stories about Alan Hansen, Kenny Dalglish, Graeme Souness and Stevie Nicol driving down to Liverpool after games and stopping and getting a fish supper on the way. That's where your memories are made as a football player. The time afterwards in the car with your pals when you are caning everybody else's performance. Without fail, there's always somebody in the car saying, 'I never played. I am not going back.' Despite the late-night drive, I would also look forward to going into training the next morning. Invariably there would be five or six lads who had been away with various countries, so everybody comes back with different stories and gossip, talking about the players they had played against and comparing notes.

Fiona and I were getting married in June 1999, but before that there was another double-header. Away to the Faroes first, then on to Prague to try and exact some revenge on the Czechs if possible. The first match ended in disappointment. We led for most of it through Allan Johnston's goal but then conceded a headed equaliser right at the death. Matt Elliott took the brunt of the blame afterwards for getting sent off, but we should still have been able to see the game out without him and his aerial prowess. Craig was furious with Matt. The worst thing you could do in his eyes was to let your teammates down and let yourself down by being sent off needlessly. I never saw Matt's altercation with Todi Jónsson, the Faroes' best player, but I heard it. It was the loudest crack because Matt was a big lad and he must have caught him perfectly. Some people said it was a slap and others an elbow afterwards, but it definitely sounded like a punch to me and I can't imagine big Matt slapping somebody. We were all pretty down afterwards. We knew that two points dropped in a game like that in June could be the difference between qualifying and not qualifying.

Matt's red card meant he was also suspended for our meeting with the Czechs and their two towering strikers, Vratislav Lokvenc and Jan Koller. Yet we started superbly, taking the lead through a Paul Ritchie header and going 2-0 up just after the hour when Allan Johnston scored another good goal. Then the roof caved in on us. They got a goal back through Tomáš Řepka then took

Lokvenc off and put Koller on, which was like replacing a giant with an ogre. Lokvenc was massive and you thought you had just come out of the woods and then they brought a bigger one on. They equalised and Koller scored the winner for them right at the death. It was a free kick swung in and a header basically and I remember thinking before it, 'We are hanging on here, a good ball and we are in trouble because with the right delivery, there's not a lot you are going to be able do with this guy.' I remember having a bad, bad feeling about it. With hindsight, that was the pivotal game of the campaign. You wouldn't expect a Craig Brown team that is 2-0 up after an hour of an international game to lose, but we suddenly had an issue with conceding goals.

When our campaign resumed in September we needed to win over Bosnia in Sarajevo and did so with a good overall perform- ance and goals from Don Hutchison and Billy Dodds, yet it was a trip I remember more for the signs of war all around us than what happened in the Kosevo Stadion. Sarajevo had been a city under siege during the Bosnian War from 1992 to 1995 and it still showed. It was only that summer that the Nato bombing of nearby Kosovo had ceased. Horrific things had happened, like the mass rape of thousands of Bosnian Muslim women by Serbian soldiers and various other war crimes and the people were still numb, trying to put their lives slowly back together. Landing at the airport and getting the bus to the hotel, we were just driving through a battlefield basically. They were cemeteries everywhere and buildings which bullets had obviously rained over. It was like a movie scene. Horrific. I wouldn't say there were tanks aban- doned or anything like that, there was still life going on, but it was as if the war had just ended and I suppose it had in historical terms. It seemed like you had just stumbled on this place where the people were just coming out of hiding after living in terror for several years.

The hotel we stayed in was fine, but being there put football firmly into perspective compared to what had gone on. Footballers can sometimes be hermetically sealed off from the reality of where we play. We land at the airport, get on our bus, go to our hotel, go to the stadium, play our match and then go home again. That game did broaden our minds, purely because we couldn't miss it. I have been on some trips, like to Athens with Rangers, where we have gone to see the Acropolis and be tourists, but this wasn't like that, this was like you were subjected to it, whether you liked it or not and that affects you as a person for good or bad. You could just tell that not everything had been as easy in life for the people who were serving you in the hotel as it had been for you. You could see in their eyes some of the stuff they had been through.

We then drew in Estonia, another slip-up, before beating Bosnia 1-0 at Ibrox in a forgettable match settled by a first-half penalty from John Collins. At least we were keeping clean sheets again and we secured a place in the Euro 2000 playoffs with a convincing 3-0 win over Lithuania as we returned to the completed Hampden. The thing that struck me that day was that as well as a new stadium we also had a new team. Just over a year after the World Cup the team that had played in it had gone. Besides myself, the only other survivors from France the previous summer in our starting line-up were Craig Burley, Paul Lambert and Christian Dailly.

England were also in the playoffs and it was almost inevitable we would be drawn against them. There was huge hype and plenty of banter at Everton in the build-up, although if anything the Scots outnumbered the English among our players back then. Myself, John Collins and Don Hutchison were all regulars in Craig's side at the time and we were all looking forward to it immensely. These are the sort of games you want to take part in during your career, after all, the sort I had dreamed of participating in when I used to go and watch them at Hampden with my dad or watched the games from Wembley on television.

The England side we would face was managed by Kevin Keegan and packed with good players – Tony Adams, Sol Campbell, Paul Ince, David Beckham, Alan Shearer and Michael Owen, but Paul Scholes was the pick of the lot for me and the one who did the damage in the first leg at Hampden, ghosting into our box to score two first-half goals and silence the crowd. Going through my career, Scholes was the best I played against based on his consistency and what he did in big games at big times. He's very quiet on the pitch. I have met him a couple of times and he's like that off the pitch, too. Yet he's aggressive and a proper football player. A pros' pro if you like. He's just a wee ginger guy, almost Scottish in appearance, but he's the real deal.

Beckham's delivery for one of the goals was also from the top drawer. We missed Paul Lambert, who was out with a fractured jaw sustained in an Old Firm game around that time and had developed into an accomplished defensive midfielder after a spell at Borussia Dortmund before returning to Scotland with Celtic.

It was a deflating defeat after the big build-up, but we didn't have time to feel too sorry for ourselves or dwell on it, as it was a quick turnaround for the second game. Craig never let us feel like we were out of it, he still had you feeling like you had a chance, that you were well in it. You look at it now, coldly, and you have lost the game 2-0 at home and are going away against the same opposition, so your chances should be pretty slim, but I guess we couldn't afford to think like that at the time. Instead, we went down there believing this was the last throw of the dice and we had nothing to lose.

This defiant mood was reinforced when we scored seven minutes before half-time. Neil McCann created the chance with a fine run and cross and Don rose to nod it in. England couldn't get the ball off us as John and Barry Ferguson excelled in central midfield. Barry had come into the squad with a big reputation as something special, but he was quiet and respectful around the place, just learning the ropes and not really making a big impact at first. His performance against England was probably when he announced himself and did what everybody knew he was capable of.

Their own crowd started to turn on England. It definitely felt like they were running on empty, that was the impression I got. You could see in their eyes they were really struggling with the expectation. We began to suspect that if we could score a second and force extra time then they would crumble. You just got the feeling they were on the ropes. I always say to people if we had scored we would have gone on to win, but it is the easiest thing in the world to say that. The fact is we didn't score. We almost did with a Christian Dailly header late in the game which unfortunately went straight at David Seaman and allowed him to make an instinctive save, when if it had gone a yard either side of him it would probably have been a goal.

At least we had salvaged a bit of pride after the first game and done ourselves justice in one of the last matches played at the old Wembley, but overall it was an opportunity missed. Qualifying at England's expense would have made us all legends. Games like that are career-defining. In the second game, we played really well, created chances and maybe just never got that wee bit of luck you need to turn round a 2-0 defeat away from home. It was another addition to the canon of Scotland going down with all guns blazing, yet going down all the same.

I hadn't been at Euro 96 obviously, but the team had become accustomed to qualifying so it was a wee bit of a slap in the face that we hadn't. You could tell the media was turning on Craig at the time. It had been Andy Roxburgh then Craig, down that school-teacher road as some saw it, the Largs mafia, and some in the press at the time seemed to want some new-fangled approach and coach. It's funny to recall what we were judging ourselves on then, whereas now Craig would probably be getting a knighthood for his achievements. He was bringing in new players like Barry Ferguson and Neil McCann, both of who had been excellent in the game against England at Wembley.

Longevity seems to breed success and probably if we knew then what we know now, Craig would have stayed in the job for a bit longer because he was gradually reshaping the team and he was getting good results in difficult places like Germany and England. Although we never qualified for the tournament, there was an evolution of the team. Yet it did feel like the knives were out for him and probably not naturally, probably a wee bit forced in some quarters. The players wanted to protect him from that because he was really fair with us and all the lads that were there were players he had brought in and given their caps. It wasn't as though they were other people's players, so there was loyalty towards him from the squad.

We were determined to put things right by qualifying for World Cup 2002, to be held in Japan and South Korea, and felt we had a good chance of making it from a group which had accomplished sides like Belgium and Croatia in it, but none of the traditional heavyweights of Europe such as France, Italy or Germany. Our friendly results in the spring after the playoff had been encouraging. We lost 2-0 at home to France, but they were the best side in the world at that point and about to add a Euro 2000 triumph to their World Cup win of 1998. We then drew 0-0 with a strong Holland side containing Dennis Bergkamp, Edwin Van der Sar and Frank de Boer in Arnhem and went to Dublin to beat the Republic of Ireland 2-1. It looked like we had rediscovered our former resilience on the road, which augured well.

We certainly needed it in our first World Cup qualifier away to Latvia. They played us off the park that day and were much the better team. In the summer Lucas was born and I'd also had Achilles and hernia operations and just got back to fitness. Fiona picked me up from the hospital having had Lucas and I couldn't walk or help her with him. We were all just out of hospital. Fortunately, my mum and dad came down to help us out. I remember the Latvia game because I got a kick on my Achilles that cut it open and I had to come off at half-time. I thought I had damaged it again, but fortunately it wasn't as bad as it looked. Their forwards, Andrejs Rubins, Marians Pahars and Andrejs Stolcers, were all wee nippy guys who caused us problems. Igors Stepanovs, one of their defenders, was about to sign for Arsenal and I am sure Arsène Wenger was at the game to watch him. My recollection is that we stole it through a goal from Neil McCann two minutes from the end. Nevertheless, it was precisely the sort of result and performance which had typified Scotland's previous successful campaigns under Craig.

We followed it with a 2-0 win in San Marino and were allowed a couple of beers afterwards in Rimini, the Italian resort we were staying in. We got into this bar or club that had a relaxed door policy and Archie Knox, who was Craig's assistant at the time, was patrolling outside trying to get everybody out. We all had jeans on but Archie had a tracksuit, so they wouldn't let him in, or maybe they figured they would be losing our custom if they let him in to march us all out. You can picture the scene with Archie getting increasingly agitated and us out of his reach but in full view enjoying ourselves. The whole squad was there and it was a pretty lively night. There was a good atmosphere because we had won two away games to start the campaign.

Our next assignment was a tougher one as we travelled on to Zagreb to face Croatia. Robert Prosinecki was their playmaker and star turn and was out of this world in that game. I can remember him doing a stepover about six times and us all laughing at the state he left whoever was marking him in at the time. He couldn't run or move much and he played as if he was having a fag, but he was still some player. They started well and scored through Alen Bokšić but we replied quickly through Kevin Gallacher after a typical Colin Cameron surge into the opposition box. Although Prosinecki later curled a shot against our post, it was much more like the sort of disciplined away performances which had become Scotland's trademark under Craig, who was sent to the stand that night after some heated dialogue with the French referee.

Our good run was ended by a 2-0 defeat by Australia in a friendly which I chiefly recall for the antics of Kevin Muscat, who was later to play for Rangers. Muscat was able to mimic the referee's whistle and used this tactic repeatedly during the match. He had a bit of reputation in the game for wild tackles and I didn't take to him, although his teammate Danny Tiatto, the wee bald left-sided guy from Manchester City, was all right, as I discovered when we travelled back down to the north-west together afterwards. Craig was trying to rebuild and used that game to give Dom Matteo his debut. He was at Leeds, who were doing really well at the time. Matt Elliott, Dominic, Neil Sullivan, Don Hutchison, were all effectively Englishmen playing for Scotland and that was a talking point, but they were all definitely adding to the team and being a big part of it, so we had no problem with it. Apart from anything else, they were all bigger than us. It is almost like the English lads are all big men and Scottish lads are wee boys, like our genetic code has to mix with someone else before we get to be a decent size.

All four of them were in our starting line-up in the spring of 2001 for what proved to be the pivotal game of this campaign and perhaps proved a turning point in the history of the national team when you consider the decade since. We were 2-0 up against Belgium at Hampden after half an hour. Billy Dodds scored both, the second from the penalty spot after Eric Deflandre handled and was sent off. We were playing some good stuff and looked comfortable, but after half-time they were a different side with Marc Wilmots, their captain, setting the tone with an amazing performance in midfield and a goal just before the hour. He was their best player, but they also had quick forwards like Bart Goor and Émile Mpenza who stretched us. They were a good team, but we had the game won. Moments before Wilmots pulled that goal back, we should have gone 3-0 ahead when Dom Matteo picked out Barry Ferguson with a ball into the box but Barry couldn't quite steer his finish past Geert de Vlieger, their goalkeeper.

Collectively, we should still have closed the game out but instead found ourselves under siege after Wilmots' goal. I remember the free kick they scored from in stoppage time like it was yesterday. It all seemed to happen in slow motion, Wilmots taking it, Daniel

Van Buyten, who was a big guy and talked about at the time as something special, winning the header and the ball going into our net. Until that point, Matt Elliott had been heading everything away, but it was a bit like a rerun of the loss to the Czechs in Prague except with Van Buyten doing the damage rather than Koller and us conceding even later this time.

Colin Hendry had won his 50th cap against the Belgians, yet his next proved to be his last in yet another instance of a distinguished Scotland career ending amid controversy. It all looked good for Colin as he scored twice in the first half of our 4-0 win over San Marino at Hampden, but then he elbowed Nicola Albani, who had just come on as a substitute, in frustration at having his jersey pulled in the final minute of the match. The referee missed it, but Colin was subsequently hit with a three-match ban by Fifa which effectively ended his international career.

It was around this time, too, that Kevin Gallacher was also approaching the end of his. The two of them were close from their time together at Blackburn and had always come as a bit of a package around the squad. Craig used our next friendly, a 1-1 draw in Poland, to try out a host of new faces, trying to cap as many players as he possibly could to reward them for turning up when many others had called off.

Despite the draw with Belgium, we were still in reasonable shape as we approached the conclusion of our World Cup qualifying campaign in the autumn of 2001. Another double-header, this time at home to Croatia and then away to Belgium, would decide whether we qualified automatically, went into the playoffs or missed a second consecutive major tournament. The first game against the Croats on a grey, September afternoon proved a non-event as they used their experience to get the 0-0 draw they needed.

So we headed to Brussels with a great support, some 12,000 of the Tartan Army, in tow and requiring a result to stay in contention. Unfortunately, we got a bit of a doing and the first defeat of the campaign effectively ended our hopes. We started cautiously and allowed them to take the lead. Then, as we pushed for an equaliser, they hit us on the break in the final minute and Bart Goor scored. They were a good team but we knew we had let them off the hook at Hampden.

We were all but out and Hampden was only half full for our final match at home to Latvia. To reach the World Cup playoffs we had to win by six clear goals and hope Belgium could win in Croatia. In the event, neither happened. The Latvians were lively again and took an early lead with Andrejs Rubins scoring. Dougie Freedman, who played at Crystal Palace with Rubins, equalised with a header just before half-time on his debut and eight minutes into the second half I scored my one and only Scotland goal with a downward header. I was out of control that day, actually, as I got myself booked as well.

It also proved the last goal of the Craig Brown era, as he stepped down as manager after eight years in charge. Craig Burley made a nice speech in the dressing-room and all the players recognised how good Craig had been with us and for us. As I said, he had brought every single one of us into his team and given us our caps, so there was definitely an affinity with him and it was really sad to see him go. I think there was a feeling we had let him down a bit, too. You should question yourself when you don't qualify. You are playing against Croatia, Belgium and the Czech Republic, after all, teams you would consider yourself on a par with and knowing you have got to beat them in order to qualify and we weren't doing that regularly enough. We were doing all right against the lesser teams, we were picking up results there. The Latvias and the San Marinos and all the rest of it, but we just weren't winning enough of the big ones. The Czech Republic one would have been a great result with a young team, but the Belgium one at home, when we had got ourselves in a position to win with what was by then an experienced team, was worse in a way. That was the moment in the campaign when I felt it turned against us.

I now began to truly appreciate what we had before and again that I'd got to a World Cup basically without doing anything. The years were starting to creep by and we now realised how difficult it was to get to a finals. The team Craig had got success with was an established team, but you didn't feel like that yet with this team. It was still evolving and we had missed a couple of tournaments along the way now. We'd lost two big playmakers in Gary McAllister and then John Collins and a lot of experience had gone out of the team. Within the campaigns, it always seems there is one game that lets Scotland down and we can't afford that one slip-up. That game, whenever it comes along, is our chance and we have to make sure we take it. The difference before was getting the results in those pivotal games. We had just lost the habit of seeing the games out and winning the must-win games.

That probably stemmed from losing the experience of McAllister, Collins, Colin Calderwood, Colin Hendry and so on, boys that had been round the block and had had a wee taste of the major championships. The supporters don't see and don't appreciate what these guys bring when they are calling for them to be replaced by younger alternatives. It then becomes a self-fulfilling prophecy because if you don't qualify, you don't get that experience.

You got the feeling that the mood around the place was to go down another route. What Craig had created had gone. We knew the search for a new manager would start, but I don't think as a player you are too opinionated about it – you have got to trust the people in charge to make those decisions. It is usually a cock-up when players are consulted, the lunatics running the asylum and all that. I have never been consulted over a manager in my life and I wouldn't expect to be. I knew we hadn't qualified for two major championships and that there would be consequences. In an international team the players can't change, but the manager can. Yet it proved to be a case of be careful what you wish for.

7

Lost in translation

MY FALL out with Berti Vogts cost me more than two years of my international career and maybe 20-odd caps, but his appointment as manager at the start of 2002 set Scotland back much more than that as a force to be reckoned with in international football. You could argue the international team is still recovering today. People think I hate Berti, but that's simply not true. In many ways, I felt sorry for him back then and still do now. You could not argue with his achievements as a player and later as a manager. He won the World Cup with West Germany in 1974 as the former and Euro 96 as the coach of the by then unified Germany. Yet all his expertise didn't matter a jot when he took the Scotland job because he simply lacked English good enough to do it properly. I still find myself asking why Berti didn't have a translator to help him deal with the players and the press. It would have helped him a great deal because poor communication seemed to be at the root of all his problems, including the chain of events which led me to stop playing for my country.

I haven't told this story in full before because, perhaps mistakenly, I didn't want to put a knife into Vogts to defend my own actions when he was still Scotland's manager and later, when I returned under Walter Smith, it seemed better to look forward rather than back. Yet it's now time to answer a few of my critics, including the one who sent me a a letter describing me as 'a rat' fleeing a sinking ship and a couple of columnists who told me not to bother coming back. Funnily enough, when I later did, they didn't mention this to me. There was also some criticism from within the Scotland camp itself and that hurt most of all. I feel anybody who was part of that regime and knew what was going on, should have known better because everybody was saying the same things. I did what I did and I am not saying I want a medal for it, but I would have expected more from them.

The Svangaskard stadium in Toftir is a remote outpost in the international game. Playing football at any level on the Faroes is something of a feat in itself. It has been known for referees to order players to crouch to avoid being gusted away by the North Atlantic winds which regularly batter the archipelago and whole stands have disappeared during the night. So you have to admire the ambition of Niclas Davidsen, president of B68, the local club, who raised £1.3m to build the venue where my international career seemed to end on 6 September 2002.

Using 50 tonnes of explosive, workers razed a cliff face behind this village of 1000 people, a church and a fish factory to create the playing surface. Nevertheless with rocky outcrops and grazing sheep in the background it remained a quaint venue, although not to Scottish eyes. We approached it with apprehension and not only because of the hair-raising descent to Vagar airport, the only stretch of land on the islands which was wide and flat enough for a runway. Just.

We had drawn 1-1 there in June 1999, a result which was already up there with Scotland's worst days in international football, and hoped we had seen the last of this spartan place, but the draw for Euro 2004 threw it up as the venue for Vogts' first competitive match in charge of Scotland after the worst run in the international team's 130-year history to that point, five straight defeats from five preparatory friendlies against France, Nigeria, South Korea, South Africa and Denmark. The only win was against a Hong Kong XI, a match Fifa refused to recognise as a full international. By then, many of us on the inside had seen enough of Vogts to know this just wasn't going to work.

Initially, his appointment excited me. I admit I thought he could teach us something by bringing a fresh eye to our football. He decided we would only learn from playing against the best so our first game was away to France, then preparing for World Cup 2002 having just won the previous two major tournaments, World Cup 98 and Euro 2000. It was one of the finest national sides the game has seen, with the likes of Thierry Henry and Zinédine Zidane to top it off and with world-class players in every position really. On the morning of the match, Berti told the boys to go into Paris and have a walk around and get a feel for the city. To footballers, normally cooped up in hotels when abroad, it was an offer we couldn't refuse. So we went walking around Paris unsupervised for hours, had a coffee and a walk down the Champs Élysées, thinking to ourselves, 'This is obviously how the German team won European championships, so why should we be in our beds resting?' You're thinking, maybe naively, we better give it a go. I never went into the game thinking, 'We shouldn't have gone for a walk this morning', but looking back now you see it maybe wasn't such a good idea. Walter Smith allows us a bit of sightseeing time now, but we always do it as a group with the coaching staff around, too, and that, to me, is a sensible compromise between being too strict and too relaxed.

In Berti's defence, given the level France had reached at that time, it probably wouldn't have mattered how good or bad we were on that particular occasion. Nevertheless, the communication problem was already evident. Berti spoke pre-match to the press of how nervous young Kevin McNaughton was, thereby leaving the young lad to live with that label for the rest of his career.

He played Dougie Freedman, a striker, wide on the right of midfield, after asking him if he thought he could do a job there. If it meant turning down a cap for his country, Dougie was hardly going to say he couldn't, was he? During the chaotic match that ensued, Gary Holt was put on and then taken off again because nobody on the bench could understand what Berti was trying to do. At the airport afterwards, Rab Douglas, who thought he'd been told he'd get a game in goal if he came along, had an argument with Berti about how he had been treated in full view of everybody, including the press. It was not an auspicious start at all.

Yet we were still respectful of Vogts' achievements and believed his expertise would soon reveal itself. Next up were Nigeria, also preparing for the World Cup, where they had been drawn in a tough group with Argentina, England and Sweden, and with some extremely talented players like Jay-Jay Okocha and Nwankwo Kanu in their ranks. Although we lost this one 2-1, things seemed to be improving. A tour of the Far East was planned at the end of the season and although we would be without Barry Ferguson and Paul Lambert, the two midfielders Berti said he wanted to build his team around, it was a chance to get to know the man and his methods better and also, if I am brutally honest about it, a chance to pick up a few more caps and move closer to the 50 which would take me into the SFA's Hall of Fame.

Now this jaunt was a real eye-opener, but for all the wrong reasons. We flew first to South Korea, where we ran into the super-charged team that Guus Hiddink was about to unleash on the World Cup. They had been preparing for months at a special fitness camp in the mountains. We were still jet-lagged from a long flight. The advice is that you are supposed to leave one day for each time zone you cross before playing. We crossed nine and then played within 48 hours. Just off the plane with few experienced players, we were like lambs to the slaughter. They tore us apart, winning 4-1, and giving a hint, largely ignored, of the high-tempo style Hiddink had successfully coached into them ahead of the finals. Hiddink was the real deal and spoke impeccable English to get his message across clearly, something that Australia and Chelsea later benefited from.

Next stop for us was Hong Kong, where we were due to play in a triangular tournament against the hosts and South Africa. The setting was spectacular. Our hotel was beautiful and the food, in particular, was amazing, but it was incredibly humid outside and the time difference was still playing havoc with our body clocks. People were catching up on their sleep and missing meetings as a result. I remember being in one of the team meetings and Berti was standing up giving his speech about what we were going to do and nobody could really understand him. The late Tommy Burns, then his assistant, fell asleep and all the players were sitting there nudging each other, grinning and pointing like naughty school-boys while Berti chuntered on oblivious. In fairness, Tommy made a habit of falling asleep and later did it in one of Walter Smith's meetings as well.

You could understand Berti to a point, but you couldn't get the detail he was trying to put across – if there was any. Maybe that was his way, but it felt to me like he was constantly frustrated by his lack of English, that he couldn't communicate what he knew to us. Jim Jefferies, for instance, wouldn't be a great tactician or a great theorist on how the game should be played, but you would certainly know what he was trying to say, whereas with Berti there was a bit of ambiguity as to what he was saying or where you were actually playing. At international level, the devil is in the detail and players need to trust what they are being told and take it in.

This was such a contrast for me with the clever and humorous way Craig Brown would make sure he put his points across. He had this brilliant knack of describing opposition players to you, particularly helpful to defenders. As I explained, he would take a player you knew well from Scotland or England and then slightly adapt them so you knew what you were up against. It would be 'He's a skinny John Robertson' or 'a tall John Robertson' or what-ever. Buried in his reports would be little jokes which he would later bring up to make sure you had read them in full or listened to what he was telling you. It was done in a light-hearted, subtle way but also in a professional one, so you felt properly prepared for the games. Craig also had a nice way when you were playing against the better teams of downplaying their best players, to give you a boost. It would be things like, 'People say he's a great player but not for me', just belittling them a wee bit to make you more confident. Somehow Craig always made you feel good about yourself. It was a knack he had that was so important for us.

That had gone under Vogts for me. There wasn't any enjoyment any more. It was like a different culture getting imposed on you and I don't think you can do that as quickly as he tried to. Maybe gradually you can do it. If you are there for five or 10 years, but it seemed to be overnight we went from something that worked to a certain degree to something that obviously didn't. Compared to Craig's style, it was all so artificial and forced. We had to go down for a beer in the bar at 11pm on the night before games, whether we wanted to or not. After training we had to do two laps round the pitch, 'Two rounds, two rounds, everybody,' Berti would shout, although it was difficult to see the point.

He threw caps around much too freely. Let's be honest, there were a few who won them without having reached a level with their clubs to deserve the honour. Again, it was such a contrast to Craig's time, when you had to earn your chance by turning up for the squads, then getting on the bench and, finally, once you proved you could be trusted at international level, you might get a game. Under Vogts, it felt like, if you were Scottish you got a trial, and a lot of them felt precisely like trial games, there were so many friendlies and so many players used in them. There never seemed to be any coherent strategy in what was going on. As a player, that's not your issue, you go out and play to the best of your ability while you are there and everybody did that, but somewhere along the line you have got to feel like you have a chance. You can only do that for so long before you say to yourself, 'Lambs to the slaughter'. You weren't getting the necessary help you needed.

Berti annoyed me with how he devalued the currency of a Scotland cap and that also applied to the captaincy. Something which is a childhood dream for many Scots seemed not to mean much to him. During the Far East tour, with Barry Ferguson and Paul Lambert missing, he called me, Christian Dailly and Scot Gemmill together to discuss who would captain the team. This was something I had dreamed of. I had seen that picture of Craig Levein with the armband on and in his Scotland strip and said to myself, 'I want that to be me one day.' Berti, though, didn't seem to have a strong opinion on it. I wondered if he was sitting there looking at the three of us, saying, 'Eeny, meany, miny, moe' to himself before choosing Christian because he had one more cap than me. Fair enough, if he had said, 'I am making Christian

captain because he's a great leader, a great player, great professional' or whatever, but it just seemed he hadn't given it too much
thought. I thought then it was perhaps the one chance I would
have of that honour in my life and that's how you get picked to be
the captain of your country. To me, that was just terrifying and I
should have probably seen the dagger coming before it was
plunged into my back after the Faroes debacle.

We were terribly briefed on them by Berti and set up in an
incredibly naive fashion, with players way out of position in a wide
open 4-2-4. I felt for Paul Dickov, a good player and pro, who was
on the wing rather than in his preferred position of striker. Inside
of him, Kevin Kyle, a novice, started simply because Berti was
determined to find a big target man. Maurice Ross and Stephen
Crainey, our full-backs, were just starting out with Rangers and
Celtic and had been pitched in way too early and without much
protection in front of them. It didn't help that their right-winger,
Jakup Borg, was probably their best player and the supply line to
John Petersen, the schoolteacher, who scored twice in the first 12
minutes. You think to yourself this isn't what international football should be about, this isn't what I signed up for. Playing in the
middle of nowhere, with nobody there. I found myself wondering,
even before the game, have we got enough to win this? Myself,
Christian, Barry and Paul were the only four experienced players,
but we should still have enough to beat what was basically a part-
time team. As the game starts, you start to think to yourself, 'Jeez
this is going to be one of those days.' It felt like going playing Mull
or something. I can remember doing that with Hearts or Falkirk
and that's what it was like, playing against lads who didn't look like
players, weren't shaped like players, but they sensed our apprehension and tore into us.

A myth has been allowed to go unchallenged that it was Paul and Barry who took charge at half-time that day. That was just nonsense. Everybody was speaking, so Paul probably did speak, but in regards to tearing a strip off people and so on, that's just nonsense. It just didn't happen. Not when I was in the dressing-room, although it more was like a school classroom from my recollection – one where the teacher wasn't in control of the class. Berti wasn't coherent, he couldn't communicate. You could tell he was angry, but it wasn't a matter of him getting a board up and saying, 'This is what we need to do, you come off, you do this.' That's what Craig Brown or Walter Smith would have been doing. Instead, it was chaos. Utter chaos.

Paul was a guy I liked, but Berti put him on a pedestal because he had played in Germany, almost like he was separate from the rest of us. Paul became more like one of the management than one of the players in this period to my mind, perhaps because he was already thinking of becoming a boss – something he has since done successfully with Norwich City. I am in a similar position now, and much older than he was back then, but I still want to be one of the lads, part of the team. Maybe I am wrong and Paul was right.

It was poisonous post-match. Berti was legitimately asked if he would resign. Fair question. Yes or no answer. Move on. Yet he took great offence and maybe even at that moment started to think of potential scapegoats. A peculiar thing about the Faroes is that you have to get a ferry before you get to the airport, which is on another island. The press and the players shared the same boat but it wasn't a happy ship. The recriminations started to fly. Some of the younger players, who had never experienced the good times under Craig, started to get their retaliation in early for the reports, already filed, which would slate us the next day. It was just inexperience on their part but I think the last people the players wanted to see right then were the press and the feeling was probably mutual.

The flight home was muted and when we got off Davie Provan, the former international and an accomplished Sky Sports journalist, was waiting to 'doorstep' Berti with his microphone and the cameras rolling as he emerged from the airport. Berti was furious at this. He was starting to feel the heat now all right. Maybe he thought Scotland would be all fishing and golf after some of the criticism he'd had in Germany, particularly from *Bild*, the leading tabloid there, but he was now beginning to understand how much Scotland's international team meant to the country.

Personally, I was disillusioned by how quickly we had deteriorated under him. It wasn't fun any more. I was spending a week or 10 days away from my family and returning demoralised to my demanding, and Scottish, club manager. Then came the final straw. Berti did an interview in Germany in which he blamed Christian and me, his two experienced centre-backs, for the Faroes result. I am pretty sure he knew it would soon filter back to Britain and that he could then claim the 'lost in translation' excuse which is so regularly trotted out. To me, it was a cynical attempt to shift the blame from himself onto a couple of his senior players. We had played badly, I do not dispute that, but we were far from being the only ones.

'The older players like Christian Dailly and David Weir, who play in England, have already disappointed me,' he was reported as saying. 'They were to blame for the first two goals, it wasn't the youngsters.' It felt like you were being singled out. Fair enough, if that's what he thought, but you say it in the dressing-room first and it wasn't said in the dressing-room. We read it in the papers first. That's not how a dressing-room should work in my opinion and it sort of snowballed with all the other things that were bugging me. If he had come and said to me man to man, 'You never played well there', I would have said, 'You're right, I never played well.' That never happened and then you read what he thinks of you in the papers some time afterwards. I even phoned a couple of journalists to check the authenticity because I was obviously not happy about it and I had it confirmed to me.

Berti then phoned me and basically tried to say he hadn't said it but he didn't convince. It is the same old story – it still happens now, when a lot of the foreign lads go back and give interviews to their local press and don't think it will come back to bite them on the bum in Britain. I phoned Christian to say I wasn't happy and to let him know what I planned to do, just to make him aware, so I didn't hang him out to dry. Christian wasn't happy either but he decided to play on. Christian played in the next game in Iceland and scored. The story I heard was Berti was going to leave us both out of the next game anyway, but somebody went down injured the day before the game and Christian not only played but scored and went on to get a lot of caps.

David Moyes was furious with how Berti had behaved towards me. He pulled me into the office at Bellefield, our training ground, and said, 'He is out of order.' He had watched the game obviously and said it wasn't a great game, that I never played well and all the things you would expect him to say, but he still kept saying, 'He's out of order, I am going to come over to the next game just to show that I am behind you.' I appreciated his support but had to tell him I didn't plan on being there myself. He asked me if I was sure that's what I wanted to do. Gary Naysmith and Faddy, because they were at Everton at the time, and were my friends as well as my teammates, were saying, 'Don't do it', as were a few of the veterans of Craig's backroom staff like Stewart Hillis and Stewart MacMillan. Even when I was out, Gary and Faddy were always asking me to come back, although they also admitted that nothing had changed.

When I phoned David Taylor, the SFA's chief executive back then, he tried to play it down and said, 'Have a think about it', but that's not really in my nature once I have made my mind up. I wouldn't really reach a decision like that without going through that process anyway. He tried to downplay it, to minimise it, saying, 'Well, you don't want to play for this manager', but I was of the opinion I just wanted to end it and get out of it. I probably could have been cleverer about the way I did it in hindsight, but I was conscious I didn't want it to be seen as me against Berti, which it probably was to be honest. Taylor kept saying 'so you don't want to play under "this manager" again or "this regime" again and I was like, 'No, I just don't want to be available for selection for the national team.' He then asked me to put that in writing and send it to him, which I did, and that was when they announced it. My letter was short and to the point, 'Due to the circumstances, I don't want to be considered for the national team.' Taylor basically told me what I needed to write, or I asked him, then I wrote it and sent it.

I got a letter back from Taylor but I didn't keep it. I got a few more letters afterwards, too. It was a woman who wrote the one I mentioned which described me as 'a rat'. They went to the training ground at Everton and anything that came with an address or phone number I replied to. I can remember phoning somebody up and saying, 'Why do you think that?' That's the way I am. I just said, 'How can you say things like that, when you don't know the circumstances, you don't know what I am giving up in order to do it. Until you put yourself in my shoes, you shouldn't be saying things like that and writing letters like that if you don't know the circumstances.' I was determined to confront my critics.

My most important conversation should have been with Berti, but it was completely undermined by his lack of English and my lack of trust in him by this point. At times he was incoherent and he also went round in circles as we spoke. You couldn't really communicate with him. It was frustrating to not be able to clear the air. With Walter or Craig it would never have happened in the first place, but if it had, you would have had a meeting and you would either come out of it saying, 'We have to go our separate ways' or 'I have maybe been a bit impetuous here', but there was none of that.

I know players who have said to subsequent Scotland managers this isn't for me, I am not enjoying it and I don't want to play again and they have quietly left them out. I wish it could have been like that for me, too. It could have been, 'Let's just say, I have not picked you for the next two squads, you go and have a think about it and if it is not for you we'll leave it at that.' If it had been put to me like that, I might have considered it. I know for a fact it has happened subsequently and it has been handled a lot better. Players I know well have been out and then back in again. I was out for two and a half years, which is a long, long time.

I never disliked Berti personally, I just felt he didn't behave professionally towards me. He was a nice man, you couldn't dislike him on that level, but just felt you were swimming against the tide with him as a manager. It's not like I did it after one game. I felt I had given it a fair crack of the whip and turned up for all the friendlies but it felt like it was going to get worse rather than better and I was probably getting worse rather than better as a result and it was best for everybody. If he'd come back to me a year later and things had changed and he needed somebody, then being me I would definitely have thought about it. You don't want it to end like that, that is in nobody's best interests because it stays with you. I will always be tarred with it to a certain degree and I knew that at the time.

I had a lot of conflicting emotions when Scotland played their first match after my decision, in Iceland. As it was an international weekend, the gaffer gave us a few days off which was unheard of for me. I had not had a weekend off like that for such a long time it was a weird feeling, but I remember thinking to myself we are going to get away and enjoy this, make the most of it, so we went to Bath with Lucas and Jensen and stayed at a beautiful hotel. My family was also a big part of my decision and was just taking shape. Jensen had just been born and Lucas was two and a handful. It's a big commitment when you go away for seven to 10 days at a time when your kids are that age and I have always been family-orientated. It felt like playing international football was compromising everything else in my life at that point. It was compromising my family, compromising me at Everton as well. I was coming back without confidence having not played well and then having to get back up and running in the team there with various young centre-backs trying to take my place. It always felt like I was having to work really hard to stay in the Everton team or get in the team at that point. If you write a list of why you do it and why you don't want to do it, there was playing for your country on the 'for' list and nothing else. My mum and dad were sick of reading all the stuff about me. They just weren't having it and they felt I was making the right decision, too.

I couldn't watch the Iceland game. It was all still too raw for me at that point. We went just went out with the kids for a walk through Bath. A normal Saturday afternoon in many ways but it was horrible, not a nice feeling. I was basically killing time until I could get back to reality, back to Everton and back to work. I just wanted to get away, to get my mind off it, and not watch the game. I had mixed feelings because my friends were playing. You want them to do well, you want your country to win, but there's also a bit of you saying, 'I hope it all falls apart.' I wish that wasn't the case but I am afraid that's human nature.

I got the stories back from the boys about what was going on in my absence. Things people wouldn't believe. International footballers going onto the pitch not knowing where they were supposed to be playing. That happened regularly. It wasn't just once. After my initial reaction, I would always watch the games and it would be painful viewing because we would be losing a lot of them and getting ridiculed. Charlie Nicholas would be on Sky slating Scotland and you would see James McFadden or Gary getting interviewed afterwards and you could just tell how much it was hurting them from their faces. They were getting bullets fired at them for representing their country and I knew what they were giving up. In fairness to Vogts, Scotland made it through to the playoffs for Euro 2004 and then beat Holland 1-0 with an excellent performance at Hampden and a brilliant goal from Faddy, but they were then annihilated 6-0 in the second leg in Amsterdam by Dick Advocaat's side and when they lost their next friendly heavily, 4-0 in Wales, the knives were out for the manager and were never really put away again after that.

Yet while the manager is being well-paid for what he is doing, and will also get a good deal to go, the players are sacrificing everything, compromising their family, their club performances. Maybe

I am being a bit cynical about it, but the reality of international football in the cold light of day is that it compromises everything else and it takes someone special, like Craig Brown, to create something people want to be part of. When we were at Everton, there would be lads from several countries there and the English boys would be telling us what they were getting financially and how they would get treated, cars coming and picking them up, taking them to the game, then waiting after the game to take them straight home. Everything was done fantastically well, no stone was left unturned. The Danish boys used to get really well looked after, too. In that era, it always felt like ourselves and the Republic of Ireland lads were the poor relations, the amateurs.

Several players have retired prematurely from England's squad, too, the likes of Paul Scholes and Jamie Carragher. I think what happens is players rationalise things more as they get older. When you are younger, you think, 'Playing for my country, great.' As you get older you start thinking more about it and having stronger opinions and taking less shit frankly. You become a wee bit more selfish probably, saying to yourself, 'What am I getting out of this in the big picture?' You have done it for so long, it becomes the norm, but when you sit back and look at it, you start to think, 'I am killing myself here.' I never missed a squad. I know a lot of players wouldn't fancy it and just wouldn't turn up. Fair enough, that was their decision, but that wasn't me. That wasn't the way I operated. That's why I probably went from one extreme to the other. I went from the guy who turned up for everything, sat on the bench and all the rest of it, to the guy who threw the toys out of the pram.

International football is still great because it is your country. You can't replicate that. A Saturday at Hampden or a midweek night there, you can't beat it, the atmosphere is fantastic. That, in itself, justified all the bullshit that went along with it, but eventually was the only reason you went at times. Standing there, listening to the national anthem, getting a result that made everything else worthwhile because everything else was a pain in the arse. Staying in a hotel for seven to 10 days, it was like being in the army. Doing training, and wondering if you will play or not, constantly aware of the possibility of getting injured and then losing your club place. All the things you didn't think about when you were younger.

I do think international football needs to restructured to make it more appealing to players again. They should make it one game at a time like it used to be and scrap the double-headers in my opinion. Play for your club on a Saturday, an international in midweek and then go back to your club, even the Friday night/ Tuesday night they have introduced recently is an improvement. I also think gathering to play one game would allow countries to name smaller squads. It's part and parcel of football that you are not going to play every game or be the best player in every game or the manager's number one choice in every game, but it creates a situation straight away when so many players report for international duty knowing they are just there to make up the numbers. The team is named, the subs are named and there are guys walking out the dressing-room in a huff or on the phone to their agents. That's human nature, that's how it operates. If you can take that out, then you would be taking a negative out of the equation as it is a hard, hard situation to deal with for the manager. I think if you can keep it as small as you can and there's nobody left out, then that's better for everybody. There's nothing worse as a player than going to a game, especially an away game, and sitting in the stand thinking to yourself, 'Why exactly am I here again?'

I would have come back in an emergency if the call had come. For instance, Berti was short of centre-backs for what proved his final match in Moldova. It came after a home defeat by Norway at Hampden in one of those dreaded double-headers. Faddy was sent off for a handball and Norway scored the penalty and saw it out for a 1-0 win. The 1-1 draw in Moldova proved an undignified end for him. He was spat on by so-called supporters after he was sat in a section near them, a situation the SFA officials, sat safely in the stand opposite, should never have allowed to happen. It was wrong. That sort of thing shouldn't happen regardless of how angry people get at their team's results and the manager. Berti didn't deserve that. You can't justify that behaviour in any shape or form. It may have been a shambles – it certainly sounded it from stories I got back from the other players – but the manager being spat on was completely unacceptable. It just makes you sad when you hear things like that because that's not what you sign up for when you go away and play for your country. It was a sad end for him, a public humiliation almost.

It was as if he was getting put out of his misery after fighting a losing battle for a long time. Everybody seemed to be against him and things weren't getting better. If anything, they were getting worse. It just seemed to have come to the stage where it needed to stop. I think he was a proud man, a genuine, passionate football guy who just couldn't communicate his passion and ideas to us.

He got respect for his record and what he had done in the game and when he came in everybody wanted him to do well. Everybody thought we have got a chance here with these great new methods, this is going to be fantastic, but a bit like Paul Le Guen at Rangers it simply didn't work out that way. It always seems like a coup getting these managers but, for me, communication is the key.

Somebody has to be in charge, but the players also have to feel they are listened to and they are important as well. That they are being treated like adults and that their opinion matters. With Vogts, and Le Guen, too, from what I have been told, they had their theories and said, 'This is what happens.' To come into a group of players that had never worked under those circumstances, it was just not going to happen for them in my opinion.

That's how national team managers go, they have a limited lifespan. It's the same with England. They go for the foreign manager, he gets a couple of tournaments, and as soon as he has a bad tournament or a bad run then they want an English manager again. Then they give him a couple of tournaments, and want to go back to a foreign manager again. It's just seems to me managers have a limited shelf-life before people want something different or think that the grass will be greener after a change. Watching England at the World Cup last summer and particularly Fabio Capello struggling to articulate himself in media interviews after matches, and then reading stories leaking out of the players' disenchantment, it did remind me of what Scotland went through in the Berti period. Basically, when a manager can't communicate what he wants properly and clearly, it is a get-out clause for the players and, as David Moyes always says, 'Be damn sure you don't give the players any excuses because if you give them an excuse they will use it. If you give them a way out, they will find it.'

For Scotland, in particular, it seemed crazy to go down the foreign route when we had so many good managers of our own. Ironically, Walter left Everton just after Berti was appointed or we might not have. At the time of writing, six of the 20 managers in the English Premier League are Scots, if we count Owen Coyle as Scottish even though he was capped by the Republic of Ireland, a higher representation than any other country in the world. Sir Alex Ferguson, Kenny Dalglish, David Moyes, Alex McLeish, Paul Lambert, Owen and Steve Kean. We may have stopped churning out players as we once did, but we still produce top-class coaches and managers. People have talked about changing the rules so that national coaches have to qualify as players do to represent their country and I think in an ideal world that would be the case. You couldn't argue against it, you can definitely see the logic behind it, but like I said there is a limited lifespan and people seem to want something different every so often.

Scotland's search for a new manager eventually narrowed to two men, Walter Smith and Gordon Strachan. I had heard good things about Strachan. He had a good reputation with the players I knew who had worked for him and I thought he would make a good Scotland manager, but obviously my personal preference was for the manager who had taken me to Everton and who I had enjoyed playing for there. I thought Walter would be perfect for the job and I was delighted when he was chosen for it. I definitely thought the appointment was right because I had worked with him and knew what he had done in the game previously in Scotland. I knew he could make a success of the Scotland job and make it enjoyable again for the players.

If I am being honest, I also hoped a phone call was coming for me as soon as he did get it. When he did call, I was sitting in a wee room at home that was like my den and it was not a particularly dramatic conversation. Walter said, 'You probably know what I am on the phone for, would you be interested if I asked you to come back?' I replied, 'If you asked me to come back, I would definitely come back' and that was it. I don't know if he knew I would say yes, but I was always going to. If I had said no, it wouldn't have become a big issue. Nobody would have known about the phone call, because that's the way Walter operates. I knew there would be issues when I did go back, but I would just have to take that on the chin. A few people had a pop at me when I quit, but I have to say I didn't have a single problem with a player when I returned. Not at all.

You can never change history but I am so glad, especially when you have family and all the rest of it, that things turned out as they did for me. I didn't want my children to grow up and think, 'My dad played for Scotland but that's not a great story.' Those thoughts kind of put things in perspective for you. It turned around from giving up partly because of having a young family, to partly going back for them, to make them proud of me and set the right example to them. I did think about it in that sense, that I wouldn't want the kids to think I had given up and just walked away because you are always telling them not to give up, not just to walk away and I suppose you are contradicting yourself a wee bit if you act differently. I don't regret my decision to stop playing for my country, but I am grateful I got the chance to return.

8

The art of Moyes

WHEN Walter Smith lost his job at Everton in March 2002, I felt responsible. It's the worst feeling you get as a football player, when your manager loses his job. Walter was the man, after all, who had brought me to to the club and showed such great faith in me. I wanted to say sorry to him, to apologise that we hadn't done more as players to protect him with our performances, because he had certainly sheltered us from the financial problems at the club.

The manager never really transmitted that to us, although subsequently we found out. He would have a meeting with the bank every Thursday or Friday, depending if we were home or away. The club was going from week to week, but we didn't know that. The manager was very good at keeping all these things away from us. Even now at Rangers you don't feel you are in an environment where all that is going on. It is in the papers, but it is not in your face. That was the case at Everton. It never really affected our working environment, but it must have had an impact on his ability to manage the club properly.

When people criticised him for being too defensive, they failed to take that into account. Yes, we would play five across the back with me as one wing-back and David Unsworth as the other and things like that, but he was trying to keep the team in the Premier League basically. It felt like you were on a cliff face and that if Everton had gone out of the League, they could have kept going, like a Man City or later a Leeds. There was definitely that feeling about the place back then.

Bill Kenwright had inherited these problems from Peter Johnson after completing his takeover at Christmas 1999. Everton were definitely under pressure to sell players each summer at this stage. At the start of what proved Walter's final season we sold Francis Jeffers and Michael Ball, two of our best young players, to Arsenal and Rangers for large fees. Nowhere near as much went back out on bringing in Alan Stubbs and Tomasz Radzinski to replace them, yet Stubbs, in particular, would go on to prove an excellent player for Everton. Similarly, Lee Carsley, who was Walter's last signing, would go on to be a stalwart in the side that David Moyes subsequently built.

We started 2001–02 slowly, with yet another League Cup exit on penalties, this time at home to Crystal Palace. We all knew it was getting bad for the manager, that things weren't good. We were away at Stoke in the third round of the FA Cup and he was under pressure until we managed to win 1-0 through a great free kick from Stubbsy. There were a lot of Everton fans there and you got the impression if we hadn't won, then the vultures were circling a bit. Then we went on a wee roll. We won our next League game at home to Sunderland then drew at Tottenham, when I scored the best goal of my career, one I still show my kids proudly on YouTube. A volley from the edge of the box that flew into the net after Gazza crossed to me. Les Ferdinand scored for Tottenham just before it with a great header and had beaten me to the ball, so I was probably trying to make amends.

This mini-run also took us past Leyton Orient and Crewe Alexandra and into an FA Cup quarter-final at Middlesbrough, but we lost 3-0 there and that was the game that finished the manager off. Walter just went immediately, but Archie stayed on for a short time and I remember going and speaking to him and saying I am really sorry about what happened and I was. I never got that opportunity with the manager. He was always on a pedestal, for me anyway, so it would have been harder to do that with him. Archie was more on the shop floor, in amongst the players more. I remember walking in that office to see Archie and thinking, what do I say to this man when I have contributed to him losing his job.

I never met Bill Kenwright, the theatre impresario who had taken control of the club, never had any dealings with him at all. He was your typical showman, with an air of drama about him. He was obviously a big Everton fan, you couldn't dispute that it ran through his blood. He would be out before the games at the main entrance talking to punters and handing out tickets. He showed a touch of class I thought when he invited Walter back to a dinner a couple of years after he was sacked. It was in St George's Hall, a stunning building in the centre of Liverpool, and Bill stood up and made a speech.

He said Walter had a mixed reputation with Everton fans, probably because a lot them didn't properly recognise the circumstances he was working under. He spoke about him in glowing terms and said, 'The club wouldn't be where it is now, if it wasn't for this man. He kept us in the League when we probably shouldn't have stayed in it.' Bill did a great job of trying to correct the image of the job Walter had done working under difficult circumstances, which was to his credit. At the dinner, the singer was Leo Sayer and he walking about singing, coming round the tables. The boys were all blanking him but I gave him a high five and the boys were giving me pelters for weeks after that for being Leo Sayer's biggest fan.

David Moyes made a mark on us all at the club right from the start. He was younger than I am now when he became manager of Everton and must have been nervous. You could tell that when he came in. He spoke well, don't get me wrong. He's a good speaker about football because he knows it, you can't dispute his knowledge. He captivated us that day all right but you could tell he was nervous, that it was a big step up for him, a big job. He had managed Preston excellently and deserved his chance, but didn't have to deal with your Gascoignes, Gravesens or Fergusons there. One of his first acts was to make Duncan captain again, and although I was deposed from a role I had taken on in the final months under Walter, I couldn't really argue with his logic. He'd come in and wanted to create an impression and by making Duncan captain then everybody was up. He also described Everton as the 'people's football club' at his first press conference, which went down well. I think he was trying to get the best out of Duncan and work the crowd a wee bit as well.

It certainly worked as Duncan scored in his first three games. In the first, we beat Fulham and David Unsworth scored after 27 seconds. Then we won 4-3 at Derby. We were well up, but they came back at us and we were hanging on. After that, I went away and played against France with Scotland and lost 5-0 in a friendly at the Stade de France. Then Gary Naysmith and I flew straight back to play for Everton at Newcastle and we lost 6-2, so we conceded 11 goals in about four days!

Gary was a young boy when I was at Hearts, then he came into the Scotland squad so I tried to look after him, although he'll maybe tell you different. There was an international game, I think it was in Croatia, and Gordon Strachan was about to sign him for Coventry City. Gary was talking to me about it, saying it was almost done. He played well for Scotland and when I went back to Everton, Archie asked me about him. I said he was about to sign for Coventry, and Archie said, 'Phone him and tell him not to sign for anybody.' So I did what I was told. I called Gary and said, 'Everton have told me to tell you not to sign' and it all happened very quickly after that. His agent was Jim McArthur, who used to be my agent. Jim must have gone away and done the finances and when he got back to the hotel they were staying in at Haydock, Gary asked how much he was getting. When Jim told him, Gary asked, 'Is that a week or a month?' 'That's a week, Gaz,' Jim replied. For me that summed Gary up – he wanted the move not the money. That was the icing on the cake. It made me smile because it reminded me of myself at his age.

I noticed a distinct change in how the new manager dealt with defeat after we lost at Newcastle. Archie's answer would have been punching people and having them up against the wall, but Moyes came in, much calmer, and said, 'It's gone, lads, we've got a battle on our hands here and we need to move on and make sure we get the next game right. Forget about that, we can't change it.' He was dead positive, which probably wasn't his natural reaction, but he was lightening the mood and playing a role and it worked as we bounced back with a win at home to Bolton and stayed up in the end by seven points. When Walter was the gaffer we would always go to London on the bus. It would be like five or six hours on a Friday. As soon as David Moyes came in, we would be on the train or we would fly. I don't know if he came in and had a wee bit more power, but we were suddenly in nicer hotels and travelling with a bit more style and comfort. It seemed the board had upped the ante a bit.

If the club had survived comfortably under the new manager, I wasn't so sure I was going to. When he first arrived, he had a meeting with everybody individually. I remember my meeting, at one of the hotels we stayed at in London. I just said what I thought, that we were struggling a bit at goalie and we were having a hard time here and there elsewhere, but he said to me, 'I think we need to bring in another centre-half.' I can remember him saying that to me and he did bring in a centre-half – Joseph Yobo was his first signing, so he wasn't bluffing or anything. He was very clever. He had obviously prepared for the job and planned what he was going to do and how he was going to act. He also said, 'Everybody tells me, you and Stubbsy are the best players here, or you kept them in the League, but if I had my full-backs tucked in as tight I could have played there.' I don't think that was an attempt to motivate us at the time, I think he genuinely believed it. My impression was that he didn't realise our value until maybe later on. I think Joseph came in and was the big signing and I always got the feeling it was me or Stubbsy afterwards. I never felt comfortable that I would play. Up until then, I never thought I wouldn't play. It was never in my head throughout my career. Once I was in the team that was me. That was probably the first time I thought I might not play on Saturday. I had been lucky to get to 32 or 33 and not have that in my head.

My partnership with Stubbsy was probably the best of my career, although I also had a good one with Carlos Cuéllar at Rangers. Although we were similar, we somehow complemented each other and played well together. Stubbsy had a great ping on him and I enjoyed playing beside him and his company off the pitch, too. He was a good lad. Steve Watson was another good friend in that period. He was a Geordie who liked a pint and just loved being in the dressing-room and organising the nights out and games of golf. Eight to 10 of us go and play at least once a week and have the occasional night out. It helped create a great spirit.

Bellefield was the kind of place you didn't rush to leave after training finished. You were so secluded, the youth team wasn't even there. It was the first team and their staff and that was it, so you could spend a lot of time there, no problem. Myself, Kevin Kilbane, Gary Naysmith, Steve Watson and sometimes James Beattie would all share a car into training together. We would meet at the nearest services from Hale and Wilmslow and the surrounding area. Someone would bring coffees and we would all drive in together for 40 minutes or half an hour, whatever it was, having a real good time. We used to say to James McFadden when he arrived that he would have to earn his place in the car and he always used to bite on that.

Then, on the way back, we would always be moaning at each other, 'Are you staying late today?', but we'd all be in there having our lunch and a laugh together for ages. We would sit in the canteen with Andy Holden, the reserve coach, who we called Taff because he had one cap for Wales, Jimmy Martin, the kitman, Jimmy Comer, the masseur, and Tony Sage, the other kitman. Tony is a Celtic fan so gives me plenty of stick by text.

Taff would say, 'Cup of tea, lads?' and we would all go up and sit upstairs for hours watching the horses and playing darts. It was like being in a wee youth club again. You really didn't want to leave, it was that sort of place. All the young lads loved Taff, the likes of Leon Osman and Tony Hibbert. They were all his babies. He's the sort of guy every club needs, someone the players can turn to when they are a bit down. He always used to talk about his own career, playing for Joe Royle at Oldham when he was the only player who wore studs on the brick-hard astroturf at

Boundary Park. Joe's team talks would always end with him saying about the opposition's main threat, 'Taff, discourage him.' He also had a great knack for predicting what level young players would end up playing at as they emerged, saying, 'He'll make a living out of the game.' When you go into Finch Farm, Everton's new training ground, it is still all the same faces sitting there in the canteen.

If I wasn't convinced the manager rated me, I had to admire his ability to weld a team together. He had three different sources for players – those he had inherited, those he signed and the best of a promising batch that had been coming through consistently from our youth system. He got most of his calls right and was able to marry them altogether so they brought the best from each other. The key player at the club for me was one who had tried to back out of joining it when he heard Walter Smith might get sacked. Walter had signed Lee Carsley before losing his job and Lee wanted out of the deal to go back to Coventry, but the deal was done. He flourished under David Moyes. What a job he did for us. He held the team together. He was outstanding, a great player and a funny lad. He was a Brummie and used to get pelters for looking like Harry Hill, but had the best sense of humour, so blunt with great expressions that could knock you down. He also got on really well with the staff and was the life and soul of the place. He helped me, and he also helped the likes of Tim Cahill and Gravesen, in particular, to do their job and Kev Kilbane and Gary Naysmith. He covered everything, a multitude of sins, the gaps that everybody else created.

The complete opposite of the selfless Carsley was David Ginola, the French winger who Moyes quickly bombed out of the club as he sifted through the squad. You got the impression with Ginola that he wasn't interested, that he was doing you a favour just coming in. He wasn't part of the group and I remember him not being happy at all for the last game of the season at Arsenal. That was going to be his last game in English football, or so he felt, and he couldn't believe he never started, he was really unhappy with the gaffer and threw a major strop. Everybody else couldn't believe he was even on the bench.

The new manager had also made it clear that he would have a look at young players in the first team if he felt they could do it. Nick Chadwick, a young ginger-haired centre-forward who I liked, came in and scored a few goals at the end of that first season. There seemed to be a production line of strikers coming through, in particular. Francis Jeffers was a good player but a bit fragile and a bit of a scally. He was a Liverpool lad, not unlike Robbie Fowler. A very good finisher, good movement and was sharp, but just very slight and the club got a decent fee when he moved to Arsenal. There was also Phil Jevons, another decent prospect, and then Nick, but it turned out the best of the lot was about to emerge.

We'd all heard about this young lad of 14 or 15 coming through the ranks. I saw him in some of the FA Youth Cup games and he was on the radar throughout that run, basically carrying the team to the final. He was considered a bit special, but you hear that in football clubs all the time. Yet when Wayne Rooney joined the first-team squad at the start of the 2002–03 season, still two months short of his 17th birthday, we all knew he was one of the best players there and he would be in the team and we didn't mind because he was so down to earth and never caused anybody a problem. I really liked him.

If we knew how good he was immediately, then the rest of the world didn't have to wait long to see for themselves. In October, we beat Arsenal 2-1 at Goodison and Wayne got the winner with a 30-yard shot that had David Seaman clutching at thin air and went in off the underside of his bar. To put it in perspective, this was the Arsenal side that hadn't lost any of their previous 30 League matches. It was also the start of six straight wins for us, a run which lifted us up to third in the table. We were in the top six all season after that, only slipping to seventh and out of the European places on the final day, when we lost at home to Manchester United.

The only blackspot was an FA Cup defeat at Shrewsbury Town. The gaffer had been a player there, so that was a sore one for him. We must have left our cars somewhere and met the bus en route. The gaffer had his car at Shrewsbury and told us beforehand he would take us back up the motorway. So it was me, Gary Naysmith, Steve Watson, I think, and Kev Kilbane who were in the car with the gaffer after the game and it was the most uncomfortable drive I've had in my life. He was fuming and we obviously weren't happy either. I don't think it was even an hour, but it felt like for ever. He was devastated, asking us what had gone wrong and we didn't have any answers for him.

Nevertheless, he won the League Managers Association Award and deserved it for how he had turned the club around. He handled Wayne's emergence expertly, using him mainly as an impact substitute in that first season because the senior strikers at the club, probably spurred on a bit by his arrival, were all playing well. The main partnership was between Kevin Campbell and Tomasz Radzinski but Brian McBride also came in and did well for us.

With Tomasz, you always felt like he was working his ticket, that there was an endgame in his mind all the time. He played for Canada but was more Belgian, his other nationality, as a person. He was that kind of lad, more continental, more European. He was really friendly with Alessandro Pistone and scored a lot of goals for us, using his pace to good effect. Pistone was a great player, left foot or right foot – you couldn't tell which was his best. He was also a great athlete who could jump over the crossbar, but was a wee bit temperamental and would miss games occasionally for not a lot. He wasn't really in love with football. He loved his cars, his clothes and his poker. He loved the lifestyle, but wasn't really in love with the game.

Brian, in contrast, was a good player and a great lad. He came in and did really well for us and we had the option to keep him. I think they thought he was maybe too old, but he went to Fulham and became a crowd favourite there. He was a proper target man, who could score a goal, an honest player who just made the team better. It was the sort of team with a lot of steady players in it and the sum added up to more than the parts. There was real synergy in the squad with guys like Mark Pembridge, the left-footed Welsh international, who had great delivery of free kicks and corners, and Niclas Alexandersson, a hard-working Swede. Niclas was very methodical and you just wanted to give him a wee kick up the backside to speed up sometimes.

Not every signing worked out for the manager. He took Rodrigo, a Brazilian lad, on loan for a year and paid a decent amount to get him, but he blew his knee out after four or five games and never kicked a ball. They also brought over a couple of Chinese lads because of the club's sponsorship with Keijan, Li Tie and Li Weifeng. Li Tie, in particular, was a cracking guy. He didn't have any English at all, but tried really hard to integrate and be part of it. He played quite a bit and played well, he was a proper grafter and a team player and he started 28 games in that season, one more than me.

That was a lot more than I played in the following season due to injury. I hurt my knee on 1 November 2003, and didn't really come back till April 2004, apart from one game at Fulham in January. It was a frustrating period because I hadn't started that season as first choice. It was Yobo and Stubbs and then I came in and started playing and we weren't really conceding goals, so I must have been doing all right. Then against Chelsea at Goodison I dawdled on the ball a wee bit, Frank Lampard took it off of me and immediately hit a shot. I blocked it and knew I had hurt myself straight away. My knee was stretched to block the shot and it took the force of it and basically opened up and stretched my medial ligament. I knew my knee wasn't right, but the game was carrying on and I was still playing and desperate to not come off. I remember Mick Rathbone, Everton's physio and a really good operator, saying if I had made a tackle in that period it would have ruptured it completely, but instead I had only torn it to a degree.

I was out for a while, and I wasn't used to it. I came back and played that one game at Fulham and then I played in a reserve game against Man United at Altrincham to get my fitness up and did exactly the same thing again. I was in tears getting stretchered off in this reserve game after being out for two or three months from November to January. I had very rarely been injured and the team was going through a bad time, so it wasn't a great place to be. Eventually, I got back in the team and played the last four or five games but we were getting beaten right, left and centre. There was a bit of a watershed when we lost 5-1 to Man City in the final match of that season. The manager was in the depths of despair. He couldn't believe what had happened and the players had turned against him a bit at that point. There was almost an 'us and them' feeling at that time.

We had slumped to 17th, although we were still six points clear of the three relegated clubs, Leicester, Leeds and Wolves. The bleak mood wasn't improved when Wayne starred for England at the European Championships in Portugal in the summer of 2004 and a move to Manchester United gathered momentum afterwards. Wayne broke his metatarsal playing against the hosts in the quarter-final and I was in Gavin Laidlaw's house, a pal who is a dentist, watching the game because as Scots we couldn't go to the pub to watch it. Nevertheless, I wanted Wayne to do well and when he came off injured I knew it had to be something serious as he doesn't come off often. Then my phone rang and it was Wayne. 'Hiya, pal, are you all right?.' 'I have broke my foot,' Wayne said. He must have phoned me from the dressing-room having had it diagnosed. My mate was sitting there and I am saying, 'Keep your chin up, you never know' etc. I put the phone down and said, 'You'll never guess who that was?' and he said, 'Who?' 'Wayne Rooney' and he said, 'Yeah, right.' The game was still going on, it was a surreal moment.

It was made out that he agitated for the move, but I got the impression that situation had been manufactured to protect the club and it hung Wayne out to dry a wee bit. He had not done a lot wrong. He had an opportunity to go and play for Manchester United and the club were getting well rewarded. He was an Everton diehard, and I am sure he still is, but people outwith football don't grasp that it's your career as well. As players, we didn't hold anything against him. We realised he needed to go to the next level.

As a manager, it is maybe different, because you want to see the benefit to your team, but as a player you see it slightly differently and he needed to leave and that was the perfect place for him to go. When he was at our place he was brilliant, so there was no animosity.

People thought we were going back to being a side that flirted with relegation, but, to his credit, time has proved it was just a blip in Everton's progress under David Moyes. He had signed the promising Richard Wright to be our goalkeeper, but wasn't completely convinced, so then brought in the experienced Nigel Martyn and he quickly established himself as number one. He was an excellent keeper, probably the best I have played with. He was a down-to-earth Cornishman and very genuine and normal. Not a flash footballer, but a consistent one who didn't do daft things. Kicking was his only problem, I think due to a foot injury that eventually finished his career. That was his only downside but he was always in good positions to make saves. He played so well for Everton there was talk of him getting back in the England squad, but he was very much a family man.

When James McFadden arrived from Motherwell, I felt like I was his big brother, that I wanted to look after him. He moved to near where we stayed in the Warrington area, so we would see a bit of him and tried to look out for him. He always had this thing that he hadn't got enough money when he came down to Everton, that his wages weren't good enough due to the deal his agent had done and he was always fighting to prove himself. Faddy felt he would be the first one out of the team or the first one substituted. He wanted it today, not tomorrow. He was hungry and wanted to be a part of it immediately.

I think the manager saw him as sort of having the potential to develop into a good, good player but he never seemed to get a settled run at all. He fitted in well, though, got on with the likes of Leon Osman and all that crowd. He loved a laugh, loved the banter, but was very respectful. James had come from nothing but had been brought up the right way, he wasn't a Jack the Lad or a chancer in any shape or form. Everybody liked him at Everton. He could change a game at any time, Faddy, and he almost became a better substitute when he was there because the manager knew he was the kind of player he could throw on and who would get you a goal or create one. The fans at Everton veered between loving him and not being sure about him. He's that kind of player, one you either love or you don't. He really divided opinion.

For me, it was almost like you needed to leave him in the team and say, 'You have got eight games, play for eight games.' He's one of those players who tries too hard if he thinks people don't rate him. He thinks people are against him and he's got to prove something with every pass. He did that for Scotland against Liechtenstein last year because he had been challenged beforehand by Craig Levein, but he's really not that type of lad, trust me. He's not selfish. He wants to do well, score the goal and be the special player, but then he comes back in and is the same lad among the group. He's not got an ego in any shape or form, which I think is a nice quality. So even though he's perceived as being an egotistical player, as a person he is nothing like that. I know David Moyes rated him highly. Since Faddy left Everton, I have heard him saying, 'We should have kept him, we shouldn't have let him go', but they got a big fee for him from Birmingham and Faddy wanted to play regularly.

Kevin Kilbane was another good addition who also became a good friend. He was such a hard-working team player, someone who often made the team better at the expense of himself. He helped his full-back a lot if he was playing wide in midfield. I know Gary Naysmith loved playing with him. You could just tell that whoever was playing against him wouldn't have a good game, that's the type of lad he was.

When Wayne departed some of the other young players at the club came out from his shadow to become key players. Tony Hibbert, for example, was always bracketed with Wayne because they had the same agent and when Wayne signed his contract at Everton it was live on Sky and Hibbo was stuck on the side of the table. Not that it would have bothered him, but he was always tagged with Wayne when they were coming through. It was unfair on him, but it wasn't a problem. Hibbo was a tremendous defender one on one, nobody could get past him. Leon Osman hadn't really made it, then he went to Derby on loan and had a really good time and they were desperate to buy him and that probably swung it for him. They brought him back, put him in the first team at Everton and he has been there ever since really. He's another really good team player. Moyes was clever, he would always organise nights out with the wives and players and karaoke to bring us all closer. Naysmith and Osman would be up singing all night, Kev Kilbane would love it. Those nights created an excellent atmosphere about the place.

The manager turned his attention to the top end of the team in the summer of 2004 and made a couple of inspired signings for a fraction of the Rooney fee. Plenty of clubs had looked at Tim Cahill but he was the one who took the plunge and bought him from Millwall for £1.5m. Tim made a big difference to the team with his goals, energy and mentality. The term winner can be loosely bandied about in football, but he had a real winner's mentality. It was quite a hungry, up-and-coming team and he was a big part of that. Tim fitted in immediately, although it was an easy dressing-room to fit into. The squad was smaller and tighter now than when I'd arrived and I think that became a strength rather than a weakness.

The signing of Marcus Bent may have surprised some of our supporters but also proved an incredibly astute one on the manager's part. He had a great period, playing in the majority of games in 2004–05, and he really was top drawer that season. He was up front on his own all the time and did an incredible amount of work and an incredible job for the team. He had pace like I had never seen before. I remember he gave Gareth Southgate five yards' start in a 10-yard race against Middlesbrough and still won it before scoring. He absolutely burned him. I just remember watching it and thinking, 'Jeez, I am glad I am not playing against that', and he just continued that through the whole season and played a big part for us.

That win put us third in mid-September and we stayed there through the autumn and then went second with a win over Liverpool at Goodison on 11 December. Lee Carsley, our unsung hero, got his reward as he scored the winner. There is a great picture of Tim Cahill with all the boys piling on. It looks a bit like that iconic image of the American soldiers planting the flag at Iwo Jima and is a photograph I am always happy to sign for Everton supporters. Unfortunately, buried at the bottom of the pile of bodies is the goalscorer himself, something he never let us forget. Lee really was the life and soul of the place, the fulcrum of the team from the other players' standpoint because he did so many jobs well.

With Lee providing protection in front of us and Nigel secure behind, myself and Stubbsy had a great season together. You need to have a strong defensive base to do anything in the Premier League because there are so many strikers out there who can hurt you if you don't. Alan Shearer was the best striker of that generation probably. He could finish, he was physical and loved a fair fight. He could score from inside and outside the box, headers, tap-ins, the lot. He didn't have lightning pace but could work the channels well. You just knew you would be in a game with him. He almost carried that Newcastle team to a certain degree, he was like the figurehead. He wasn't likeable on the pitch, he would do anything to win and had no banter, which was fair enough. Teddy Sheringham would have banter, he was more of a Jack the Lad, but Shearer was just all business. You knew if the ball was there and you were there, you were getting smashed. There wasn't any grey area and that was fine.

Les Ferdinand was another big, physical guy. An absolute monster, so powerful. Thierry Henry was different. He was lightning quick and a good finisher, but I saw a different side to him when he tried to do me with a bad tackle at Goodison one day. He never made contact and I wasn't hurt. It looked a lot worse than it was. Michael Owen was another flying machine with good movement, who always played down the side of you or in around you. Jimmy Floyd Hasselbaink would shoot from anywhere and was aggressive and would take no nonsense from you. He'd want to fight you and all the rest of it. He had a big personality and an absolute hammer of a shot. You always got a laugh with Jimmy, he was funny. Mark Viduka came across as being a bit thick, he was always laughing at himself and not too serious. He would walk out the tunnel with you like he was walking down the street, not as if going out to play. Technically, though, he was a very good player.

Robbie Keane was another really clever football player. Always thinking, always looking for a quick free kick. You knew you had to be switched on all the time against him. I really liked him. He was almost like a Kenny Dalglish player with his back to goal or on your shoulder and he would run back towards play as well. He always came short to go long. Ole Gunnar Solskjaer was another clever player, while Andy Cole was just a finisher, a penalty-box predator, who was very serious and moody, with a chip on his shoulder all the time. Always moaning at referees and teammates, moaning if you kicked him. The world was always against him.

There were also guys like Fabrizio Ravanelli, Gianluca Vialli, Alen Bokšić and Juninho at various points. It was like a who's who. John Hartson was a handful and had a good career, but I was never worried about playing against him. Never felt I couldn't match him. He was physical, first and foremost. You just had to stand up to him or he would bully you. You got the impression if he sensed a wee bit of weakness, he would go for it. Paulo Wanchope was one player who often caused me problems. He was so unpredictable and had such a big physical presence, always making it difficult for you or you would guess the wrong way and end up with his elbow in your face. Dion Dublin was like that as well. They were hard people to play against, without looking particularly fantastic for their teams.

In midfield, guys like Roy Keane, Émmanuel Petit and Patrick Vieira were proper men when they were playing. Sometimes you look at the teams now and you think they are boys turning into men, but they were hardened, seasoned international and Premier League players right at the top of their games. They just had an aura about them.

Ryan Giggs was one of the best and most popular players in the Premier League in this period. I have met him a couple of times and he comes across as very normal, as do a lot of the Manchester United players. Like Scholes, like Phil Neville, when he came to Everton and was an excellent influence, like Darren Fletcher – they are all the same. They have just been brought up to be normal and that has become the usual thing at their club. Giggs comes across as the leader in all that. He, Gary Neville and Scholes are the ones that set it in stone.

You were almost watching Giggs when you were playing against him. He just made it look so easy and covered the ground so gracefully. That was the general consensus. Scholes was the other one you wouldn't find anybody saying a bad word about. He is someone people in the game have a genuine affection for, a good professional who promotes the game and does it the way it should be done. All the players that played against him, like Barry Ferguson and Thomas Gravesen, all these people, say he's the one. The hardest to play against and the best.

Yet in that 2004–05 season we weren't in awe of anybody. I don't know if it was my best season at Everton individually – I won a couple of Player of the Year awards in earlier seasons – but definitely as a group it was our most successful season when I was there. We were third or fourth nearly all season, always punching above our weight. Everyone was waiting for us to drop but we didn't.

We lost Thomas to Real Madrid but Mikel Arteta arrived from Real Sociedad to replace him as our playmaker. Mikel was so tidy and so easy on the eye, beautiful to watch, a very natural player. He had been at Rangers and had perfect English and adapted to the culture no problem. He wasn't one of these foreign lads who are temperamental and want to go back home all the time. He just fitted in like a British player. His set-piece delivery was superb and he was also so nimble and cute he used to win more free kicks than anybody I have seen in my life. Opposition players used to get really frustrated with him. Mikel has been unfortunate not to get capped by his country because he is of that generation of brilliant midfielders they have produced, including Xavi, Andrès Iniesta and Cesc Fàbregas.

To add an edge to things, Liverpool were chasing us for the fourth Champions League spot and we lost to them at Anfield in March as the race between us intensified, but we then pulled a home win over Manchester United out of the bag. Big Duncan scored our goal when Mikel picked him out with a free kick and was incredible in that game. He pulverised Rio Ferdinand. Gary Neville was sent off for kicking the ball at a fan and Paul Scholes was also red carded. It was a big win for us and when we beat Newcastle at home with three games to go, we were almost over the line. We won 2-0 and I scored our first with a header from another free kick delivery from Mikel before Tim Cahill made sure. We only needed one point from our final two League games now to clinch a place in the Champions League qualifiers, but we didn't even require it when Liverpool couldn't win at Highbury the next day. The gaffer had already authorised a night out if that happened and was on Sky drinking a glass of champagne at his house after the Liverpool result came through. To be honest, myself, Kev, Gary and all that crowd were already out in Wilmslow having a few beers anyway, but we really went for it later that night. The extent of our celebrations, players and staff, probably showed when we went to Arsenal on the Wednesday night and lost 7-0.

We also lost our final match at Bolton 3-2 but nobody gave us stick. We hadn't been out of the top four since September, had finished in Everton's highest league position for 17 years and above Liverpool for the first time in 18. They went on to win the Champions League after that dramatic comeback against Milan in Istanbul. That created a problem for Uefa because there was no precedent of the winners not having already qualified to defend their title. There was a story that they weren't going to let us or them into it, but thankfully common sense prevailed.

It was great for Everton to get back into Europe after so long. It was something to look forward to through the summer but there was still a conspiracy theory going around that the draw for the qualifying round would be harsh to prevent England having five teams in the group stage. I am not so sure about that, but we certainly didn't get it easy. We were sitting in the canteen at Bellefield and the one team we probably didn't want was Villarreal. I remember Mikel there with us and he immediately said it would be tough. They had Juan Román Riquelme, Diego Forlán, Marcos Senna and Joan Capdevila in their team, some really good players. Our team had changed – Stubbsy fell out with the club over his contract. He wanted two years and the policy at the time was you only got one year if you were 30-plus. He ended up going to Sunderland, while Lee Carsley was injured and missed almost the whole campaign. The dynamics of the team changed a wee bit, although Stubbsy came back to us from Sunderland six months later.

It turned into a really difficult season and maybe that was a result of going out of Europe so early. It can have such a big impact. We played really well in the games with Villarreal. They won 2-1 at Goodison, so it was going to be tough for us to turn the tie around.

We went over there and they scored again, when Juan Pablo Sorín's shot deflected off me and went in, but we got a goal back from Mikel's free kick and we knew if we got another one it was going to extra time and we were really pushing. Pierluigi Collina, the famous Italian, was the referee and Duncan scored with a header from a corner and he disallowed it. That happened all the time with Duncan because of his size and the way he played, but it was the wrong decision on this occasion – there was no getting away from that. It felt similar to Scotland's game against England at Wembley in that we had lost in the first game but now had the impetus and if Duncan's goal had stood we would have won the game and the tie. We kept pressing but the winner just never came and then they broke to make it 2-1 through Forlán in the final minute. We'd played well over the two games but they were a top-level team. It was a fine line.

Our subsequent Uefa Cup elimination by Dinamo Bucharest, on the other hand, was an absolute disaster. It was just one of those games where everything they hit went in and we never played well. It was similar to Celtic's game against Artmedia Bratislava, which they lost 5-0. Dinamo scored, then Joseph Yobo got an equaliser. It was a poor stadium and pitch but it was 1-1 at half-time, which was a decent result. Then, in the second half, they seemed to score every time they went forward. It ended up 5-1 and never in a million years were they four goals better than us. Coming back to Goodison we still felt we had a chance. Tim Cahill scored relatively early and you thought, 'If we can get another one here, they'll fold', but we never managed to get another one. It was a big disappointment. From being in the Champions League qualifiers and having a chance to go into the Champions League proper we were out of Europe completely within a month and the season just never really recovered from that. We had a small squad and probably couldn't have coped with a European campaign, but we were obviously desperate to stay involved in it.

That second-leg victory over Dinamo was one of only two wins from our first 14 matches. We improved dramatically after Christmas and challenged for a Uefa Cup spot but ultimately finished 11th. The 4-1-4-1 system we had perfected the previous season wasn't working as well with Lee injured and it also relied heavily on the single striker. Marcus Bent had handled that burden brilliantly and the manager had also brought in James Beattie to give him another option but it was a demanding role. The manager had obviously been a defender when he played and when it was him and Alan Irvine together, he would always take the defenders and Alan would take the forwards. It was as if that wasn't his forte. He had his ideas on what he wanted and how he would like to play and he would go through that in detail but probably came at it from a defender's perspective.

The strikers also struggled with the pressure of their transfer fees. James would have been the highest transfer fee in the club's history when he joined and later Andy Johnson would have been the highest. It was big money in Everton terms, probably all the manager's budget, and you could sense he felt the pressure of spending that money well and that almost loaded the pressure onto the players, too. I know Beatts well and Andy Johnson and they both felt like they had this burden on them. They never felt like they were free to go and just play. Andy Johnson did well at various points. He was a proper handful and a top player when he could stay fit and in the team and get on a run, but you just felt the manager was never convinced by him.

You have got to be an exceptional player to play up front on your own and the way our system was you had to work really hard. Probably the best, over a period of time, was Marcus Bent in that good season we had but you could only play four or five games at that level, with the workrate the manager wanted, while trying to score goals and then you needed a rest. We needed a Didier Drogba or somebody like that, but those players are few and far between. Marcus made a great fist of it, Beatts could do it but I don't know if he could do it for a length of time. He had come from Southampton, where he scored spectacular goals but usually played in a pair. Andy Johnson could do it, but it was hard for them all to keep doing it consistently.

Andy arrived in the summer of 2006 and so did the player who would eventually replace me. The manager had tried a few times and I had kept playing my way back into his plans after Yobo, Per Krøldrup and Matteo Ferrari arrived, but when Joleon Lescott joined us from Wolves I knew I had a real fight on my hands.

I had options to leave that summer and the manager was good with me about it. 'Go and see what you want to do but there is a contract here waiting for you if you want to stay,' he said. I went and spoke to Birmingham and West Brom, who had both been relegated to the Championship, and he also mentioned Stoke to me. It was all Championship clubs, but good Championship clubs. That was always in my mind, that I didn't want to go to a club where I would be pissing against the wind. Birmingham were desperate to get me. Karren Brady, their chief executive, was on the phone, saying, 'What we can do to make the deal go through, is it financial?' It wasn't, but I should have said it was. 'We'll get a box for your family, we've got a great school for your kids,' she told me, 'they will be well looked after.' They couldn't have done any more for me, they were absolutely desperate to get me and I'll admit I was tempted.

Nigel Martyn and Duncan had retired, Steve Watson had gone, Gary Naysmith was injured and people like myself and Kev Kilbane probably thought our era at Everton was coming to an end too. I went away at the end of the season to Japan with Scotland weighing up whether to move to West Brom or Birmingham, who were both offering me two-year contracts. I visited both clubs and their managers. I went down to Birmingham and met Steve Bruce at his house and liked him, but then went to the training ground and wasn't impressed at all. I also knew it was too far to commute and it just wasn't right for me football-wise. I went to West Brom's training ground, too, and really liked it. I got a good feeling about it. Bryan Robson came to my house in Cheshire and came across really well, but I just wasn't ready to leave Everton. I wanted to give it one more go. They were both Championship clubs at the time trying to get up and I felt I was a Premier League player, that I could still offer something at that level. I was maybe 90 per cent sure it was time to leave, but wanted to be 100 per cent certain. I probably stayed too long but I needed to be sure. West Bromwich and Birmingham weren't the right ones. They were good in a lot of aspects, but I had just seen so many players move for not 100 per cent the right reasons and then regret it. David Moyes always used to say there's not many players leave Everton and go on and do better and to be fair, maybe apart from Wayne, he had a good argument.

The season started and I wasn't in the team again. Although that was nothing new, I knew it would be harder to change this time. I liked Joleon as a guy, although I could see straight away he was coming in to challenge for my position and that can be really awkward as a footballer because it is your job, your livelihood. He was dead respectful. Even now he's at Man City he's the same lad – a genuinely nice guy who just bought into being at Everton. There was a nice atmosphere and he just came in and added to it. It also helped that he was a really good player. When he was in the team ahead of you, you didn't have a complaint. Maybe with Joseph Yobo at times I would think, 'Why am I out of the team?' but not with Joleon, he was top drawer. He scored goals, he stopped goals, he could play left-back, he could play centre-half. He was a proper player so I never had an argument and that probably played a part in my decision to leave. The manager had finally got it right with him and later Phil Jagielka and Leighton Baines as he rebuilt his back four. He'd gone through Krøldrup, Yobo, who for me never really set the place alight, and Matteo Ferrari but Joleon was probably the one that came in and I said to myself it's going to be hard to get this guy out of the team. I have not really got as good a case now. Whereas I always felt with the rest of them that I did.

I only started a couple of games and was then subbed at half-time at Portsmouth a fortnight before Christmas 2006 when we were 2-0 down. That was the final straw for me, that was when I said to myself, 'Right, I can't be here any longer.' I didn't want to stay and just pick up a wage if I wasn't playing and I wasn't ready to stop completely. My era at Everton was at an end but I will never forget the eight happy years I had there. I used to love running out to the *Z-Cars* theme, getting a wee sense of history from it, of what the club was all about. At Bellefield, there were always people coming in, people trying to sell you stuff like meat, fish or even a suit. It had a charming, old-world environment about it. Tommy Griff, Duncan's pal, was a regular, an older guy who had been in Liverpool all his days who Duncan would go out for a pint with. Everybody had a laugh with him. It was all these sorts of characters who seemed to be around about the club. You always had a sense that the club meant a lot to a lot of people. It still means a lot to me.

9

Three shades of blue

RETURNING to play for my country would also lead to me return-ing to play in Scotland for Rangers, but I didn't know that when I turned up at the Mottram Hall hotel at the beginning of February 2005 along with the other players selected by Walter Smith. I was just grateful to be back on board and hoped I could help him repair the morale in the squad and the reputation of the national team, both of which had taken a bit of a battering. If Mottram Hall was a short journey from my Cheshire home, then we faced a much longer haul to reach the 2006 World Cup finals in Germany. Heavy friendly defeats, 4-0 in Wales and 3-0 at home to Hungary, had suggested Scotland would struggle when our qualifying group started and so it proved as we drew at home to Slovenia, then lost at Hampden to Norway before drawing 1-1 in Moldova in what proved Berti's last match as manager.

With just two points from nine, it was going to take a minor miracle for us to reach the finals and the initial task was to become hard to beat again and get back a measure of self-respect. Yet before we could get to that, the mood in the camp had to change. Mottram Hall was about making it fun playing for Scotland again, about lifting the gloom that had settled on our gatherings and the siege mentality which had turned into 'them and us' between the players and the press. It was a minor masterstroke on the part of the manager, the basecamp from which we began our climb back up the Fifa rankings.

The gaffer immediately identified what was happening and what he had to do to turn it round. The first thing was to get everybody together and let them have a game of golf and a drink, but away from Scotland, away from that environment we had come to dread. We hardly trained. He just brought everybody together and basically said, 'These are the best 25–30 players Scotland have and and this is going to be the group. I won't discard you unless you don't want to be involved. If you don't, come and see me and we'll have a chat. Otherwise, you are in the group and you will remain in the group.'

Straight away he created a sense of unity and of an elite, whereas before every game had been like a trial match and you constantly felt you could pay for one bad performance with somebody being plucked from obscurity as your replacement. We all stayed up late and had a drink together. Ally McCoist and Tommy Burns were there, too, and it was just good fun again, an enjoyable environment to be in. Everybody knew it wasn't going to be like that every time we met up, but it was a fresh start and I think we all appreciated that. Tommy had been Berti's assistant and was admirably loyal to him through all the criticism, but he had always been good with me and I knew there wouldn't be a problem between us when I returned.

Tommy always used to remind us of what it meant to get a Scotland cap. 'I never got to a World Cup, I never got many caps, I had to win three Leagues with Celtic before I got a cap,' he would tell us all. It was done with humour but was also a reminder of the significance of playing for your country, which was right on his part. We had lost that and Tommy was trying to bring it back. The gaffer spoke about the team and the tactics, while Coisty and Tommy were in amongst the players. Not having a laugh and joke all the time, it wasn't like that, but definitely the mood was better straight away. If you were two minutes late it wasn't the end of the world. We just worked on changing the dynamics of the squad and the atmosphere.

Part of that was making the team hotel less open to the press. With some lads, it was almost like they were living in a hotel with you and you couldn't breathe. I suppose results dictate everything, but some of the criticism had become personal and that was a big issue for the players if I am being honest. It had become a barrier they felt was contributing to the team not being successful, the little vendettas between certain journalists and certain players. It was taking your eye off the ball of what you were really there for. On the flipside, the manager reminded us we had to act like internationals and that speaking to the press was part of that, whether we liked it or not. He designated certain days as press days and expected everybody to do their bit and act like adults, both players and press. It was another smart move on his part.

We also had to find a shape which suited us and the manager initially settled on a 4-1-4-1, which was similar to the one I was familiar with at Everton. He used this in his first match away to Italy in March 2005. They went on to win the World Cup the following year under Marcello Lippi and we lost to two deadly free kicks from Andrea Pirlo, but gave a good account of ourselves. We went for a supervised walk on the morning of the game as a squad in our tracksuits, but it was very relaxed.

The gaffer likes Italy, he's influenced by their football in the way he plays and thinks, so he really enjoyed pitting his wits against Lippi. I can remember going to train at the San Siro the night before the game. Tommy and Coisty went away early with the cones and the markers to set up the training pitch and get everything right for us getting there but when we arrived there was no sign of them. They had managed to get lost en route. With a lot of managers that would be the end of the world, but the gaffer was delighted. It gave him mileage to say to the players, 'This is what I have got to work with.'

It was a decent counter-attacking performance, very much setting down the style the manager would use with Scotland and then Rangers in the years ahead. Kenny Miller had a couple of chances to score and although we lost we were in the game and had a threat. Barry played well, Paul Hartley played well on the right of midfield. Gary Caldwell played in front of myself and Steven Pressley to keep an eye on Francesco Totti and did well, too. We had solid players like Lee McCulloch and Nigel Quashie in midfield helping to protect the defence. There is always a freshness with a new manager, but you got the feeling it was going to last, that the job suited the manager and the players liked the thought of him being the manager. Obviously I was biased, but that was my impression. It was fun again and you were looking forward to it. You knew there would be a togetherness and the spotlight wouldn't be on you for the wrong reasons. You weren't on tenterhooks all the time.

We continued our progress in June with a win at home to Moldova and a draw in Belarus. It wasn't spectacular but we were at least more solid now and kept clean sheets in both the matches. It gave us a chance going into the autumn of at least rescuing a playoff place from the campaign. That feeling grew when we took four points from six in a double-header at home to Italy and away to Norway at the start of September. Kenny Miller scored all three of our goals in these games and was flourishing in the role of a solo striker, a role he would also later replicate at Rangers. We now had a solid defence and a threat on the break. We had redressed the defeat at home to the Norwegians at the start of the campaign under Berti. You were back in a team that was capable of getting results from difficult games in difficult places against decent teams.

Nevertheless, we let ourselves down in our next match at home to Belarus. We needed to win but lost a goal after five minutes and couldn't get our momentum back for the remainder of the match. A second-half downpour made it a miserable day all round and it was a reminder that we were still a work in progress. If you have ambitions to qualify, you've got to win games like that. Walter addressed that with us afterwards. He always saw the big picture of the campaign, and he always used to point to that one, long afterwards, and say that was the game where we let ourselves down. It just seemed like it was never going to be our day but it was still a big disappointment, especially losing to a side we should have been good enough to beat.

At least we got a reaction when we travelled to Slovenia for our final group game, turning in another really strong away performance and winning 3-0 through goals from Darren Fletcher, Faddy and Paul Hartley. Faddy's was particularly sweet as he had taken one journalist to task beforehand for describing him as a 'bearded oddball' and 'a conundrum wrapped in a riddle, caped in an enigma'. We all knew he was furious and was going to pull the reporter concerned aside at the team hotel and he did, pointing out forcibly that it was fair to comment on his performances but not on his appearance. My other memory was that there was a toboggan run right outside that hotel and on the day of the game, while we were all confined to our rooms and trying to get a kip, you could just hear the staff flying down on these things screaming their heads off. They were out enjoying themselves, while we were lying on our beds with our curtains shut.

Finishing so strongly gave us hope for the Euro 2008 campaign to come and the manager used a home friendly with the USA to have a look at some of the young players who were starting to break through. We drew 1-1 and it was a proper game, as it always is against the States. They play flat out to win whether it is a friendly or not. Our depressing run of a decade without a win in a Hampden friendly continued when Switzerland visited the following spring and beat us 3-1, but an end-of-season jaunt to Japan for the Kirin Cup tournament proved much more rewarding for all involved.

First, we beat Bulgaria 5-1 in Kobe with Kris Boyd and Chris Burke scoring two apiece. We then caught the bullet train to Tokyo and held the hosts, who were preparing for the World Cup, 0-0 at the Saitama stadium. We weren't great, but we hung in and it was a good feeling to lift a trophy as captain and take it back to Scotland. We also received a £100,000 cheque which the SFA must have forgotten to mention to us. We stayed in central Tokyo in a skyscraper hotel with glass windows in the restaurant. You would be looking out of them at the city's fantastic skyline when somebody would come up behind you and give you a shove and scare the life out of you. A few of the boys, me probably being one of them, didn't like being so high up, but it was a brilliant place to explore from and the gaffer gave us a chance to enjoy it as a reward for making the long journey at the end of the club season.

We all ended up going out for a drink after the last game. We were leaving to come back the next morning and it was an absolute shambles. There were bodies everywhere. I was rooming with Gary Naysmith and had got up for breakfast and came back to the room to find he was still out the game. I remember Professor Stewart Hillis, one of the team's medics, coming in and us packing his bags and getting him dressed and downstairs. Honestly, it was like getting a wee kid out to school in the morning.

We got on the bus and half the players and half the staff were in the same boat as Gary. I'll not name names, but we were actually carrying the staff into the hotel. People were running over cars and stuff, which obviously didn't go down too well with the local constabulary, and there was a need for some skilled diplomacy to smooth things over. It was similar to the night out we had in Hong Kong under Berti four years previously, which ended with Faddy missing the flight, but the difference this time was that we all somehow managed to board the plane back to Britain the next morning along with the Kirin Cup.

We took the winning habit into our Euro 2008 campaign, despite a daunting group which contained Italy and France, the World Cup finalists of that summer, and Ukraine, who had reached the quarter-finals. Victories were essential against our old friends from the Faroe Islands and Lithuania, who completed the section, in our first two games and we started with a 6-0 rout of the Faroes at Celtic Park. The manager picked an attacking team with Kenny Miller, Kris Boyd and James McFadden all starting and it paid off handsomely as were 5-0 up by half-time. Darren Fletcher scored the first, then Faddy made it two before Boyd was brought down and put away the penalty. The match is probably best remembered for Faddy and Boydie squabbling over who should take the second penalty, but Darren intervened as captain and instead gave it to Kenny, who was having a bit of a drought at the time. It wasn't the best penalty, but their keeper dived over it and with Boydie scoring again and Garry O'Connor adding a late sixth after coming on as sub we had the start we were looking for.

Our next match was in Lithuania, where we had failed to score on two previous visits. I won my landmark 50th cap, making it into the Hall of Fame, which I thought I would miss out on when I stopped playing for Scotland, and was also captain for the occasion. More importantly, we won the game despite a poor pitch and losing Nigel Quashie and Faddy to first-half injuries. Christian Dailly put us in front with an emphatic header after a corner from Gary and then Kenny scored a good second goal. They pulled one back with five minutes left but we held on to make it a perfect start of six points from our first two games in the group.

It was all positive afterwards but our next match was a little bit tougher, as we welcomed France to Hampden. We rode our luck as they dominated the first half, then snatched the lead through Gary Caldwell from a corner midway through the second half. Craig Gordon, who had emerged as an excellent goalkeeper, made some good saves as we protected our lead through to the final whistle. It was probably in that match that Scotland first developed the mentality of soaking everything up and being defiantly defensive, the same system Rangers later developed as well. That game, for me, was the start of it. It was a great atmosphere. There was a Uefa coaches forum at Gleneagles that weekend and I remember walking into the dressing-room afterwards and Alex Ferguson and Andy Roxburgh were there congratulating the manager. The whole ambience was good. It was a big Saturday game at Hampden and we produced, so it was one of those special occasions. You don't get many of them with Scotland, but that was definitely one where it all went right on the day.

We didn't have too long to savour our success as we were

immediately off to Kiev to face Ukraine. We didn't play particularly well and went down 2-0 with Andriy Shevchenko scoring the second from the penalty spot. Steven Pressley had already been sent off for a foul on him just before that. They had good players so it was disappointing but not the end of the world as nine points from the first 12 meant we were still on target for qualification. José Mourinho was there and spoke to me afterwards. He struck me as someone players would play for. He had an unbelievable aura about him, a star quality. You could see people just watching him with their eyes popping out of their heads. It was like royalty had just walked through the place.

The games were good for me as I wasn't playing much at Everton at this point, although I did get a couple for my club when I returned from those internationals, against Sheffield United in the League and Luton in the League Cup. Nevertheless, I increasingly felt that if I wanted to keep playing first-team football regularly I would need to move somewhere else and this was confirmed when I was subbed at half-time in what proved my final match for Everton at Portsmouth on 9 December.

Matt Taylor scored that wonder goal from the halfway line, which sailed over my head and then Tim Howard's head. Kanu added a second and the manager was furious and changed our system at half-time. Myself and James Beattie were taken off and I just remember sitting in the dressing-room at half-time and saying, 'It's time to go', that was like the penny dropping. I had probably left it too long. I had waited six months to give it every chance, but that was like the final straw, knowing I couldn't do this any longer, being on the periphery and being the one to drop out if things went wrong. I never played for a month after that.

I had made my mind up to leave but probably didn't know what

I wanted to do. I had been to Birmingham and West Brom the previous summer, but wasn't sold on them. My career has always been like that. If I wasn't sure about something, I wouldn't do it and I wasn't sure, so I never left. Then I made up my mind it was time to leave, but there wasn't a club sticking out for me and then the Rangers thing happened with Walter getting the job and I thought, 'That's the right club.' It just kind of fell into place for me. It was perfect.

Rangers had brought in Paul Le Guen the previous summer amid much fanfare but it simply hadn't worked out. It was a bit like Berti Vogts in the national job in that an attempt to impose a foreign way of doing things on the Scottish mentality ended in disaster. It was a culture clash and the most obvious manifestation of it was in the deteriorating relationship between the Frenchman and Barry Ferguson, his captain. When he dropped Barry for a match at Motherwell just after Christmas, it was clear one of them would have to go and with results poor it was Le Guen who made way.

Sir David Murray turned immediately to Walter and, while I was obviously disappointed that the manager was leaving Scotland, I could understand the situation and why he would leave, although that wasn't everybody's opinion at the time. It almost happened at the same time, thinking it is time to leave and seeing him getting that job and hoping the two things could marry together somehow. I remember going into David Moyes' office at Everton and saying, 'This isn't happening for me, you know I am not the type of person to bang doors and rock the boat but I need to leave.' He understood, and said, 'I was waiting for you to come and see me. We won't stand in your way, you have been a good servant and we would be happy to keep you here as

long as you want to be here, but if you don't then I will do everything I can to make that happen.' He even said, 'I'll phone Walter
for you if you want', and he always said Tony Pulis at Stoke was
keen on me. I said, 'I don't need you to do that but I appreciate it.'
I think by that point I had either spoken to Walter or my agent
had spoken to him. It was in my mind by that time anyway and I
thought I am going to try and force this a wee bit, but to be fair
David Moyes was brilliant about it.

Initially, I thought, 'from now to the end of the season' about
joining Rangers. Ruben had just been born, was only four or five
months old, and anybody who has kids will you know what it is
like with a new baby – it's hard work. Family life was good, but
football-wise it wasn't so good and Fiona knew that, she's always
been supportive that way. She said, 'Do what you want to do, you
need to be happy at work.' She was probably getting the brunt of it
when I came home at weekends and hadn't played.

You can't hide it. Monday to Thursday is okay but on Friday,
when the manager goes through the set pieces, the team for
Saturday becomes pretty obvious and you know you are not in it.
You come home but you are not in the mood to chat and enjoy
your weekend. I would go in on the Sunday and work, so I would
be up early morning to get into the gym at Bellefield and just
trained by myself for an hour. I did it because I was out of the team
and I knew I needed to keep myself fit.

I was conscious that I didn't want to let myself down if I did get
a chance. I was also conscious I was getting older and needed to
train if I didn't play on the Saturday. You don't train on the Friday
because you might play on the Saturday and if you don't train on
the Sunday then you have not trained for four days. I was conscious
I couldn't afford that. Going in on the Sunday was probably the last

thing I wanted to do but I did it. Often Mick Rathbone, the physio, who we called 'Baz', would be there. I would go on the treadmill and do a 12-minute run at level 16 or along those lines and my leg weights, which I thought was a big thing for me. Then Baz would get on the treadmill after me and do a run at level 18 for half an hour. I thought I was working hard and keeping myself fit, but he was wiping the floor with me.

Nevertheless, I was glad I had maintained this routine when the chance to join Rangers came up because it meant that I was ready to play as soon as I arrived. My debut was at Dunfermline in the Premier League aged 36 years and 236 days, the oldest outfield debutant in Rangers' history, but still a mere boy. It was soon after Rangers had lost 3-2 there in a Scottish Cup tie. That was Ian Durrant's game in charge, his one and only, as he still gets reminded by the lads at Rangers. I played with Karl Svensson, who was getting a hard time, but he played well that day and was a lovely lad. Rangers were getting hammered on their defending generally, with particular criticism of their inability to deal with aerial attacks, but we kept a clean sheet there to win after Charlie Adam scored an early goal.

It was significant because it was my debut but also because it was probably one of the last times my dad was able to watch me play before his condition deteriorated. It means a lot to me that he did get to see me play for Rangers. My recollection was he probably wasn't at his best by then, but I can remember him going to that game. We didn't know it was Alzheimer's but we knew he wasn't right. At the time, he was still aware because he went through and watched the game, so he was still operating at some level if not at his peak. He probably went along with my uncle Douglas as it's not far from Falkirk to Dunfermline.

We knew something was wrong with him when I was still at Everton. Dave Whelan, Wigan's owner, had a charity golf day and after it there was a big evening do at the Wigan stadium. Mum and dad had come down to babysit so Fiona and I could go along. I was playing with Stubbsy at the golf day and I went into the clubhouse with my dad, and another couple of lads, and saw Kenny Dalglish sitting there and was absolutely starstruck, I couldn't even speak to him. It was a pro-celebrity thing, but dad came along. I wanted him to just walk round with me, but he was always agitated and easily bored. After five or six holes he said, 'I'm off', and I thought, 'Oh no, I hope he gets home all right.' He went off and I continued playing golf, came off and phoned and they said he hadn't come home. He was going back to our house, which was only 20–25 minutes away via the motorways, and my mum was there with Fiona and the kids. He never got back all day, so we phoned the police and they went looking for him.

They obviously deal with situations like that all the time and they found him and said, 'Look, he's got issues with his memory and has obviously got confused.' He had just been driving around the motorways in the area. It is a crossover of the M60, the M61 and the M62 and it can be confusing, but anybody else would have stopped and phoned or figured it out. Dad was now at the point where he couldn't and that hit us like a hammer blow. We felt so helpless. We got him back eventually and he was still at the stage where he was embarrassed about it. It came and went. He knew something had happened, but didn't really know how it had come about. He would have been properly diagnosed after that. We had probably already diagnosed it ourselves but you don't accept it until reality kicks in. You don't want to accept this is happening to someone you love so much.

If coming back to Scotland meant I could see a bit more of him and mum, the obvious downside was that I would be spending less time with Fiona and the kids. It didn't help that shortly after I joined Rangers we endured an armed raid at our home. I had returned from Scotland and had bought some new strips for the kids and they were all trying them on. Fiona popped out with Ruben, who was just a baby at the time, to see one of her friends nearby and I went upstairs for a shower and left the other three downstairs with their strips. Suddenly, I could hear them scream-ing in real distress. Any parent will know the difference between a child's cries and it was immediately apparent this was something more than a fight between Lucas and Jensen, who were around six and four at the time. I rushed downstairs and found the kids in the kitchen with four men all clothed in black and wearing balaclavas. One of them had a huge machete that looked like a pirate's cutlass, but I was so angry they had come into our house and upset the children so much I punched one of them, who I could see was tall and skinny. I guess you don't how you will react to something like that until it happens to you.

They told me to think of my kids, took my watch and made me lead them to other valuables upstairs. I think what they were really after were the keys to my car, a Mini, which were in my pocket, so I threw them at them. As we came downstairs, I whispered to Lucas to make a run for it and tell Fiona and he did. I was still holding Jensen's hand and had Kenzie, who was just two at the time, in my arms. They took the rest of us back inside and then a few minutes later, took off in the car. When I rang Fiona, Lucas wasn't with her, and I was frantic they had taken him to stop him raising the alarm and cursing myself for telling him to run away. It turned out he had gone to a neighbour who lived nearer than where Fiona was, one of his own friends' houses, but had told the family to lock the door and not answer it if anybody came to it. The people, rightly, wouldn't answer the door to me, but they then called Fiona to let her know Lucas was safe. Our gates were open that day and there may have been an element of opportunism in the robbery.

The police were quickly on the scene, but the kids were quite shaken and it did make it harder for me to leave them afterwards. When you have been through a burglary like that, it is always with you. We made the house more secure and Rangers even offered me a security guard, who would sit outside watching Fiona and the kids, but we discussed it and decided it would be better just to try and get back to normal as quickly as possible. The security would have to stop at some point and we didn't want to start depending on it too much.

Fiona was very good about it – it probably helped that she hadn't been there when it happened – but we were very worried about the effect on the kids and I still sometimes worry about that aspect of it. I had to balance this with wanting to keep playing and knowing that I wanted to give it a go at Rangers for a few months and see what happened from there. Our results were decent and you could sense the same momentum gathering as we had previously had under the gaffer with Scotland. I wanted to be part of that again as the mood was similar. You were treated like adults and expected to behave accordingly.

When we played Hapoel Tel Aviv in the Uefa Cup in February we all went for a walk on the beach in Israel together and then sat and had a coffee. It would have been cold back home but it was lovely there and I remember thinking, 'This is what European football should be about.' David Lavery, the masseur, who is a big Rangers fan and an absolute diamond of a person, got some stick. He had either forgotten or run out of his massage oil and typical of Disco he went to somewhere in Tel Aviv to buy some, but instead came back with coconut-scented shampoo. Something got lost in translation, so he was massaging the boys with this coconut shampoo. The whole team was stinking of coconut before the game. It was an enjoyable trip although we lost 2-1, but it didn't matter as we won the second leg 4-0 to progress in the only trophy we still had a chance of winning that season.

There was a strange mix in the dressing-room. The Scottish lads were good but there was also some of Le Guen's signings like Filip Šebo, Libor Sionko, Karl Svensson and Saša Papac. Saša was very quiet and a nice lad but Šebo and Sionko didn't try a leg in training, didn't like getting tackled and didn't work hard enough in my opinion. Barry was always moaning at them and with some justification. Whatever you think about Barry, he always wanted to win. He trained at a high tempo, worked really hard. He took it seriously and they didn't. That was their culture, they didn't seem to care if they won the games. There was an edge to training, with some lads who did take it seriously and some who didn't. You didn't want them on your team because you knew if they were on your team you weren't going to win. Some people cared and some didn't and you sensed that. If we were going to be successful these people had to move on – that might sound harsh but that was the truth of it.

I liked the young Scottish lads at the club a lot, boys like Charlie Adam, Alan Hutton and Allan McGregor. They were playing under a lot of pressure with things going badly but you could see they had a bit of character and ability about them. They had all come through the ranks at Rangers and it could have been, 'Who does he think he is?' when this old guy arrived from

Everton to join them, but they weren't like that at all. I just got a good feeling that I liked them and they liked me. I enjoyed working with them and thought there was a lot of talent there, that they all had a great chance. A lot of people had said to me England to Scotland would be a step down, but looking at them it didn't feel like that. There was a lot of talent there and they were also young and daft and I liked that. I'm not saying I saw myself in them – it was a different era – but it did make me feel young again and fresh. They used to make me smile and laugh with their antics, especially the goalie.

They were in a really tough environment and hadn't known anything different – Charlie maybe had to a certain degree after being out on loan, but the others perhaps didn't realise how tough a place it was to work, but they handled it well. They obviously made mistakes and you felt a wee bit sorry for them in certain respects as they were under the spotlight, but there were also a lot of benefits from that. I remember we beat Hibs 2-0 at Easter Road at the start of March and Charlie scored a couple of great free kicks, including one he put cleverly under their wall. It is easy to say it now, but I remember thinking that boy has talent but also thinking he was potentially a bit of a time bomb, too. His level of talent was right up there with anything I had seen in England or at international level, though. He did a lot of things in that season that were special.

That set us up for our first Old Firm game since Walter's return. He'd had a great record in the game from his previous time as manager but it was a different era and a different Celtic now, so people were eager to see if he could still do it. Celtic were in the ascendancy, there was no getting away from it. They had a thing over Rangers at that point. They had won the League previously but we went there and won 1-0 and I think that was a wee bit of a marker for us and them. We went to their place, their ground, and beat them. Ugo Ehiogu scored our goal with an overhead kick. The gaffer had brought me, Ugo and Andy Webster in to address what he perceived to be the problem with the team at centre-back but Andy was injured in his first training session by accident when he was hit on the knee by a shot from Sebo. Ugo was straightforward, a good lad to play with, and scored a great goal that day which will be remembered for ever. There's a great picture of us celebrating that goal, where you can see the delight on our faces. It was a big thing for us at the time.

Unfortunately we went out of Europe to Atlético Osasuna the following midweek. We had drawn the first leg 1-1 thanks to a great goal at the death from Brahim Hemdani, a rising shot from the edge of the box. Brahim didn't really fall into either of the two camps in the dressing-room. He was a very good professional and he spoke to people fine, but you could tell it was a job to him, that was the impression you got, that he was fulfilling his contract to the letter. Nothing more and nothing less. He was the same on the pitch, where he did his job as an accomplished holding midfielder, particularly in our European games. We lost the second leg in Spain 1-0 and once we went out of Europe that was effectively our season finished. We couldn't win the Scottish Cup, we couldn't win the League. It was just about trying to get some consistency in the remaining games.

We beat Celtic again in the final Old Firm game of the season with goals from Kris Boyd and Charlie Adam. Again, it was significant for us that we had beaten Celtic twice although the results would not stop them winning the title again. They had been used to being champions and we were the new kids on the block. They had a big lead when the gaffer got the job and he was just trying to put a few markers down, I think, to show that we were back and capable of beating them.

I also remember the game because I ran into my old pal Thomas Gravesen, now with Celtic, in the tunnel beforehand. It is always very tense in the tunnel before Old Firm games, nobody looks at each other or shakes hands or anything like that but, of course, Thomas was the exception to the rule. As I walked out, he boomed: 'Hello mate', then looked down at his boots and added: 'Look, new shoes!' I was like, 'Bloody hell, welcome to Scotland, Thomas.' Then, when we were coming off at half-time, Barry turned to me and said, 'What about that Gravesen, he's off his head', as we were walking in. Apparently, Thomas had been asking him during the first half, 'Are you going out for dinner tonight, Barry?' I can hear him saying it. He's just nuts.

Alex McLeish had become Scotland's manager and maintained the momentum we had in our Euro 2008 campaign. Maybe we had been a little bit lucky at home to Georgia in March, where we won through a late Craig Beattie goal, and we then lost 2-0 to the world champions in Bari. Luca Toni, the Italian centre-forward, did the damage that night by swooping onto a couple of crosses to score, but Alex was upbeat afterwards and said we were still very much in the mix.

That was his way. He was always putting positive thoughts into you and repeating a positive mantra. He was getting that across to the players all the time and he had a belief in it, too. He is a big, gallus guy, and a likeable one, too. You could have a laugh with him and his two assistants, Andy Watson and Roy Aitken. Andy was harum scarum to a degree but they were all serious about their football and a good mix together. Alex was very good. He won seven of his 10 games as Scotland manager and always seemed to be able to get a result, by hook or by crook, that was my impression of him. He always gave his team a feeling you could come away with a win. You saw that in Birmingham City's League Cup final win over Arsenal earlier this year. He gets a reputation for being lucky, but it can't be luck. He's obviously got a talent and a temperament for big occasions and he gets his thoughts across to his players.

He is a different character to the other managers I have played for. You can tell that he takes on a different persona when he is working. He's thinking about it, you can almost see the cogs turning. I really liked him as a guy and as a manager. I have not got a bad word to say about him. I used to watch him as a boy – I remember my dad taking me to games and telling me to watch him closely. I thought he was a great player, someone you aspired to be as good as. Things like that stick with you and you wonder what they are like as people. I recall not being disappointed at all with the way he was.

It was a good time to be a Scotland player and we finished the season with a couple more wins. First we went to Vienna and beat Austria 1-0 in a friendly with a goal from Garry O'Connor. We stayed in a lovely hotel on the river and Vienna struck me as a particularly beautiful city. Garry scored again as we returned to the Faroes once more for a qualifier. Back to Toftir, where I thought my international career had finished five years previously. Shaun Maloney also scored, with a free kick, and to go there and win 2-0 at the end of a long hard season was a good result after draws on our previous two visits.

It was a satisfying end to the season and I had also done enough to ensure a contract for another season at Rangers. There was plenty to look forward to as I spent some time with my family that summer. I felt Rangers could make a tilt at taking the title from Celtic in the season to come and that Scotland were in with a chance of making their first finals since World Cup 1998. I was about to embark on an incredible season packed with matches and memories.

10

The season that wouldn't stop

I PLAYED 66 games for Rangers and Scotland in 2007–08, some of them among the biggest of my career. Rangers played the final nine matches of their 68 in just 24 days in May, a run which included a Uefa Cup final, a Scottish Cup final and the title run-in. It was an epic campaign and, ultimately, an exhausting one, with the games simply coming too thick and fast for us by the end.

The season which would finish with the Scottish Cup final against Queen of the South on 24 May 2008, began on 31 July 2007, with a Champions League qualifier against FK Zeta of Montenegro. These games are always awkward and this one proved no exception. There was an element of good fortune when we took the lead and I scored what I claim as my one and only Champions League goal. The ball came out to me and I lobbed it back into the box, their keeper came running out as Nacho Novo tried to get there but neither of them did and the ball just trickled on into the net. Lee McCulloch, who had just joined us from Wigan for £2m, scored another one late on and we completed the job over there with a 1-0 win.

There were two qualifying rounds to get through which for me, with bad memories of the Champions League qualifiers at Everton, was a bit of a worry. Next we played Red Star Belgrade. I had been there before with Hearts, so thought I knew exactly what it was going to be like, but it was twice as bad as I remembered it. We were there two hours beforehand and their fans were already in bouncing up and down. They were proper Ultras, the real deal. Going down the tunnel after our warm-up, there were things flying about our heads. It was a dangerous atmosphere, the most intimidating I have played in.

We had won 1-0 at home and went away needing a result. It was a backs-to-the-wall job and that was the start of Rangers showing the obduracy that would carry us so far in Europe that season. A case of going there and hanging on to what we had in a 0-0 draw. As we pulled away from the Marakana stadium afterwards through the deserted streets of Belgrade we could see little pockets of their fans with rocks in their hands lurking behind trees and we were sure our bus was about to get stoned. Yet all that made the feeling of coming away with a result all the sweeter, a real rush of euphoria as we progressed at their side's expense. It was a big game, with a big prize at stake of getting into the Champions League, a proper pressure game, with Rangers struggling financially.

You find out about the people around you in games like that and I discovered that Carlos Cuéllar, my new centre-back partner, was top quality. Carlos played really well and I really liked him as a person, which helped, and we started to develop a relationship from there. He was a natural defender, someone who enjoyed stopping strikers scoring. I thought to myself I'll enjoy playing with this guy if I get the opportunity. We had played against him when he was with Osasuna the previous season and I remember Ian Durrant talking about him then and saying he was a good player, the sort we could do with.

We paid £2.37m for Carlos and he was probably the pick of the new signings as the manager reshaped the squad over the summer to one he felt could challenge at home and abroad. He shipped out the likes of Libor Sionko and Filip Šebo and the net effect was to make us more physically robust. Lee was obviously part of that process. He also signed two strikers from French football that summer, Jean-Claude Darcheville and Daniel Cousin. Darcheville was always smiling. I don't think he played 90 minutes for Rangers, but he was explosive and strong. You could tell he had all the attributes, but you almost felt he was at the wrong end of his career and trapped in an older man's body. The willingness was there, but he just kept breaking down. When his body didn't betray him, he was powerful and probably one of the quickest players I have seen. I really liked Cousin, I thought he was a top-class player. He always played well in the big games but unfortunately was just the kind of lad who picked and chose when he wanted to play. He had to be up for it to be at his best and that wasn't the case sometimes.

There were also several Scottish lads who were all young, athletic and versatile, what you might call modern footballers. This group of signings included Kirk Broadfoot, Steven Naismith and Steven Whittaker. I would say the penny had dropped with these guys early that they have to look after themselves to benefit their careers, if anything Kirk does too many weights sometimes. They are not monks by any means, but they do the right things to recover after matches and probably not the sort of things I was doing at their age. They are a new generation in that respect and have all become important players in our squad.

The pick of them has probably been Steven Whittaker, who is two-footed to the point where you couldn't tell what his good and bad foot is. He can jump, he's quick and flexible and gets to balls he shouldn't get to. For me, Steven could go and play in the Premiership tomorrow and make a good career for himself down in England. If anybody asked me who I would sign, I would say Steven Whittaker because he's good player and versatile and would play most weeks wherever you needed him to.

Steven had followed Kevin Thomson from Hibs. Kevin was more of a specialist than the others. Kevin's a good footballer, it is just staying fit and staying on the park that have held him back. A bit like Olivier Dacourt at Everton, he would pick up a lot of bookings and would be suspended or pick up a wee injury and never get a clear run in the team. He was a typical Edinburgh lad for me, they are definitely a wee bit different. They like the horses and their golf, while the Glasgow boys like the pub and the football more. I always thought Kevin could go and play at a good level. He was an important player for us and you wanted him to be in the team. He always used to say I have never lost against Celtic and stuff like that and certainly wasn't short of self-confidence.

As well as reaching the Champions League group stage we made a decent start domestically, too, by winning our first four Premier League matches. This run included a 7-2 win over Falkirk at Ibrox. It was only 3-2 with 15 minutes left and then the goals started flying in for us and I remember feeling almost sick for Yogi and Brian Rice, who were my pals, as they did. Up until that point, they were in it and had played really well. It was really cruel on them.

With things going well at club level, I could report for international duty at the start of September with a clear head and focus on Scotland's bid to reach Euro 2008. It was a double header, against Lithuania at home and then off to Paris to face France. We knew the first game was the tricky one, the one we were expected to win, and that the second would take care of itself if we took care of Lithuania at Hampden. We took the lead through Kris Boyd but they equalised from a penalty from Tomas Danilevicius after

Saulius Mikoliunas, then with Hearts, dived when challenged by Darren Fletcher in the box. Mikoliunas got battered for that afterwards, it was a cumulative thing as he already had a reputation for trying to fool referees but it basically ended his career in Scotland. There was too much moral outrage about it for my liking. Players here do it every week and it's not just foreigners. I couldn't help but think a Scotland player would have been hailed as a hero for nefariously winning a penalty in a decisive qualifier, just as Joe Jordan was when Scotland beat Wales to qualify for the 1978 World Cup.

It didn't matter in the end as we won 3-1 with late goals from Stephen McManus and Faddy. It was a good goal from Faddy, who doesn't really do tap-ins, but the one he scored in our next game against the French means he will never be forgotten by Scotland supporters. We had defended well again but the game's deciding moment came in the 64th minute out of nothing. A long clearance from Craig Gordon found Faddy in the middle of the French half, with four home defenders between him and goal. He controlled the ball with one touch, turned and let fly from 30 yards with a dipping, swerving shot that Mickaël Landreau could only parry on its way into the top corner. The French were stunned. They hadn't lost a home qualifier since 1999 and that was their only competitive defeat in qualifiers since 1994 until our two wins against them.

The game had gone to the atmospheric Parc des Princes because the Stade de France was being used for the Rugby World Cup and it was a special, special night for us. Another case of getting absolutely battered yet we had belief because we had beaten them already. We knew we would need some luck again, but were determined to hang in there and not get beaten by four or five as we had by France in the past. We had good players – Paul Hartley, Stephen

McManus, Barry Ferguson, Graham Alexander all played well for us, Stephen Pearson did a great job after coming on for Darren Fletcher and, on the right flank, Scott Brown and Alan Hutton outplayed Éric Abidal and Florent Malouda. I remember going out for a walk on the morning of the game and sitting in a café with the whole team. It was similar to how we had prepared under Walter and I don't know whether Alex picked up on that. Going back to that Berti story, when we lost 5-0, then we were running round Paris, in and out of shops and all that rather than relaxing. This time, we watched the world go by with a coffee rather than behaving like frantic sightseeing tourists.

The whole country seemed to go crazy afterwards and we were lauded left, right and centre in the days which followed. It was one of Scotland's greatest results and people genuinely believed we were going to qualify for the finals, but I came back down to earth with a bump on the following Saturday when Rangers lost 4-2 to Hearts at Tynecastle.

We were then straight into our Champions League group, another glamorous but tough section containing Barcelona, Lyon and VfB Stuttgart. I must admit to sitting like a wee boy at Christmas before the draw began, writing out the teams I wanted on a piece of paper, and what we got wasn't too far removed from my wishlist. It was an exciting period for Scottish football, a heady time with the national side performing well and both Rangers and Celtic in the group stage of the Champions League.

The German side visited Ibrox for our first match in this section and took the lead through Mario Gómez but we came roaring back with Charlie Adam scoring a great equaliser after Alan Hutton created the chance with a driving run from right-back. That was the game that really marked Alan's emergence for me. He charged down the pitch, beat a few men and the ball landed with Charlie, who came inside nicely and curled it home with his right foot. Charlie also scored in the return with Stuttgart and was fond after that of asking the rest of us at Rangers how many goals we had scored in the Champions League.

Hutton was a bit special or certainly having a period in his career when he was special. He definitely announced himself in that win and it was another of those runs of his which led to our winner. He was brought down in the box and Darcheville converted the penalty. Alan is probably the best athlete I have played with in my career, an amazing specimen physically. His performances in the Champions League that season did not go unnoticed and Rangers couldn't refuse a £9m bid from Spurs for him in January. It was a fair fee but also an ominous sign the club could no longer resist bids for its best players.

We had a good start but were to play even better in our next game away to Lyon, recording a 3-0 win over the French champions which ranks with the best results Scottish clubs have achieved in Europe over the years. It was a night when our counter-attacking tactics worked to perfection. Daniel Cousin told me beforehand that he felt he had something to prove to a few people in France who had written him off for coming to Scotland to play, and it showed in his performance, which was excellent. Lee McCulloch put us ahead with a header, then Daniel made it 2-0 before setting up the third for DaMarcus Beasley. We wanted to play every week in France at that point and again returned to much praise and a League defeat, this time to Hibs at Ibrox.

Next we had to make sure that we didn't slip up at home to Ukraine or away to Georgia after our win in France. We managed the first part of that task fine at Hampden, beating the accomplished Ukrainians 3-1. We started the match superbly and were 2-0 up inside 10 minutes through Kenny Miller and Lee McCulloch, then wobbled slightly after Andriy Shevchenko pulled one back for them before Faddy scored yet again midway through the second half to ease the tension.

A win in Georgia and we would be just about over the line in this demanding group but we somehow squandered our chance. That was the turning point for us. Georgia had a young kid in goal and a young kid up front and I can remember heading the ball from a corner and it hit him and went in. It was just prior to an Old Firm game and much was made of Alan Hutton and Scott Brown pulling out prior to the Scotland game and then playing 90 minutes on the Saturday lunchtime for Rangers and Celtic. I am not saying they weren't injured, but it was almost like you had a choice playing in one or the other, which probably tells you everything about priorities in Scottish football. We are what we are in that respect, I am afraid. I don't think you can change 100 years of history and say we'll do what other countries do. You can't nail people for being injured either, you have got to take their word for it, but there is no doubt it affected the camp. They were the legs of the team. Hutton was the best right-back in Europe at the time, in the Champions League team of the week and so on. He was unstoppable. Scott Brown was at his best as well. With their combined athleticism, you would take them against most people and we definitely missed them.

Rangers won that Old Firm game 3-0 with Nacho Novo scoring two goals, the second a penalty, to sandwich a goal from Barry. Nacho was an intermittent starter for us and an unpredictable player, both for the opposition and for his own teammates. We were sure Nacho didn't speak Spanish but also couldn't make out a word he said in English. He seemed to have combined the two languages into his own dialect. Nacho was a law unto himself. He needed and wanted people to like him and everybody did like him, but he was still self-conscious with not a lot of self-confidence. For me, he was the ideal sub, especially at Rangers because the supporters loved him and just seeing him warming up could get them going.

He was frustrating for other players because he would go from the sublime to ridiculous, sometimes in the same game. Yet he scored wonderful goals too often for us for him not to mean it. He would always go in the huff if he wasn't playing but soon came round, usually after a cuddle from Paul Jackson, the team doctor, who he was friendly with. Paul was one of these people that every club needs, someone all the players could turn to if they or their kids were ill, which must have been particularly reassuring for the foreign lads with families. I have never seen a player with more pairs of boots than Nacho. He had a box above his locker packed with them. He used to get them specially made and sent over from Spain and was never out of Greaves, the sports shop in the centre of Glasgow. Nacho was great with kids and my boys used to marvel at his collection of boots.

It was another important win for us over Celtic, our third on the trot. At that stage, it was like we beat them every time we played them and the more I played in the derbies, the more I realised the significance of them and the ramifications of them. It was an important sequence for us psychologically as a new side growing in confidence and learning about each other.

Next we faced Barcelona at Ibrox and we were unashamedly defensive. After our wins over Stuttgart and Lyon we knew a point would leave us just one win short of the 10 points usually required to reach the knockout stage of the Champions League. Afterwards, Lionel Messi famously described our tactics as 'anti-football' and he was probably right. With the way we played, a 0-0 was the best we were going to get but that had been a Scotland thing and a Rangers thing and it had worked for us so what did he expect from us? We weren't kicking people or acting like thugs or anything like that. For me, defending well is a skill in itself. When you go on coaching courses the first thing they ask is if you are hard to beat. Is it hard to win against your team? It's a like a game of chess and they have got to overcome that. If we go and play Barcelona straight up, we will get beaten 5-0. Arsène Wenger talks like that some-times, too, but teams aren't going to play to suit him. They are going to make it as hard as they can for him and they have got to use whatever means they can within the rules to try and win. That's what sport is about. It's not about a level playing field and playing the way the other team want you to.

We adopted the same approach in the second leg but lost 2-0 at Camp Nou. They scored their goals early and then went easy on us to be honest, conserving their energy. Myself, Lee and Barry had organised a plane to take our families across for the game. My two boys went and Barry's sons, so there were six or seven of them on the plane and they had a great day. They were picked up and taken to the square in Barcelona where all the Rangers fans were and the boys were kicking the ball about with the fans and then flew back after the game. When we were going back into the airport we saw them and the boys were saying, 'Just come home with us', but I didn't have my bags, so I said I would drive down in the morning.

I went back to my flat in Glasgow and went to bed but couldn't sleep, which is quite common after games, so I got up at 3am and decided I would drive down to Cheshire. It wasn't the smartest move on my part as I fell asleep at the wheel just before I made it home, on the M6 near Haydock Racecourse. I hit a lorry, spun round and was parked on the hard shoulder facing north when I was heading south with cars flying by me at six in the morning. I couldn't have parked it any better but the car was battered on the passenger side and I had literally come within inches of losing my life. I was so lucky as part of the car had come flying in at me. I am not a dramatic person, but if the car had spun into the motorway somebody would have hit me and I would be dead. It felt like somebody was watching over me.

I was taken to hospital in an ambulance with a massive cut on the top of my head but I thought 'I'm all right, how lucky am I?' and never phoned Fiona. However, she got a call from somebody we know who is in the traffic police saying there had been an accident involving my car so she phoned me and I told her I was in the hospital but all right. I said I'd crashed the car but not to worry. I was picking the glass out my hair for days and weeks afterwards. I had a really bad cut and was covered in blood but I just wanted to get home. I had a bag with me so I managed to change and make myself look respectable. For weeks afterwards, I had a bald patch and I remember worrying about that and going to the doctor and him saying, 'It will grow back eventually, it has been a trauma to your scalp.' The hospital just put stitches in like they would with any other lad.

It happened 10 days before we were due to meet Italy at Hampden in our final Euro 2008 qualifier, the biggest game Scotland had played for years. I can remember meeting up with the squad and telling the medical staff I had crashed the car. They told me to be careful in training, not to head the ball and they would leave it as late as possible before deciding if I could play. On the Friday before the game, the final training session, I remember thinking, 'I am going to have to head the ball some time, I need to know.' So the first chance I got, I headed it and I knew straight away it had completely burst open again. I was thinking, 'Oh for God's sake, here we go again.'

I should have known Professor Stewart Hillis would come to the rescue. He smuggled me into the Western Infirmary in Glasgow. They didn't want anybody to hear about it, so we entered by a side door and Stewart got one of his friends there to sort me out. He put in this thread that was like fishing line and you just knew immediately it wasn't going to split again. I was just sitting in this ward with people in with all kinds of real problems and conscious that this shouldn't be happening, that I shouldn't be in there jumping the queue, but as soon as I was stitched with this stuff I knew I was going to be fine to play.

There was also a meeting on the day before the game with Gordon Smith, then the SFA's chief executive, in Alex McLeish's room at the Cameron House Hotel beside Loch Lomond to thrash out our bonuses if we qualified. It was probably not the ideal time to be discussing it, but that's how football operates. We weren't due the money until we qualified, but wanted to know what we were getting if we did. We wanted it cleared up and to be fair to Gordon that's what he did. That's typical of football. I have signed bonus agreements at motorway service stations on the way to the first game of the season because in England you have got to sign them before the season starts. The captain had to sign them to make them binding and I did that at Everton.

I didn't agree with the idea of giving up our match fees and bonuses for a one-off qualification fee. I always feel playing for a bonus adds an edge for professional footballers and it's something they are accustomed to at club level. As I said earlier, the match fee was also significant for those in the squad who weren't on huge wages and made you feel you were being treated properly. A win bonus created the right environment for success, whether it was playing for Scotland or with Bo'ness.

We needed a win to reach the finals after our defeat in Georgia, although there was an outside chance that a draw would be enough if France lost their final match away to Ukraine. It was a special occasion and everybody was really excited beforehand. There had been no domestic football in Scotland the week before, so there was a huge build-up but it fell flat as they scored after 76 seconds. We were caught sleeping, me included, as they took a quick throw-in on our right and Luca Toni scored against us again. We gradually played our way back into the game and Barry equalised for us. We then tried to win it but were stung right at the death. Alan Hutton was fouled by Giorgio Chiellini down by the corner flag but the referee gave the free kick to Italy. Andrea Pirlo flighted it in and Christian Panucci outjumped Darren Fletcher to score. You are disappointed when you lose like that obviously but you are doubly disappointed if your team doesn't turn up on that kind of big occasion. I didn't feel that was the case. I felt we played well but just weren't good enough on the day. Nevertheless, when we all look back on our Scotland careers we will think if we had got a result we would have qualified.

Rangers' Champions League campaign also failed to live up to its early promise. We lost 3-2 in Stuttgart, their winner coming five minutes from time, so we needed a result in our final match against Lyon to stay in the tournament. We lost 3-0 and it was hard to take, but Lyon came to Ibrox that night and played really well, reversing the scoreline we had achieved at the Stade Gerland.

Karim Benzema was outstanding for them and scored twice in the final five minutes. The Stuttgart game ebbed and flowed, so you always felt you had a chance in it, but Lyon won fair and square. We had no complaints about that, but it was a still another big disappointment, there was no getting away from that. It felt like an autumn which had promised so much had come to nothing for both Scotland and Rangers, yet it turned out that another European adventure was about to start.

We responded well to our Champions League exit, going on a 12-match unbeaten run domestically, and also had the consolation of dropping into the Uefa Cup knockout stages, although whether the manager really wanted that became a bit of a running joke. We drew the first leg of our last-32 match against Panathinaikos 0-0 and the story goes that when we were 1-0 down in the second game in Greece, the coaches turned to Walter and asked him what to do and he replied: 'Nothing, we are not going to do anything.' That's the story, but obviously Nacho scored and we went through on away goals. As players we were buzzing and the gaffer is clever, he would be trying to win the game all right. As players we were delighted because they were a good team and we were keen to continue our jaunts abroad for as long as possible as it certainly beat a week of training back home in the Glasgow rain. Before that game, we went to the Acropolis, did the tour and got a feel for Athens. It was great.

Next we beat Bremen at home and Tim Wiese, their goalkeeper, helped us with big errors as Daniel Cousin and Steven Davis scored our goals. That was a special result and then we went over to Bremen and got absolutely battered. Forget France and Barcelona, that was the biggest doing I have played in. We hardly got out of our own half. They had some excellent players like Diego, their

Brazilian playmaker, the big centre-half Per Mertesacker and Hugo Almeida, a Portuguese striker.

The big difference was that we had a superior goalkeeper in Allan McGregor. He made a string of excellent saves that night, including one which probably ranks as the best I have seen in my career. It took them a while to score, through Diego, and then this chance arrived in the closing moments. The ball came across the face of the goal to Boubacar Sanogo, who had come on as substitute. It was a tap-in and as he connected I remember thinking, 'That's in' and turning away, but Allan got a touch on it and I still don't know how he did. I genuinely thought it was a goal, not it was going to be a goal – that *is* a goal. I had marked it down as goal mentally and then it hit the bar and came back out and I could not believe the save and how he did it.

I am a fan of Allan. He has a great desire to win and not concede goals which he transmits to the defenders in front of him. He's similar to Nigel Martyn in that he makes saves you don't expect him to. As people, they are completely at opposite ends of the spectrum, they couldn't be any more different. Nigel would make difficult saves look easy or his positioning would be such that he didn't have to make a difficult save. Whereas Allan will make a save and you will think, 'How the hell did he get that?' Nigel couldn't kick the ball, whereas Allan is a very good kicker and keeps saying he could play outfield and take penalties – he is desperate to take them all the time. Allan has the potential to be as good as Nigel but Nigel was definitely the best I have played with, although Allan still has time on his side.

If that was Allan's game, the League Cup final against Dundee United which followed was all about Kris Boyd's scoring prowess for us. He scored both our goals in the game itself and then the decisive penalty in the shootout at the end, but I have to say we were very lucky in that game as well. United put a lot into it. Eddie Thompson, their chairman, was terminally ill at the time and they understandably wanted to win it for him and you just felt the momentum was with them because they had a cause. It was another test for us. Everybody was wanting Dundee United to win for obvious reasons and we weren't at our best. We had just played in Bremen and were a little lethargic. We were lucky in that game definitely. Kris got his goals and that kept us going. He equalised with five minutes of normal time remaining, pouncing on a back-pass from Mark Kerr, then brought us level again with eight minutes left in extra time.

Kris divides opinion in football. He always judged himself on how many goals he scored, that was all he was interested in, it was almost like him against the world. If he scored a goal it was two fingers up to the world, two fingers up to the journalists etc. I enjoyed his company and he made me laugh. He could laugh at himself as well, he never took himself too seriously. You only had to see the ridiculous moustache he had grown around the time of that final to see that.

He was perceived by some to be fat, slow and with a poor touch and it was said he couldn't do anything bar score goals. He constantly felt that the world was against him, but he could laugh at himself within that. He was also, which I liked about him, a big football fan. He would watch football all the time and if you said a player's name he would be able to tell you everything about them immediately. I don't know if it was from playing Fantasy Football or Football Manager! I still speak to him regularly and he's always watching football and thinking about football, he's a really big football fan.

It's no accident he scored so many goals with his movement and aggression in the box, even in training. If you are the defender and marking him it's a nightmare. If the ball is there, he'll be first to it, whether he's a yard slower than you or not because he wants to score a goal so badly. It is almost like a drug for him, he needs that hit of scoring a goal. That's him silencing the critics for another day – it is almost like he's reassuring himself that he can do it. He was a bit of an enigma as a player. Some of his attributes were of the highest class, while others were nowhere near the same standard. I remember one Scotland training session where he was putting everything away and Darren Fletcher turned to me and said he had never seen finishing of that calibre, which was a huge compliment when you consider the strikers he has worked with at Old Trafford.

We had our first trophy of the season but were still chasing three more. The one that probably meant the most at that stage was the Premier League title and our prospects of taking it from Gordon Strachan's Celtic, who had won it in the previous two seasons, looked good after we beat them 1-0 at Ibrox on 29 March. Kevin Thomson was excellent in midfield that day and scored the winner just before half-time. We then drew at home to Sporting Lisbon in the quarter-finals of the Uefa Cup and I got booked, which meant I was suspended for the second leg. I wasn't missed as we turned in another counter-attacking masterclass to win 2-0, with our second goal, scored by Steven Whittaker after a pass from Steven Davis, a particularly good one.

The games were really piling up for us now. It didn't help that we kept requiring replays to get through in the Scottish Cup. We needed two games to get past Hibs and two more to shake off Partick Thistle. We then squeaked past St Johnstone in the semi-final at Hampden on penalties and lost Steven Naismith to a serious knee injury after a bad challenge from Martin Hardie, their midfielder.

Our backlog of games in April also included two visits to Celtic Park in the Premier League. The games came in such proximity to each other and at the same venue that people often get mixed up with their memories of them and will tell you something happened in the first game when it was in the second and vice versa. For the record, we lost the first game 2-1 to Jan Vennegoor of Hesselink's header right at the death. Carlos Cuéllar was sent off for handling a net-bound Shunsuke Nakamura shot but then Allan was able to save Scott McDonald's spot-kick despite being injured. He was subbed soon afterwards and missed the rest of the season and Neil Alexander came on.

The fun didn't stop at the full-time whistle. I got into a fight with Gary Caldwell and we both received red cards as a result. Somebody was having a go at Nacho and Nacho was probably having a go at them and I got involved. I got called into the referee's room because I hadn't been sent off during the game and Coisty said, 'I will come in with you.' Kenny Clark was the ref and said, 'I am sending you off for violent conduct.' I probably deserved to get sent off but I still asked him, 'What are you sending me off for?' 'I don't need to answer your questions, get out,' he replied. I was flabbergasted by somebody speaking to me like that, it was disrespectful. There was no particular animosity between me and Caldwell – yes we grabbed each other, but it could have been anybody as far as I was concerned. It was just the situation. I was disappointed, so I was probably taking out my frustration. Clark annoyed me far more than Caldwell. I had never really rated him as a referee. He didn't communicate well with players, and seemed to look down on them.

When Vennegoor of Hesselink scored that goal, it was a hammer blow for us. Under Gordon Strachan, that Celtic team had the same strong mentality we had and we knew we had to try and disrupt that. Despite what happened there was a respect between the two camps at that point and the two managers handled the rivalry well, too, managing to maintain a friendship. Most of us played together for Scotland. I liked Stephen McManus, for instance, but in a game like that I was fighting with Gary Caldwell. Nevertheless, there was a professional respect between both teams.

The second game 11 days later was almost peaceful by comparison. With Carlos suspended, Scott McDonald and Jan Vennegoor of Hesselink were a handful for myself and Christian Dailly. Both he and Neil Alexander, who had also joined in January, were needed now as we lost key players to injury and suspension and our relentless schedule of two games every week continued. Christian's career often seemed to run in parallel to mine. We made our Scotland debuts together in 1997, played in the World Cup the following year together, played in England in the same era and were both criticised by Berti, of course. We both had big families and both commuted to play for Rangers, although Christian flew up from his home in London and sometimes flew back the same day after training. We were often bracketed together by people but there were differences between us, too. Christian had come through the classic football route at Dundee United and played for Scotland all through the youth levels, while my path into the professional game was less conventional. He moved for big money, while I moved for nothing or small fees. Christian was a natural athlete and very passionate about that. He was ahead of his time in things like diet and all that but he was also a good lad, somebody who didn't have a bad word to say about anybody, and proved a good addition for us with his attitude and ability to play in several positions. I think the gaffer would have kept him longer if the budget had allowed.

Neil came in for Allan and did well too. He'd had a good career but hadn't played at as high a level as Rangers and seemed to see it as a good opportunity to win things and play in big games. He had a good temperament for an understudy and probably played more than he might have expected to when he signed in Allan's absences for one reason or another.

In that second game against Celtic, I thought McDonald was offside when he gave Celtic the lead but we came back and I got lucky with a header from a Steven Davis corner and then Daniel Cousin met another one to put us ahead. McDonald equalised with a shot which deflected in off Christian and I had to go off injured at the start of the second half before Kirk Broadfoot fouled McDonald and Barry Robson scored their winner with a penalty 20 minutes from time.

It meant there was no margin for error in the title run-in and we also had a Uefa Cup final to factor in, too, as either side of the second match with Celtic we had defeated Fiorentina in the semi-final. It was another triumph based on being difficult to beat as we played out two 0-0 draws and then beat them on penalties on a balmy night in Florence. It was a classy place with a lovely atmosphere and we stayed in a really nice hotel with wonderful food. Their team was pretty tasty, too, with strikers who had moved for millions in their careers such as Adrian Mutu and Christian Vieri, but they couldn't find a way past us despite Daniel Cousin being sent off and it went to penalties. I am terrified of taking a penalty, so I would probably never have hit one, but the gaffer had left Coisty and Kenny McDowall in charge of deciding who should, so

end not foe – the players at Everton didn't blame Wayne for moving on to Manchester United.

ierry Henry and co could not find a way past alkeeper Craig Gordon at Hampden in October 06. We beat France 1–0.

Alex McLeish's positive approach as Scotland manager almost took us back to a major finals.

Kris Boyd (*left*) and Kenny Miller (*right*), two very different strikers, complemented each other well.

Dealing with Andriy Shevchenko, the £30 million man, as we defeat Ukraine at Hampden i October 2007.

lebrating with Ugo Ehiogu after he scored the winner for Rangers at Celtic Park in
arch 2007.

ir win over Lyon at the Stade Gerland in October 2007 was one of Rangers' greatest
ropean performances, and Daniel Cousin was superb.

With teammates at the Acropolis. Walter Smith let us see the sights on our European adventures.

Allan McGregor is a formidable last line of defence at Rangers. Here he stops Lee Wilkie's penalty in the 2008 League Cup final.

Our disappointment is obvious after we lose the 2008 Uefa Cup final in Manchester but worse was to follow.

Lifting the 2009 Premier League trophy with Barry Ferguson after succeeding him as Rangers captain.

Lucas and Jensen on the pitch at Hampden. The gaffer always made boys welcome whether at Murray Park, Ibrox or Hampden.

Above: I owe Walter Smith so much. Here we colle[ct] our Manager and Player of the Year Awards in 201[0].

Left: Life's a beach – I go for a stroll along Bondi Beach during a pre-season trip to Sydney.

Below: The team behind the team – Walter Smith, Ally McCoist, Kenny McDowall and Ian Durrant.

Above: Ryan Giggs and I put the 'old' in Old Trafford before our Champions League draw there in 2010.

Right: Nikica Jelavic was Walter Smith's last major signing for Rangers, and proved an inspired one.

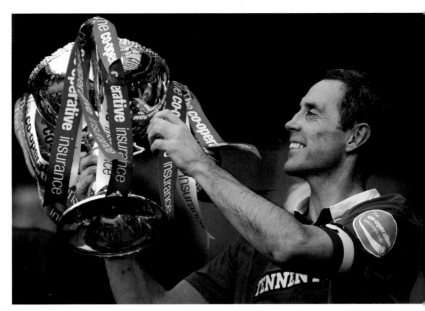

Don't write me off – a few people did before our League Cup win over Celtic in 2010.

A third consecutive Premier League title as captain convinced me to continue playing.

With Lucas Jensen Kenzie Ruben and 2010 League Trophy.

there were people like Sasa Papac walking up to score, in fairness, and the gaffer just thinking, 'What are they doing?' Barry missed for us but Vieri put his way over the bar and Neil made a good save. Suddenly, Nacho was walking up with a chance to win it for us and he did. It was one of those games where you didn't realise how close you are to the final. Afterwards, as we came through the interview zone, a reporter from Radio One seemed incredulous at a man of my age being able to play football for 120 minutes. 'Davie Weir,' he asked, excitedly. 'What DO you have for breakfast?' I am afraid I couldn't enlighten him on the secret of eternal youth.

One thing that definitely helped drive us on was that the club, perhaps thinking we wouldn't go so far, had agreed an extremely lucrative bonus structure for reaching the latter stages. There were serious sums at stake and that combined with how much we enjoyed the trips abroad spurred us on. Now, though, it dawned us that there was also a place in the club's history on offer, to be remembered and recalled in future with the same fondness as the team which won the Cup Winners' Cup in 1972.

Our achievement in reaching the final was soon overshadowed by the sort of parochial row which Scotland sometimes seems to specialise in. It boiled down to whether the domestic season should be extended to allow us better preparation to face Zenit St Petersburg at the City of Manchester stadium in the final. If you speak to a Rangers fan they will say the season should have been extended, if you speak to a Celtic fan they will say it shouldn't have and that sums it up really. It will never change because that's what drives the rivalry and makes it what it is. I am not saying it's right – it's far from right – but if anybody thinks you are going to change 100 years of madness, it's not going to happen. They talk about playing Old Firm games behind closed doors and things like that and that's not going to happen either. They would have a civil war on their hands.

So we soldiered on with our schedule. We drew at Hibs and then beat Motherwell and Dundee United at home, with Craig Levein, United's manager, livid at the performance of Mike McCurry, the referee, in the latter victory. We would take any break going by that stage as we weren't going to get one from the games themselves. We were now halfway through that period of nine games in 24 days I referred to and our next match was the Uefa Cup final. It was like it was sprung upon us. Normally before a game of that magnitude, there is big build-up and you get a chance to savour it and look forward to it, but this time it was more like, 'What are we doing next week? Oh, it's the Uefa Cup final.' You just went from one game to the next and never got the chance to appreciate the achievement.

We stayed at Mottram Hall, where, in a sense, my journey to Manchester had started when we had that first Scotland meeting with Walter in February 2005. We went out for a meal the night before the game and Sir Alex Ferguson, who is very close to the gaffer, came to see us. Yet our journey to the game itself was a real anti-climax. We drove through the back of Manchester with a police escort, saw a few fans underneath the stadium, but never got a feeling of the occasion and we'd had that throughout the campaign, a feeling of it being special. It was very clinical and sterile. If we had even driven through Manchester and seen the fans, we would have got a sense for it. You just felt like you were cut off from it and the campaign hadn't been like that at all, we had seen a bit of the world and done some travelling during it. In Manchester there's not a lot to see, but the thing that was clear was the number of Rangers fans that were there. Going out into the stadium beforehand, we finally got a feeling it was special and were reminded of the club's stature. There were Rangers fans everywhere and just a few Zenit supporters but we still felt we had lost a wee edge in the build-up and that was a shame.

Zenit were managed by Dick Advocaat, the former Rangers manager. They were a better team than us and deserved to win the final. They had players like Andrei Arshavin, Anatoliy Tymoschuk and Fatih Tekke, the Turkish striker. They had beaten Bayern Munich in the semi-final and invested a lot of money. They were a special side. It would have been great to have won, of course, we would have been Rangers legends and it would have meant a lot to me personally, too. Fiona and the boys were there and my mum. Keith had flown over from America, too. Everybody was there.

The club's name was dragged through the mud in the aftermath with a certain inevitability. The accessibility of the final for supporters meant they had attended in droves and in a gathering of that size you are always going to get troublemakers, I am afraid. Sure enough, there was a riot and pitched battles between these 'supporters' and police on the streets of Manchester. Phil Neville lived in an apartment on the top floor of the Hilton hotel in Manchester at the time and couldn't believe what he was seeing as he looked out his windows. 'What are these people doing to my city?' was his reaction. He couldn't believe the amount of people and what they were doing. As players, we got 20 tickets each to buy, but you could have got rid of 1000 tickets no problem. It was just an unbelievable amount of people who travelled to Manchester.

So the headlines the next morning were not the ones we had hoped for and we now turned into the home straight of our marathon and realised we had no kick left in our legs. On the Saturday after the final we went to Motherwell for a lunchtime kick-off and it was at Fir Park I believe we let the Premier League slip out of our grasp. That was the pivotal game. That was the day. Christian put us ahead but when they equalised five minutes into the second half we just couldn't respond by raising our game again. We were so listless but what stuck in the throat was Motherwell's players wasting time at the end of the game. I remember thinking, 'Why are they not trying to win the game, why are they playing for a draw?' I just couldn't get my head round that but, again, that's Scotland. It's all about 'get it up you' to use the vernacular and they would have done the same to Celtic. You are never going to get an easy game in Scotland. People say you do, but that summed it up for me in a nutshell. That's what it is all about. There's an attitude of 'Who do they think they are coming here and expecting to win?' Many people in England think it is easy to play in Scotland, but those who actually do find it is more difficult than they imagined.

We beat St Mirren on the Monday night but by the final day of the season it was in Celtic's hands not ours. If they won against Dundee United at Tannadice, they won the League and we knew they would. We were treading water by that time. I remember flying up to Aberdeen and we were in a crap hotel on a miserable day. It was like the writing was on the wall. That's maybe a bad thing to say, but that was the feeling among us. We had simply run out of steam by that stage. The tiredness was almost tangible and we lost 2-0, while Celtic won their match for the title.

We flew back from Aberdeen and went straight into the hotel at Mar Hall near Bishopton with less than 48 hours to the Scottish Cup final against Queen of the South at Hampden. It was like a never-ending cycle. A couple of days and then it was another game. It was almost like you wanted to get it over with. In the final we were 2-0 up at half-time and cruising, having not really played well, and then they scored two goals in quick succession just after half-time and we were thinking to ourselves we have got nothing left to give here. We are not going to score. They are on the up. They must have been thinking this was their chance to spring a surprise, but then Kris again popped up with another vital goal for us.

It was a consolation prize, better than nothing, and there was also a relief that it was all over. There was progress on the previous season, but it didn't feel like that at the end. We were going into the final two weeks of the season with a chance to be the most success-ful Rangers team of all time. We had a chance of a domestic treble and a Uefa Cup. It was an unbelievable achievement, almost. We had been to every final of every competition, we had taken it to the final game of the League. We had gone the distance and fallen at the final hurdle. If we could have chosen two trophies to win from the four, we would have chosen the other two. I think anybody would admit that, but at least Rangers had started winning again.

11

Winning

AT RANGERS you remember the trophies you don't lift more than those you do. You remember the games you lose, better than those you win. It's a fact of life that you must accept when you join the club. Most clubs go into a season hoping to win a trophy – that was the case at Falkirk, at Hearts and even at Everton, but Rangers go into each season expecting to win the League.

Ally McCoist still talks about losing the 1998 Scottish Cup final to the Hearts side I played in. He holds on to how he felt that day, he won't let it go, and I can understand why. It is a reminder of failure and its consequences, something you are constantly aware of at Rangers. When you win something it's never a big deal, it's a relief almost. If you don't win a trophy it spells the end of people's careers at the Old Firm, that's the nature of it. There's not many clubs in the world like that.

Some players don't enjoy that insatiable demand for silverware at Rangers and Celtic, some people need breathing space from what can be a claustrophobic rivalry between the two clubs. Yet I think having that edge in every game has helped me extend my career. There is no breathing space, you cannot take your eye off the ball for a second. You have got to be 100 per cent concentrated on every game, win it, enjoy it briefly, and then you are onto the next one. It's good for me and the way I am now but it's not for everybody and I understand that completely.

Maybe I get my breathing space when I return to England after each game to spend a day or so with my family before returning to Glasgow for the next game, maybe that gives me a break away from the constant expectation of success. A chance to switch off from it. Yet the summer of 2008 wasn't about forgetting, it was about remembering how it felt to lose the League and the Uefa Cup in the final fortnight of the season.

The gaffer sensed a hangover in us when we returned for pre-season. He knew there was something not quite right before we faced FBK Kaunas in the first of two Champions League qualifiers. He told us we needed to raise it a wee bit, but we didn't respond, it was almost like those two matches belonged to the season before, when we ran out of steam, rather than the new campaign. He could see it before it happened, whereas everybody else waited for it to happen and then said it was a hangover from the previous season. He was able to identify it, but he couldn't stop it because we didn't heed his warnings.

The first game was 0-0 at our place, so we went over to Lithuania knowing it was going to be difficult. We had all been there with Scotland, we all knew it wouldn't be easy. Kevin Thomson scored and it was a relief, as we knew they needed two goals to beat us, but then we gave away a silly free kick before half-time and Allan could probably have done better with the shot from Nerijus Radzius. We went in at half-time knowing the next goal would be vital. These are proper pressure games because you know financially what it means to the club, the same as the Red Star game the year before, there are numbers on it, people tell you it's worth £10m or more and jobs could be at stake. As it turned out, whatever money we made the club from Europe the club has not really seen it. They scored very late. It was a high ball forward and Christian tried to take a touch and it bobbled off him and went out for a corner. It all seemed to happen in slow motion as the corner came in and Linas Pilibatis scored with a header.

It was only the first qualifier – we would still have had another one, where I think we would have played Aalborg of Denmark, then managed by Bruce Rioch – so even if we had got through we would have had another tough game, there was still a bit of work to be done. Nevertheless, it was a big let-down and the gaffer was really disappointed. Maybe he had budgeted for getting into it and also we had such a good year the year before. We had gone from one extreme to the other. From having 19 European games the previous season to having just two. That was it and there was nothing to soften the landing, no safety net. You weren't put into the Uefa Cup as consolation.

There were no excuses, we should have been good enough to get past Kaunas, but a factor was that we lacked some creativity in midfield. The manager had completed deals for three new strikers, Kenny Miller, Kyle Lafferty and Andrius Velicka, early in the summer but was still trying to tie up the transfers of Steven Davis, who had been excellent when he joined us on loan from Fulham the previous season, Pedro Mendes, the Portugal international, from Portsmouth and Maurice Edu from Toronto to increase our midfield options. It was a case of waiting for the cavalry to arrive to an extent as we needed to freshen things up.

They all brought different things to the team. Pedro raised the level of the club. He was urbane and classy, but normal with it. A bit temperamental with regard to his body, he took good care of himself and liked to be in good shape when he played, but a top player and professional. He always said the right things and acted in the right manner. When you went to places in Europe, Pedro was the player people recognised, him and Barry.

Davo is very quiet, but a very good player. He's a Premiership player again, with a feeling for the club as well. At that time, you could go through the team and see people who had a wee bit of feeling for the club and had also played at a good level, all the ingredients you would want, and he was one of them. He ticked all the boxes for me.

Mo Edu came with quite a big price tag for a young lad of £2.6m but with no great professional experience and was moving away from home so a lot of circumstances were changing for him. He had DaMarcus Beasley here when he first came, which would have helped. He needed to become a big player for us and it was putting a lot on his shoulders given what he had done in the game. It was probably a big ask, but when he was at his best he was very good for us. Mo's a real athlete who gets about the pitch and nips in front of people. He often gets injured because he gets to places he shouldn't really get to. He is a typical American player, honest as the day is long, and a good teammate with a will to win.

We also had a change at centre-back with Carlos joining Aston Villa for £7.8m and Madjid Bougherra arriving from Charlton Athletic for £2.5m to replace him. Carlos was more my kind of player to be honest. Carlos was reliable and what you saw was what you got – a real defender who wanted to defend. Madjid is, well, different. He will tell me two or three times during a game he's too tired and will be staying back, then, two minutes later, he is on the right wing charging forward. He's a good player but he could be a great one in my opinion. He has all the attributes, yet maybe doesn't take care of himself as well as he should. I am not judging him, but he's got so many good qualities to build on. He's so quick and strong, he can head the ball and he is aggressive as well. He definitely could be a Premiership player. He's not signed a contract at Rangers for now but he's not made big noises about moving to the Premiership either and I think that is maybe a confidence thing for Madjid. With Carlos, you always felt he was playing close to his best in every game. Madjid is probably potentially the better player of the two but doesn't reach the level he is capable of as consistently.

As we incorporated our new personnel, we also had a tough start to the League season to deal with. We beat Hearts at home and then drew at Pittodrie, where I scored with a header at the Beach End. We didn't have a good record up there and had lost in the final game of the previous season so it was important to come away with something before our next match, away to Celtic.

We won 4-2 at Celtic Park, turning in one of the best performances I have been part of at Rangers. It felt a little like we were getting all the frustrations of the previous campaign out of our system that day. Daniel Cousin was unplayable, it was one of the best centre-forward performances I have seen. You could tell from the first minute that it was his day, he was absolutely outstanding. He rag-dolled Gary Caldwell and Stephen McManus and you could hear them complaining about him throughout the game, which is a sure sign a striker is on top in a duel. He scored a good goal on the angle, before being sent off into the bargain and sold the next day to Hull City as the club tried to recoup some of the summer outlay.

Kenny Miller scored twice, too, and a beautifully controlled strike from Pedro Mendes made it 4-1 to us with half an hour still to play. It was one of those games where we deserved to be 4-1 up. It could have been 5-1 or 6-1, but it ended 4-2 because Shunsuke Nakamura scored from a free kick with virtually the last touch of the ball. It's not very often you get the chance to enjoy an Old Firm win in the moment, when the game is still going on, but I was annoyed as I walked off the pitch that the score was only 4-2. I remember at Hearts we were 3-0 up against Hibs at half-time once and Jim Jefferies was desperate for us to kill them because he had been on the end of the 7-0 Edinburgh derby defeat in his own playing career and was constantly getting reminded of it. It's not easy, though – teams have pride and don't want to be on the end of a rout.

After Daniel's departure a productive partnership started to develop between Kris and Kenny. Boydie scored a great goal at Partick Thistle in the League Cup, a stunning volley, and he was capable of that. It was a proper partnership. The two of them playing together had a wee bit of everything. Kenny could work the channels occupying defenders, and they were constantly worried about it going over the top with his pace. Boydie was just the opposite, waiting in the penalty box for every chance to put it away.

I always thought Kenny was a top player even before I played with him at Rangers. He could do all the difficult things really well. He is quite an intelligent player and also very businesslike about his football. He had a pride in how he played, but it was like a job for Kenny, whereas for some lads it is just playing football. In our team, he was one of the leaders. He was a strong character who wouldn't take any bullshit, and an important part of the team. You always need key players in key positions and he was definitely a key player for us. He always came to meetings about bonuses, but he wasn't a team player, Kenny, in the way, say, Lee McCulloch was. Lee had a big influence on the place, similar to Lee Carsley at Everton.

Lee McCulloch talks to the young lads and makes everybody's life a wee bit easier. Kenny wasn't like that. He helps people and speaks to them, but his job and career are foremost. Later, when Boydie left, he kind of metamorphosed from this guy who worked the channels and was getting battered all over the place for not scoring goals into the guy who stood and scored. It was almost like he had turned into Boydie, his number of goals went up and he became the top scorer in the League. He definitely changed the way he played and became more of an individual and less of a team player. To be fair, Kenny probably identified he had been doing all that work for years, sacrificing himself for the team, so he stayed in the penalty box and scored 20 goals a season instead. He changed the perception of him as a player and also became a better finisher.

My Scotland career had resumed again. I was initially left out when George Burley succeeded Alex McLeish as manager, but it became a little like my situation latterly at Everton where David Moyes would come back to me after trying younger alternatives. I always made myself available and wanted to play. I enjoyed the Scotland games and as I got older I appreciated it more again. I played in the Northern Ireland friendly in August 2008, but wasn't even in the squad for the glamorous Argentina game in November, which was a huge disappointment. For me, that's how you reward players. A Scottish cap is a great thing but, as I have said, you are away from your family, you are not getting paid, you are stuck in a hotel, there are all those downsides, but the upside is the game itself and there's no bigger upside than playing against Argentina with Diego Maradona as the manager. That's your reward. Craig Brown or Walter would see that and select the lads who had done well for them and allow them to enjoy it. I am not saying I had done well for George, but that's how I would see it as a manager.

Between those two friendlies, our World Cup 2010 campaign had started. I had been left out for the first two games, a defeat in

Macedonia and a win in Iceland in September, but was recalled for the match against Norway at Hampden in October. It ended 0-0 but John Carew gave me and Stephen McManus a hard time that day and they probably deserved to win. The main talking point afterwards was a glaring second-half miss from Chris Iwelumo and Kris Boyd's decision to stop playing for Scotland after he stayed on the bench when Iwelumo and Steven Fletcher were introduced as substitutes 10 minutes after half-time.

Beforehand we felt we had talked Kris out of it, by saying much the same things people said to me when I stopped – 'Don't do that, you'll just get in bother, you'll regret it, it will be all over the papers and you will get stick. If you don't want to be in the squads you can just say you are injured or do what countless other people have done and not go along for a wee while.' We thought we had talked him out of it, but he phoned a journalist after the game and basically did it while still in the huff. He phoned me later to say, I have told them I am not going back. He felt he was Scotland's sixth-choice striker and added: 'If I am not going to get a chance when it is 0-0 at home, when am I going to get a game?' I could understand that but with my experience of what had happened to me, I was trying to say to him, 'I agree with you, but you have got to be a bit more sensible and clever about it.' Yet when I had made up my mind I couldn't be swayed, so I respected it was Kris's decision even though I knew the fuss which would ensue.

We had heard only good things about George Burley from the lads who had played under him at Hearts, they held him in high regard. We were all looking forward to working with him, but I always felt George wasn't completely comfortable in the position of Scotland manager. He was more like a club manager and it is just a completely different job. When he got up and spoke in front of us all, it was so apparent how nervous he was. Everybody could see it, not just the more experienced people in the group. He always used to say 'y'know' and the lads were on that straight away in typical footballer fashion. He wasn't at ease. He was a quiet, normal and decent guy, but to be the national team manager you need a real edge to you. You always got the impression the press weren't really buying it either, probably because he was preferred to Graeme Souness. The former Rangers and Liverpool manager had made it clear he was interested in the role and maybe Scotland missed a chance there, looking back now.

At Rangers we were steady rather than spectacular and defeats at Tynecastle at the end of November and then at home to Celtic just after Christmas were definite setbacks for us. Scott McDonald scored the only goal at Ibrox and it was a good finish. Any Old Firm game you lose is a blow, but particularly at home after beating them so well in the previous game. We knew then the title race was probably going to go the distance again.

We managed a 0-0 draw at Celtic Park in the League in the middle of February but then lost the League Cup final 2-0 to them in extra time at Hampden a month later. Darren O'Dea scored with a header in the box from a set piece and Boydie kind of lost him. Coisty was angry with Boydie afterwards. Their relationship perhaps wasn't as close as people on the outside imagined it to be or as close as Boydie would have liked it to be. Kris felt Coisty could have helped him more. Boydie would have grown up with Coisty being his hero. I can imagine Boydie having pictures of Coisty on his wall and I think he maybe hoped they would hit it off and be closer than they were. Coisty had also been a great goals-corer for Rangers, whose overall game had been criticised, so Kris maybe expected there to be an empathy between them. Instead

Kenny and Coisty were the ones who gelled better. Kris is probably louder, but Kenny is more confident in himself, more like Coisty probably.

Celtic got a second goal from the penalty spot when Kirk Broadfoot brought down Aiden McGeady and was sent off but the game was already over by that point. It was a sore one for us and, as it turned out, stopped us winning the treble. Despite the disappointment, I made a point of staying to watch Celtic lift the trophy. I just felt it was the right thing to do, to show a bit of good grace in defeat. Half of Hampden empties and it is all a bit surreal. I can understand that, I wouldn't expect the fans to stay, but as a group of players I feel you should.

I wasn't included in George's Scotland squad for the double-header against Holland and Iceland which followed, but the events of the 'Boozegate' drinking session at Cameron House after the squad flew back from a 3-0 defeat to the Dutch in Amsterdam on Saturday, 28 March, would impact directly on Rangers and on my own role at the club.

It had happened throughout my Scotland career that when you came back on the plane from a game you were allowed a couple of glasses of wine. When you got back to the hotel if you wanted a drink, especially if you were coming home after a night game, you were allowed to have a couple of pints and something to eat. That was authorised. The lads would have couple of drinks and then Omar or later Richard Simpson would come up and say, 'Bar's shutting, the gaffer wants you into your beds' and that's the way it worked. They would have sorted out what became Boozegate, but I don't think Richard was there. He had his faults, yet he also had good points. He was the point of contact for the players and good at dealing with all the things which could have become a distraction for us, such as sorting out flights and tickets for people. He was also a useful interface with the manager, someone we could trust to pass on messages on our behalf. He was an important part of the set-up at that time, and would take pride in situations like that not happening on his watch just as Omar had before him.

Don't get me wrong, Richard had pints thrown over him and all the rest of it for going into similar situations but in this instance nobody did that. Nobody told them they were going over the score or ushered them out. The other players involved in the session went to their beds, eventually, but Barry Ferguson and Allan McGregor didn't. You can't excuse what they did, they had too much to drink and stayed up too late. I think there were hotel guests coming down for their breakfast and they were still going strong. It should have never happened. They were stupid, but it wasn't made black and white for them as it should have been and had been in the past. It wasn't 'Go and have a couple of beers and then go to your bed', and 'Richard, you stay with them and if they are not going to their beds come up and see me' from the manager. It wasn't like that on this occasion.

They were supposed to be training the next morning but Allan got carried to his bed basically toward lunchtime. The manager found out about it and said he was going to send Allan and Barry home, but the players amongst themselves tried to talk him out of that. I would imagine guys like Darren Fletcher, Gary Naysmith, Faddy, Kenny Miller and Gary Caldwell went to see him and said, 'You can't send them home if you don't send the other lads home because they were there drinking as well.' Darren would be very pro the players and stick up for the boys. They were just making the point that it's got to be fair and that he can't do this to the team. If it comes out, if you make it as public as that, it is going to reflect on the whole team was their argument. Of course, when Barry didn't appear as captain at the pre-match press conference, it came out anyway.

The one silver lining in the whole business was that Darren emerged as a respected leader within the group, although that was probably already the case. I like the way he is. There's no edge to him at all. He's just a normal guy and I don't see why we expect him to be any different just because he plays for Manchester United. He genuinely loves playing for Scotland. He used to turn up rain, hail or snow for games. Sometimes he would come injured or go back injured and that put him under pressure. He would be told not to come back injured by Sir Alex Ferguson and would go back with a knock.

I remember he was going through a time when he thought he was leaving Manchester United at the end of one season because he was becoming peripheral. He got a hard time from the fans at Old Trafford for a long time and had almost resigned himself to leaving, but decided to give it one last go and that was when the penny dropped with the United supporters of what an excellent player Darren is. He would have been a leader in that situation and strong for the players as well. The players could trust him, they knew there wasn't an agenda or that he wasn't the teacher's pet. He wasn't trying to curry favour with anyone, he was doing it for the right reasons.

At a previous squad gathering during George Burley's time, when I was selected, there was an issue with Steven Pressley along similar lines to Boozegate. George must have allowed us a couple of beers and we were in the same bar at Cameron House. It was common to come back there and have a drink, as I said. Some lads would take a bottle of wine back to their room and have a cigarette, thinking they had got one over on the teacher. That was always how it worked. So we were having a drink just after George got the job and it had been said 11pm was bedtime, although it wouldn't have been quite as formal as that.

Pressley came up to us and said, 'You need to go to your beds', yet I am older than him and had played with him. Barry, Scott Brown, Gary Naysmith and a few others were there. He was standing there, but we just ignored him. Half an hour later, Terry Butcher, George's assistant, who was far more popular with the players, came up and said, 'How can I come up here and tell you lot to go your bed? I have been in your position, I have done it and I was worse than any of you.' He sat and had a pint, then he had another pint and chatted away, then stood up and said, 'Time for bed, eh, lads?' Five minutes later, everybody else got up and went to their beds. Terry didn't have to say anything to make it happen, he just had our respect. He had the authority and if the manager had come up he would have had the authority as well. He would have said, 'Lads, get to your bed' and we would have gone. Terry didn't even have to say it, he just had the presence and aura about him, but I am afraid Steven Pressley didn't. I still don't understand why George brought him into his backroom staff when he was still playing. It is a really hard position to be in, trying to tell guys you have played with how to behave and it was never going to work out.

Walter phoned Allan and Barry after it all came out and and told them to make sure they kept their heads down, come back to the club and he'd sort it out. He had spoken to them directly and told them not to do anything stupid and take it on the chin but they then made those infamous V-signs at photographers while sitting on the bench at Hampden before the Iceland match on, appropriately enough, April Fools' Day. They were just trying to ruin the pictures, they weren't directed at anybody, but it was still poor behaviour. At the pre-match meal, they were talking about it apparently, saying, 'We'll just spoil their pictures.' You can imagine them talking like that, not with any great plan about what they were going to do, but just through stupidity. The most stupid part of all was that they had disobeyed the gaffer's orders to behave themselves until they got back to Murray Park and that led to them both being suspended by the club and me being asked to take over as captain. It was a big call by the manager as we were in the middle of a title race and they were two of our best players.

The consequences for Barry and his family saddened me. He was a great player over a long period time for Scotland. He missed a lot of squads through injuries and had been involved over a lot of years and never got to a major championship or into the Hall of Fame. Yet, for the length of time he played, the impact he had on Scottish football and the personality he had been in Scottish football, he should be in there. As I said earlier, he worked really hard and trained really hard. He wanted to win and he was a very good player. He moaned because he wanted the standards to be high and a lot of the lads frustrated him. I was probably a wee bit similar to him. I trained hard and liked to win in training, so I got on well with him, but I could see why some people didn't because he was extremely demanding.

The gaffer said a great thing about Barry after he had left Rangers which sticks with me. He said whatever you think about Barry, whatever your opinion was, it meant something to him if Rangers won or Rangers lost. It mattered. You knew he went home and it affected his life, whereas for some of the lads it doesn't matter. It was a big pressure on his shoulders, captaining Rangers. I thought he was the best Scottish midfield player of his generation and in some of the early European games after I joined Rangers his performances were unbelievable. I remember saying to him after one game, I had never seen a better performance from a midfield player. He was sensational. He was capable of dominating games. He was the one that would come deep and get the passes and the one that would finish moves off at the end. As a physical specimen as well, in pre-season and stuff, his fitness was incredible. He was the kind of lad who wouldn't let you see him working with the fitness coaches, he was embarrassed almost. Yet within himself he wanted to be the best and would be paranoid about what his body fat was. He wanted to be the leanest, the strongest, and he played with a lot of injuries that many other players wouldn't have played with.

Yes, I could see why some people would get annoyed with him but I think he moaned for all the right reasons. I think as a manager, I would like someone like that in my team. It meant something to him. He had a wee bit of history with the club and a wee bit of feeling for the club and he had a wee streak in him where he liked being the captain and liked the attention, a Souness sort of thing. He needed to think he was the main man. He was genuinely two-footed and that was by diligence, training and working. That doesn't happen by accident. Yet he was also the typical Glasgow boy, he loved a drink and would have a cigarette or a bottle of red wine the night before a game to relax because he took the weight of the club on his shoulders before big games. He was a complex character, but I liked him and as a player I have not played with many better.

He loved the club and the club loved him, but by the end they were killing each other. I think the manager realised that it had reached the stage where it was one or the other. His influence was so pervasive it was compromising the team. It had almost come to a natural end, but it was sad nonetheless because he is a Rangers great, there's no doubt about it, a proper Rangers captain and one of the best players Rangers have had. Yogi was a great captain at Falkirk but Barry was a great captain in a different way at Rangers. In the way he led people, in what he did to get himself on the pitch when not fully fit and what it meant to him. There are fakes in football, plenty of them, but Barry was the real thing.

It was a boyhood dream of mine to become captain of Rangers, but it was also kind of tarnished by what had happened. It was April and at that time we were going for the League and that's all that mattered to me, being captain was irrelevant. All that mattered because of the disappointment of the previous year, all we were interested in, was winning the League. It was such a big thing for us, so important. It was the be-all and end-all, so who was captain or what the circumstances were was always secondary to actually winning the League. That's the truth.

We put ourselves in a good position to take the title with a win over Celtic in the final Old Firm game of the season. Steven Davis slid in to score the only goal in front of the Celtic end at Ibrox, but we then dropped two points by drawing at Hibs as the tension increased. Invariably after a good Old Firm result, you get a kick in the teeth afterwards. Yet Celtic would also draw at Easter Road when they visited in their second-last game and that meant that unlike a year previously our fate was in our own hands as we faced Dundee United away in our final game.

This time we were favourites and Celtic were at home to Hearts and needed us to slip up. That sunny afternoon at Tannadice was the best we had played all season in the biggest game of the season. It was the mark of a good team that when we needed a big performance we got one. We won the game comfortably and exorcised what had happened the year before. Kyle Lafferty scored and then Pedro scored a second. It was 2-0 at half-time, then Boydie made it three early in the second half, so you had half an hour to enjoy it while still out on the pitch playing, which is a rare luxury. The helicopter came over with the trophy and I remember Craig Levein went over and shook hands with the gaffer before the final whistle, which was a nice touch on his part. The manager showed his compassion and man-management skills by saying I should lift the trophy together with Barry and that was already in my mind.

We went back to the hotel we had stayed in the night before and picked up some beer, wine, champagne, and just partied all the way home on the bus, having a good singsong. I was pleased to see lads like Steven Smith and Graeme Smith, who had grown up being Rangers fans, enjoying it even though they hadn't played as much. You could just tell it meant a lot to everybody at the club. Then we went back to Ibrox, as is our custom. It feels quite safe and the families are all there. There must have been 30,000 fans in the stadium by the time we got back.

Celtic were criticised for not spending any money in the January transfer window that season. It was thought that they could have buried us at the time if they had because we couldn't really respond as we were struggling financially. The gaffer had a meeting with us to keep us informed, something that had never happened previously at Everton. It wasn't put in front of us there, but now the gaffer said, 'If a bid comes in for you and it's acceptable to the club you will be going.' He told us we were all for sale basically. 'I can't skirt round the issues and tell you it's not true,' he added. He addressed it and made us aware of it, so we all knew the situation.

It never affected us being paid and we were still staying in the same hotels. There were no obvious cutbacks. We needed players in that 2007–08 season, but we had too many to be able to sustain them after that and he just made us aware of what was happening, so a year ahead we could think where we would be going and things like that. He knew they were trying to make cutbacks on the squad size, on the wage bill and on the budget.

We still had the Scottish Cup final to come and it was against Falkirk, managed by John Hughes and Brian Rice, my two former teammates. I had played against Falkirk before in a Scottish Cup semi-final for Hearts and it was a bit strange but by this stage that had worn off because I had been away so long. However, my family still lived there, so it was still relevant. My sister's husband Graeme is a Falkirk fan and so are my nephews, Douglas and Lewis, so they have an attachment to the club. Falkirk played well on the day and it was a great opportunity for Yogi and Chipper to really make a name for themselves, although they had done that anyway with what they'd achieved at Falkirk.

They had a strategy, as I discovered on a coaching course at Largs the following week. Yogi came down as a guest speaker and said, 'Our strategy was to leave one centre-half with the ball. Bougherra or Weir? Weir.' He was winding me up, but it would also be true, so I just said, 'Well, that was a mistake wasn't it?' That's how Yogi is, he would be raging at losing the final but down there at Largs days later telling you how his team played. Falkirk played really well and deserved better, but Nacho scored a wonder goal just after half-time, which was typical of him. The move which led to it was like a Craig Brown throw-in crossover play that had been practised to perfection, except we had never practised it. This time the manager told me to lift the trophy on my own, it was like he had decided that the transition between Barry and me was now complete.

The double was certainly a far more satisfactory end to the season than the previous year and it also guaranteed direct entry to the Champions League group stage. Before we got to that, I got another Scotland recall after George's side were hammered 4-0 in Oslo by Norway in August for our final group game at home to Holland. We needed to win but we lost and I let Eljero Elia in for the only goal with nine minutes to go. I treated every Scotland game like it was my last one by that point. The ball was up the other end of the pitch and was cleared toward me. I thought, 'I am not getting there, what is the best I can do, what's the worst-case scenario?' I decided I needed to try get something on it, but my header went straight to Elia, who was very fast and a good player. He got to it and finished well.

That's what happens in football, defenders make mistakes and you have to get over it. Stephen McManus was more devastated than me. He was like, 'You have been brilliant, you have played so well.' Maybe I had played well up to that point, but that's what is remembered and that is the life of a defender. You take the good with the bad and I knew that. I had done it before, after all. Stephen sent me a really nice text as I was heading home and I thought that was good of him. He's a genuine fella, who wants to do well and wants his team to do well. That summed him up for me.

The Champions League proved heavy going for us, too, as the cuts to our squad really started to bite. Our section was also a bit underwhelming compared to the previous season. Stuttgart were familiar to us, while Sevilla and Unirea Urziceni of Romania did not have quite the same lustre about them as Barcelona and Lyon. We started well with a draw in Stuttgart but I missed that game as

I had damaged my ankle against Motherwell, after a bad tackle from Keith Lasley. I went over to Germany and was desperate to play but when I tried to run around I couldn't.

It was a sound start and we then had two home games against Sevilla and Unirea Urziceni, but lost them both 4-1. Sevilla were a good team, but we had been criticised in the previous campaign for anti-football, being negative and getting 10 men behind the ball, so I think the gaffer made a conscious decision he wanted to open up a wee bit and have a go and try to answer the critics and it just never worked for us. It showed what would happen if we did that, we got exposed at that level.

The Unirea game was a funny one because we scored early but didn't play well at all. Pedro Mendes scored with the aid of a big deflection and then they scored with a couple of deflections as things went their way. 4-1 wasn't a fair reflection of the game – it was a wee bit like the Dinamo Bucharest game with Everton, when nothing went right for us and we came out looking really bad. We never played well, but I don't think it was quite as bad as the score-line suggested. Sevilla were a different level, they were a good team more than capable of doing that to anybody. We went toe-to-toe with them and came out on the wrong side of it really. Fredi Kanouté was still a top player and so were Luís Fabiano and Jesús Navas in their attack, while at the back they had Sébastien Squillaci and Julien Escudé, two French international centre-backs. They had top players right through their side. We also lost 2-0 at Ibrox to Stuttgart and went to Sevilla for our final game already out of Europe and in damage-limitation mode. We didn't want to be embarrassed again, so we were very defensive, didn't create a lot and lost 1-0.

The only bright spot of a miserable campaign was the

emergence of Danny Wilson, who gave a top-class display as we drew 1-1 in the away game against Unirea. He was still 17 and the youngest player to play for Rangers in the Champions League. There were always a few questions marks about Danny before he came into the first team. When he came in and trained with us, he would go off injured quite often and be a wee bit casual, probably because he was such a good player. We didn't know if we could trust him in the first team, if he would realise what was at stake, but he was a very confident lad and well-liked. You couldn't doubt his ability either. He had a beautiful left foot and could pass the ball, yet we always worried if he liked defending.

He played in a lot of big games very quickly and his performances silenced all those doubts. You just knew he wasn't going to be around too long and sure enough he signed for Liverpool for £2m. I think he would come back and play for Rangers in a minute because he's not kicking a ball down there right now and I think it would be good for him, too.

Straight after losing 4-1 to Sevilla at Ibrox, we faced the first Old Firm derby of the season there. Kenny scored twice for us early on and Celtic felt they should have had a couple of penalties for challenges by me on Shaun Maloney. I thought the first one wasn't, the second one might have been, but the one later awarded against Sasa Papac I wasn't sure about either. I thought for maybe one of the three Celtic could have got a penalty.

I try not to be the grumpy old man of Ibrox but I make an exception where Kyle Lafferty is concerned and I had a pop at him as we lost away to Aberdeen at the end of November. Kyle's a likeable enough lad but he frustrates you because he doesn't do enough to maximise his talent. That day I felt he was looking for a rest in the game, when he is one of the younger players we need to bring energy for us and we couldn't afford that. I had a go at him at half-time that day and I still do sometimes. I don't know whether Kyle is listening to me, but I see it as my duty to keep telling him whether he is or not.

Sometimes you need to let off a little steam at each other to clear the air but I am not claiming credit for the free-scoring form which followed. We scored 26 goals in six League games through December 2009 with Boydie scoring five against Dundee United in a 7-1 demolition to overtake Henrik Larsson as the top goalscorer since the formation of the Scottish Premier League in 1998. It was an incredible month, where we basically picked up the points and improved our goal difference, which can play a part. That became almost like an extra point for us with the amount of goals we were scoring.

It set us up well for a visit to Celtic Park on 3 January, but Celtic battered us in that game. We took a doing but emerged with a draw. It felt like we had stolen it, that it was a point gained for us and that they had lost two points. They outplayed us and deserved to win. It was almost like the old Rangers–Celtic games, in Walter's previous time as Rangers manager when Tommy Burns was in charge of Celtic. When they finally got the goal their pressure merited through Scott McDonald, we hit back immediately with Lee McCulloch scoring with an excellent near-post header from a corner. It proved a pivotal goal in the context of the season.

Lee is definitely the next captain of Rangers in my opinion. Coisty trusts him and he is a West of Scotland boy, so it means something to him. Like the gaffer said about Barry, you know if they don't win a game it hurts them. He's a very funny boy and I get on well with him. I can relate to him because he played down in England and we lived in the same area. He knows Faddy and a lot of the people I know, so we have quite a lot in common. He has become an important player for us. When Lee was hoping to sign for Rangers in the summer of 2007, he was phoning me all the time. Every day almost. Have you had a word with the gaffer? Have you found out what's happening? He was desperate to come to Rangers. He was a fan, and was also keen to get back up the road to Scotland.

When he first arrived, he played wide left of midfield and did a good job there in our European run. He is fantastic in the air and I remember thinking he would score 10–15 goals for us in the League, I thought he would score more than he did. He got a bit of a hard time from the punters – they weren't really having him, asking what does he actually do, whereas we always valued him. He wasn't easy on the eye out there and they would say why have we not got Nacho Novo playing wide left or DaMarcus Beasley. The position he is now, sitting in front of the centre-backs, is perfect for him but he had never really played there until he was 30. The gaffer identified that in him. He's also played centre-back and he was good there. He has matured now and runs the place. He is such a big influence. All the young lads go to Lee for advice because he always knows what's going on at the club.

We beat Celtic again at the end of February in the League despite their signing of Robbie Keane on loan from Spurs in an attempt to overhaul us. Kevin Thomson welcomed Robbie to the game with one of those ferocious tackles you often see setting the tone at the start of an Old Firm game. It was similar to one Barry Robson made on Christian Dailly when we lost the League to Celtic in 2008, but now it was the other way round. Scott Brown was sent off after he and Kyle tangled midway through the second half and then Mo Edu scored the winner for us right at the end. That was the turning point where the momentum swung. The League was ours to lose after that and we never really gave it up.

Whether it's a Scotland manager, a Rangers manager or a Celtic manager, you get a feeling very quickly of how it is going to pan out. It is as if people have got their minds made up and the momentum is very hard to change and it was a bit like that for Tony Mowbray. To be fair, he wasn't very far away on a number of occasions but in the big games, the ones that really mattered, we seemed to come out on top. It is such a fine line and the Old Firm games are the ones that have the biggest influence on it. It is kind of kill or be killed for the Old Firm managers. They only get one season to prove themselves. Mowbray was sacked after a 4-0 defeat at St Mirren, but we had a similar defeat around that time, 4-1 at St Johnstone. People tend to forget about it because we went on to win the League but it was a right kick in the teeth for us at the time.

We had already lifted the League Cup, overcoming St Mirren in the final despite being reduced to nine men after Kevin Thomson and Danny Wilson were sent off. It was the same as previously in the Scottish Cup finals against Queen of the South and Falkirk. It was such a big day for St Mirren and they put everything into it. We never seem to play well in cup finals. They were the better team until Kevin was sent off and then we came into the game a wee bit more. Then when Danny went, you could almost sense they thought that was their chance and pressure went from us onto them and they couldn't handle it. The momentum swung and they thought they had to come and win the game and they didn't like that much. They started giving the ball away and feeling the pressure and we sat in and got the goal on the break as I passed to Steven Naismith and he crossed for Kenny Miller to score with six minutes left. It is one of the greatest feelings when you get a goal like that. I remember the gaffer was out directing the traffic in that game, he was really up for it. People see him sitting in the stand or standing down on the touchline and think he is undemonstrative, but believe me he is often animated at half-time and I think it is then and by changing things during a game that the top managers really earn their corn. It was certainly a sweet feeling to go down to nine men and still win, that doesn't happen very often. To go down to 10 men and win is difficult enough.

We clinched the title at Hibs with three games to go. It was less dramatic than the previous season perhaps but no less enjoyable for that. There were individual accolades for me, too, as I was voted the Scottish Football Writers' Association Player of the Year and the Clydesdale Bank Premier League Player of the Year. Another great honour was passing the record set by Jock 'Tiger' Shaw, a legend at Rangers, of 39 years and 325 days and becoming the oldest outfield player at the club since 1945. I turned 40 the day after we finished the season with a 3-3 draw at home to Motherwell, having played every minute of every League match that season. Not bad for an old man.

I received the Clydesdale Bank's award at a dinner in Glasgow. The gaffer had been named Manager of the Year and invited me out to lunch with him and his staff. It was him, Martin Bain, the chief executive, Coisty, Kenny McDowall, Ian Durrant, Jim Stewart, the goalkeeping coach, and so on. Beforehand, I thought, 'That's outwith my comfort zone', but we went to La Parmigiana, an Italian restaurant in the west end of Glasgow, and it was brilliant. No football chat, just 12 guys sitting talking and eating in a beautiful restaurant. They were good company, then we went on to the Blythswood hotel and had a couple of drinks. You got a feeling of how well the staff got on, as they were all hammering each other. You saw the dynamics of how it worked and thought this is a good way to run a football club. They are all friendly, they take the piss out of each other and have a laugh.

Then we all turned up at the dinner, sat down at the table and I saw my old pal Kenny Clark was the after-dinner speaker. I thought, 'You are winding me up.' After the way he had spoken to me after the game at Celtic the previous season he was the last person I wanted to sit and listen to and Coisty had been in the room with me, so he knew what had happened, too. Clark was up there telling crap jokes about Barry when he obviously doesn't know him one bit. I was cringing when he was talking because I knew what he was really like and I wouldn't have laughed even if it had been funny to be honest. Our whole table seemed to share that opinion, as we all just sat and glared at his 'act' without so much as a smile on any of our faces.

At every club you have a level of success. At Everton, initially, it was avoiding relegation that was success and then it was maybe getting in the top half of the table and then it became qualifying for Europe. Qualifying for the Champions League with Everton was better than winning the League because we broke into the top four at the time. Our league was basically the 16 other teams, so we won our league and more if you look at it like that. There is a context, a ceiling, for what is a successful season. With Rangers you get a trophy if you are successful, but that's not the case at every club.

I don't think I measure it by trophies, but other people do and definitely at Rangers you get measured by your trophies. You don't get measured by how good a player you were. You get measured by how many trophies you win. I bet if you asked the majority of lads they wouldn't know where their medals are. It's in your head, you know you have done it and you don't even need the medals. They are just a confirmation that you have done it, rather than the reason you do it. Yet at Rangers, or Celtic for that matter, they are a necessity if you want to hang around a little longer.

12

Rangers and Scotland, 2011 and beyond

WE KNEW it would be harder to win the Premier League last season. Celtic had improved a lot under Neil Lennon at the end of the previous campaign and we knew they would be up for it and that it was going to be an interesting season ahead. Tony Mowbray's team were perceived as one who would outplay you, whereas we knew it would be more than that with Lennon's version. More of a battle. More like being back up against Gordon Strachan's teams. There was definitely that influence again. I think everybody at Rangers was aware it was going to be a different challenge.

We started strongly, but so did Celtic. Both sides won their first nine games before the first Old Firm derby. It was almost like you had done so well, yet still hadn't created a gap, that perfection was the minimum required of you and it was a case of who would blink first. Then we won the Old Firm game and won it well, which felt like putting down an important marker for the rest of the season. They went 1-0 ahead, when Gary Hooper scored just before half-time, but I can remember the gaffer saying to us at half-time that we were the better team and would win if we just kept playing as we had been and we did. It was a message he kept reiterating to us as the season unfolded. We quickly equalised through a Glenn Loovens own goal, then Kenny Miller put us ahead. Celtic contributed to a certain degree and got a lot of criticism afterwards for perceived mistakes in the build-up to our goals, but it was a big result.

It was also the start of the various refereeing controversies which would mar the season in Scotland. Our third goal, also scored by Kenny, came after Willie Collum, the referee, awarded a penalty for Daniel Majstorović's challenge on Kirk Broadfoot in Celtic's box. It was a soft penalty when you look back at it on TV now, but Majstorović's leg was hanging out and you have seen them given many times. Celtic got a worse one of similar ilk against us in the final Old Firm game of the season, when Anthony Stokes came inside and just bumped into Steven Davis, who couldn't avoid him, but Allan McGregor saved Georgios Samaras' shot. On that fevered day back in October we thought it was a penalty straight away, but it probably wasn't one looking back at it now. People say these things even themselves out over a season and whether they do or they don't, bad refereeing decisions cut both ways, which is something I felt was largely forgotten in Celtic's subsequent campaign for 'justice'. Willie Collum, for me, is a referee who plays to the assessor in the stand, regardless of who he is refereeing.

That game came at the end of a busy start to the season in which Scotland's Euro 2012 qualifying campaign began hesitantly but Rangers made a much better job of the Champions League than the previous year. Scotland started with a 0-0 draw in Lithuania. They are always an awkward bunch but in order to qualify I think you have got to win these games. They can be the ones that cost you at the end of the campaign. The difference of two points between a draw and a win is a big margin. We had gone over there and won the last time we had them in our section, for Euro 2008, and still didn't qualify. At the time, a draw was perceived as an okay result, but I think you have to beat the teams seeded below you – home and away.

Our next match, at home to Liechtenstein, had all the hallmarks of being a disaster. They went ahead with a good goal from Mario Frick and we were really struggling to turn it round. The script was written, it was back to the days when everybody was hopeless, sack the manager and all the rest of it until Kenny Miller equalised and then Stephen McManus scored in the sixth minute of stoppage-time to make it 2-1. You are playing Liechtenstein. You are expected to win and should win, but on the day there honestly wasn't a lot between the teams. There was also an argument in the dressing-room at half-time between Faddy and Craig Levein. I felt it had been building up between them during the week. The manager said Faddy had to show he was worthy of a place in the team before-hand and, in consequence, Faddy tried too hard in the game basically. It just never happened for Faddy but it didn't happen for all the right reasons, because he was trying so hard. Trying to prove a point, rather than doing what comes naturally to him. He got taken off at half-time and he wasn't happy about it. Knowing Faddy well, I could have predicted that was how he would react to being told to prove himself. Maybe Craig picked a team he didn't want to pick but felt he could get away with in that game, it was almost like he was trying to prove a point to himself. Faddy started and so did Kris Boyd. It was like he knew it wasn't the right team for him, but everybody else perceived it to be the right team. I think he got swayed to a certain extent and maybe he moved from that to the Czech Republic, for our next game, and went completely the oppo-site way. It can click with those kinds of players, but you just got the feeling Craig wasn't convinced.

Rangers' 0-0 draw at Man United in our first Champions League game was definitely a tactical triumph because we were perceived to be going down there to get a hiding. I had been down there before in 2003 to watch Rangers play when Alex McLeish was manager. United won 3-0 that night, but it was 3-0 going on 6-0; men against boys. It was just too easy but we made sure it wasn't easy this time for United with a stubborn 5-4-1 formation. It was a new system and the gaffer had obviously thought about it a lot and it worked to perfection. There aren't many games at Old Trafford where Man United don't score – in fact we were the only side who managed to record a clean sheet there last season in any competition. Yes, it was backs to the wall and they made a few changes, but they do that a lot. We followed it with another good result, a 1-0 win at home to Bursaspor in which Steven Naismith scored a good goal and we had four points from six and a start which gave us a chance of progressing.

If Rangers had been unapologetically defensive at Old Trafford, we still fielded one striker in Kenny Miller. Craig took things to another level for Scotland's visit to Prague by using a formation which, controversially, didn't have a striker in it. When the manager tells you something you buy into it as a player, you go for it, but looking back now, going to Man United with Rangers we still had one striker, we still had an opportunity and we were still in their box at times. We didn't have chances really, but we still had a potential threat. They couldn't leave the back door completely open because there was still a worry for them, but my recollection of the Czech Republic game is we couldn't get out of our half. It felt like there was no threat at all, that we didn't have one, that was the difference and, obviously, Man United were a better team and deserved more respect. The Czechs weren't that good. Tomáš Rosický is a good player, but other than him I didn't think there was anything too special within their team. That was my take on it. Afterwards you start to think about it and analyse it, but at the time you have to be 100 per cent behind it and buy into what the manager is saying. We did that, there's no doubt, but it never worked and they scored a goal from a set piece.

The manager was clear in saying he was going for a 0-0, that was his game plan, and I remember before the game Steven Fletcher and Charlie Adam getting left out altogether, not even on the bench, and thinking they are two players that can change a game. It was almost like that was the system and there wasn't a Plan B. Kenny was on the bench, too, and the team was leaked early, which didn't help either. Everybody knew what the team was beforehand. I don't know if the Czechs prepared any differently as result, but it would have been better to surprise them.

On all the coaching courses we go on now as part of the Pro Licence, at all the talks, they say name your team on the day of the game and not before. Lars Lagerback, Sir Alex Ferguson, José Mourinho and Arsène Wenger – they all name the team on the day of the game. Players' agents can leak it if their man isn't playing, I have seen teammates texting line-ups to journalists on the bus to games, and now you have players going on Twitter saying 'not playing today'. The uncertainty keeps players on edge. David Moyes would give you a rough idea of the team on a Friday afternoon, but wouldn't name it. I always wanted to know so I could prepare properly if I was playing, but his argument was prepare as though you are playing and he was right, with hindsight. I definitely understand why people don't name teams now, yet that team was out two or three days before the game.

In our next qualifier we faced Spain, the reigning World and European champions at home. They were in control for long

swathes of that game, as they always are with their passing abilities. We were 2-0 down and well out of it, then Naisy scored to
bring us back into it and we equalised via an own goal from Gerard
Piqué. Naisy played well in all the big games last season, they seem
to suit him. He's brilliant in the air for his height and non-stop in
style. You can now see a hardness developing in him as well. Walter
always spoke about getting that winning mentality, that edge, and
with him and Steven Whittaker you can see it developing month
by month. It's interesting, almost like the nature/nurture debate –
are you like that or can you become like that? You definitely can in
my opinion, the club you are at kind of dictates it to you and it
maybe takes some players longer than others. Spain, though, won
that game, with a late goal from Fernando Llorente which we
should have stopped.

If that was another disappointment with Scotland, it was still a
good start to the season at Rangers. We drew 1-1 with Valencia in
the Champions League, meaning we had only conceded once in
270 minutes in the tournament. It was such a contrast from the
year before and the manager had addressed that failing. He had
probably opened up against his better judgement to play more
expansively and we got our just deserts for it, whereas when we
went the opposite way we had some success. Maurice Edu scored
with a header after he outjumped the goalkeeper but then unfortunately cancelled it out with an own goal at the start of the second
half. I felt we played really well in that game and deserved to win
it. If we had, we would have been in a great position to qualify.

It was around this time that the refereeing controversy gathered
momentum, too. Looking back now, it started at the game between
Celtic and Dundee United at Tannadice on the Sunday before we
won the first Old Firm derby of the season. Dougie McDonald, the

referee, rescinded a decision to give Celtic a penalty, changing his mind after consulting with assistant referee Steven Craven. Afterwards he told Neil Lennon that Craven heavily influenced his decision but in fact he realised his own error immediately and only told Lennon that to protect himself and he later received an official warning from the SFA for lying over his reasons. There was a cover-up, but I thought it was all blown out of proportion. As a club we could have made our own claims, made a big fuss out of things that happened in games, both before that and after it, but we never did. It was almost a desperation thing to me. I know I am biased, but a lot of people in the game felt it emanated from Celtic, yet nobody wanted to say so. I think that needs saying to a certain extent, but whether it will make any difference or not I don't know.

I feel sorry for the referees – they are doing a job and I am totally convinced they are not biased. I grew up a Rangers supporter, but I was desperate to beat them when I played for Falkirk and Hearts and referees will be the same. You are there to do your job and when it becomes a job, when you are getting paid for it, you simply go and do it. You don't even think about who you supported, I can guarantee you that 100 per cent. You think about your teammates, your dad watching in the stand, you want to do your best to try and win the game. The referees are the same, their families are there and they don't want to make mistakes or give decisions they don't believe are correct. They are under pressure and I think the biggest thing for the referees is that it is always known who is refereeing what game beforehand in Scotland. That shouldn't happen, it should be a surprise who is refereeing the game. In Italy they draw lots, which can be a bit of a nightmare in terms of an inexperienced referee getting a high-profile game, but it takes bribery or questioning the integrity of the officials out of the equation.

McDonald lied to Lennon but his decision was right, which is ultimately what you want. Later in the season, in the League Cup final, Craig Thomson changed his mind when Nikica Jelavić went down in the box under Thomas Rogne's challenge, first, giving the penalty, then not giving it. He felt he got the decision right, so however he had come to it didn't matter. That is the crux of the issue. Celtic won the game at Tannadice, so why try to fight battles and cause a furore, it's self-defeating. Rangers wouldn't operate like that. After the Jelavić incident, I went and spoke to Craig Thomson and asked, 'Why did you not give it?' and he said, 'I made the right decision in the end, I made the decision too quickly but it was the wrong decision, so I changed my mind.' 'So the fourth official or your assistant didn't have an influence?', I asked. He said, 'No, I made the decision', so I said, 'Fair enough, I can accept that.' I like Thomson as a ref, you can talk to him.

Yet in the autumn the row escalated, with the referees feeling their integrity was being questioned after the McDonald affair and that it was leading to increased threats to them and their families. They voted overwhelmingly in favour of a strike at the end of November, although they still remain adamant it was 'a day of reflection'. It was dangerous from their standpoint to be honest because they brought in all these foreign referees and by all accounts they did really well and they have perhaps created a precedent there. Yet I also felt sorry for them because it is impinging on their private lives and I think there are a lot of issues that have not been in public, things that have happened with regard to their personal safety and their families and stuff like that. When we have spoken to referees off the record on our Pro Licence courses, they have referred to this without actually spelling it out. I think they have been thrust into a place they don't need to be and I think a lot of that is down to them being named before the games, particularly the Rangers–Celtic games and the cup finals. I don't see the benefit of that at all, it just adds to the pressure on them.

It was a relief to get away from all the domestic squabbles in the Champions League. We lost heavily to Valencia in Spain, but I didn't think it was a deserved 3-0 defeat. We had chances before they scored, Naisy had a really good one, and it was an even game. The previous year we were getting beaten 4-1 and that was an accurate reflection of the games – it felt we were seeing out some of the fixtures toward the end, hoping to avoid another heavy loss. But in this campaign, we always felt like we were in the games and had a chance of winning them. Next we lost 1-0 at home to Man United to a Wayne Rooney penalty, and away to Bursaspor they got a draw late on when we should have won the game.

It meant we dropped into the Europa League rather than making it to the last 16 of the Champions League, but losing the Old Firm game on 2 January was a bigger blow for us. Going into it, we were perceived to be big favourites to win, and people thought that if we did, then the League was over. Celtic were at a low point, they were getting pilloried for defensive lapses and mistakes. It was their last chance. Time has since painted the picture that Celtic really played well that day and that Georgios Samaras was brilliant. That's not my recollection. I thought we were the better team until they got a goal out of nothing, after a couple of wee mistakes. Richard Foster gave the ball away and Allan came off his line too early as Samaras raced through. Looking back now, it was probably one of the better things that happened to us. It put us back on our toes and made the League more interesting. Celtic obviously got a lot of confidence from it because they were kind of on their last legs. Myths get built up afterwards, like Samaras tore us to shreds. It wasn't like that. He scored two goals and fair play to him, I am not trying to rain on his parade, but the gaffer always believed we were a better team and he doesn't bullshit you.

That error apart, Richard, or Fozzy as he is known, was tremendous for us, particularly in Europe. He's almost like an old-fashioned man-marker. He's very quick and people can't get away from him. Fozzy is the kind of lad in my opinion who could go and play for a European club. All the boys like him and he's fitted into the dressing-room and developed a Rangers mentality. It proved a sound move taking him on loan from Aberdeen as our squad size dwindled. Kyle Bartley was another player who came in on loan, from Arsenal, and got better the longer he was here. Kyle also looked like he would like to be part of it permanently. He was respectful and well-liked. I met his dad and you could just tell he was from a nice family with good values. You could see him being a Rangers player, one you would love to have at your club, although it will be hard to get Arsenal to allow him to leave. If he hadn't got injured, I maybe wouldn't have played a lot of the games in the run-in. There is definitely a chance that could have happened.

We were also drawn against Celtic in the Scottish Cup and although the replay attracted notoriety, the first game was a good one. We were 2-1 up at half-time and in that situation you have to decide whether to stick or twist. We sat back, invited them on and they played well and kept the ball. Although they had Fraser Forster, their goalkeeper, sent off for the penalty that put us 2-1 up, they looked like the team with 11 men and you have got to give them credit for that. Scott Brown scored a good goal and then celebrated right in front of El-Hadji Diouf, our new loan signing from Blackburn, who he had been having a bit of banter with during the game. Diouf is different, not your stereotypical footballer. Yes, he talks the talk but he walks the walk as well. He's not one of those who doesn't really produce in games. He's up for the fight and he's got heart, you can tell he's had to battle in life. He might not be everybody's cup of tea, but what you see is what you get with him and I would take that all day. He spat at Celtic fans while previously playing for Liverpool, which is out of order, but it wasn't a wind-up signing as some people suggested. The gaffer's not daft. He spoke to Sam Allardyce and people who had worked with Diouf and we had also played against him in pre-season in Australia. He came as a striker, I think, and then the gaffer realised he wasn't really as effective there, so he started to use him differently. He's not got pace, but he became almost like an impact player. He's a clever footballer when it comes to utilising what he has got, protecting the ball with his body and so on.

We were well beaten by Celtic in our next League encounter with them. The 3-0 defeat at Celtic Park also saw me written off by many former pros as past it. John Hartson, Derek Johnstone, Mark Hateley – all the usual candidates – but that is part and parcel of Scottish football, it goes with the territory. I am not going to say I was happy about it, but I knew the way to respond was to go and play well in the games that followed and I think I did that. Former Rangers players should know better and I had a word with Goughie about it once. I met him on the train when he was coming back up from an Everton game he had been at. I said to him, 'You are out of order, you should know better, you captained the club, you know what it is like to play for them, nobody needs to tell us when we haven't had a good result or aren't playing well.' Gough and Hateley and people like that have had better Rangers careers than I will ever have, but I just hope I am never in the position where I feel I have got to do that with a Rangers team.

I got criticised for the first Celtic goal, fair enough, but I don't think Gary Hooper got enough credit for it. That goal wasn't scored because I was slow or 40, without a shadow of a doubt. Anybody who appreciates football knows that was a great piece of skill, a great touch. I am going that way, he's coming this way and it was almost simultaneous and he left me for dead. Then he still had to finish it. I have handled Hooper better since but that situation could happen again any time. It could have happened in the next game or it could have happened 10 years ago to me when I was, supposedly, in my prime. That's how I get it straight in my head, but for everybody else that's the end of Davie Weir. It wasn't for me. Obviously I am not happy about it and I think about what I could have done better, but there's not a lot I could have. Maybe that's wrong, but that's what works for me. It was a clever idea and a wonderful touch and that makes me think all the people who were critical of me don't know what they are talking about. That sort of sums Scottish football up, rather than saying it was a good move by Hooper, it is 'How bad is Davie Weir?' That's it, maybe, in a nutshell.

It probably did us good to get away to Lisbon in the Europa League immediately afterwards. The boys were desperate to stay in Europe because they are the best games for players. The nights you really remember. You can almost recall every one of them, the games and the occasion, while many of the domestic ones blend into each other. The Champions League ones are the best, but the Europa League ones are special, too. Even the trips away. Lisbon last season, for instance, was a great trip although I suffered some food poisoning. You stay in a beautiful hotel, get a feel for the city and go to a different ground. It breaks the monotony of playing the same teams and seeing the same faces all the time.

A big thing was made of Celtic going out of Europe early last season. That was perceived to be a benefit to them, but as it turned out it wasn't. It can get to a ridiculous stage if you progress too far, as we did in 2008 or Celtic did in 2003, but last season we had 10 European games, which was just right for us. It refreshes you and gives you a reason to win the League as well. You get to know your teammates better, too, especially with the way our club is. We have a laugh. It is a tight group and you enjoy the company of the staff and the players. It's not a chore, I think it's great – one of the best things about being at Rangers for me is the European trips. People are more interested in them – my kids are. For Lucas' presentation at school the other day he took in all the foreign strips I have picked up over the years. There's a bit of mystique to it.

The food poisoning only lasted for 24 hours, although I still wasn't sure I would play in Portugal. As it turned out, I started and was then replaced by Kyle Lafferty with about 20 minutes left. They went 2-1 up with seven minutes to go but then David Healy, another sub, sent us through on away goals when his clever movement and his ball across the box allowed Maurice Edu to equalise. I watch David in training and he's got that intelligence to his game and he can finish. Probably the higher the level the more it suits him, as his phenomenal international scoring record with Northern Ireland suggests.

It was then back to the domestic mayhem. The Scottish Cup replay with Celtic. It did kick off and we had three players sent off, so you can't dress that up. Steven Whittaker got sent off for two tackles you could argue all day about. Diouf got sent off for being Diouf and Bougherra's wasn't a sending off either, but if you get three players sent off in an Old Firm game, it's World War Three, isn't it? That's how it is perceived. The confrontation between Coisty and Lennon happened at the end and again was next to nothing. I am sure, looking back, people would have done things differently but the perception is because those two have an argument, it is Protestant against Catholic, half of Scotland against the other half, or Scotland against Ireland, those are the connotations. With the same argument in any other football game, they aren't really brought into play. But all of a sudden it's a matter for the government, it's a matter for Alex Salmond, the First Minister, it's a matter for Stewart Regan, the SFA's chief executive. These things happen all the time in other places but nobody is trying to put it in a context it doesn't deserve to be in.

Our European exit eventually came against PSV Eindhoven. We drew 0-0 in Holland, which was a good result, but then lost 1-0 at Ibrox. It is easy to say now it was a good thing to happen to us, but we never felt we were going to win the tournament, that was the impression I got. We probably thought the same when we reached the final back in 2008 but we also probably learned the hard lesson that it cost us the League. If you are being honest, at the back of your mind you are thinking about the League. I think that seeped into us all subconsciously. You are never happy to go out, don't get me wrong, but you could justify it as one of those where the glass is half full or half empty and the half-full way to look at it was to go for the League.

From New Year to the middle of March it had turned round full circle and now the League Cup final was seen as our last chance to save our season and Celtic's chance to bury us. Nobody expected us to win that final. I was finished, again, Celtic were flying and scoring goals left, right and centre. They basically said they had the Cup wrapped up. That was the impression we got. The gaffer was brilliant in the week leading up to it. He employed a trick he had used before of belatedly handing out our Premier League winners' medals from the previous season. We were meeting upstairs one day at Murray Park and he went through his chat, saying, 'You know what this week means to the club, this club has been built on being winners and it has a history of winning, it takes special players to play here.' Then he added, 'I have got to hand these out and I have got to post 10 of them to people who have left', so he got his message across with some humour and still made it special. It was him reminding us we were the reigning champions and it worked. From then on, Steven Davis started to hit top form and Jelavić was outstanding. He terrorised them in the final, and although he got the penalty taken away from him, he still scored the winner in extra time. That penalty incident could have been our get-out clause, toys out of the pram, game over, but we reacted in the right way. We went and won the game, didn't moan about it, and the issue was finished there and then.

Walter paid £4m for Nikica at the start of last season. He was given an amount of money and it was how he wanted to spend it. The bank said, 'Get a few players in and boost the numbers', but he said, 'Rangers are better than that, we are not just going to sign squad players.' He's told me he had to set a precedent with regard to the sort of players who should be coming to Rangers. It was a statement and I knew straight away it was the correct decision. You could tell, even with the way Nikica was as a lad. He's just got it, a confidence in himself. We were like, 'He'll do for us all day' immediately. He was just beginning to find form when he got injured at the start of October by Ian Black at Hearts. It was little short of an assault and you knew right away it was a bad one because he's a brave lad and stayed down. I was really angry about it and a lot of our lads were. Ian Black got a bit of treatment when we played Hearts after that. The thing about Jelavić, a good player no doubt

about it, was his attitude as well. He is what you would like a stereotypical Rangers player to be, desperate to win, a warrior, hungry,
and he wants to play. He's got a lot of strings to his bow. I spoke to
David Moyes about him and he said Everton looked at him but just
weren't convinced, they didn't know if he had enough, but I would
hang my hat on him.

Nikica put us ahead in our next League game, at home to Dundee
United, but they kept coming back at us that day and we lost 3-2 in
the final seconds when we left ourselves wide open to a counter-
attack. God knows what happened, we must have had everybody in
their box bar Ricky Foster. Steven Whittaker hit their bar with a
header without it actually looking like it was going in, to be honest,
and then all of a sudden they are running up the park and nobody
was there for us. Any one of them could have scored. The manager
was very angry afterwards with us all, but he never went over the
score. He'd always said, 'I can't ask any more from you, I can't criti-
cise you', although I think it was mind games when he told the
press he thought the title had gone when Kenny Miller left us for
Bursaspor in January – I don't think he really believed that.

That defeat meant our final meeting of seven in the season with
Celtic at Ibrox on 24 April was seen as a must-win for us in the
context of the title. We drew 0-0 after Allan brilliantly saved
Samaras' late penalty but I wasn't too disappointed. I didn't think it
was the end of the League. In my perception of it, Celtic thought
they had won the League that day, with the way they celebrated on
the pitch and Lennon walking off with hands cupped to his ears and
so on. I know it was out of our hands, but that gave us so much
motivation. They were basically celebrating the League on our
pitch, rightly or wrongly that's how it looked, and that just
shouldn't happen. It wasn't spoken about in any great detail, but

everybody took note. There was a lot of stuff going on like Kris Commons claiming, 'We are younger and fitter.' For me, that phrase comes from a psychologist. It was almost like they were not convinced they could win the League. That's the impression I got, I could almost see it written on a whiteboard, as if someone was trying to convince them. Commons is a good lad, so it was almost like he had been programmed to say it by someone. From our standpoint, it was all about a good manager managing us. I am not trying to say Lennon is not a good manager, but our manager just had more experience, so he wasn't trying to be too clever or use smoke and mirrors. He was just being a good manager, trusting his players.

When Celtic lost 3-2 at Inverness, I was at Uefa's headquarters near Geneva on a coaching course for my Pro Licence. One of the lads on it came through and said it was 3-1 to Inverness. I'd actually forgotten the game was on and I asked if he was joking and if it was finished. He said there was still 20 minutes to go, then we went into a lecture and I was sitting there scared to look round, scared to look at my phone and just waiting for it to go mental at the end. There is a wee bit of superstition, you don't want to jinx things by looking at it. That was our opportunity. We didn't know if we were going to get one, we hoped we would, but I never doubted that if we did we would follow it through. Some of the lads like Davis, Lafferty, Jelavić had their best spells of the season at a great time for us. We beat Motherwell 5-0, Hearts 4-0 and Dundee United 2-0. The games were won early and there wasn't any time in any of them where you thought this result is in doubt.

Nevertheless, when it is in your hands on the final day of the season there is a lot of tension in the air. I was very nervous because the League is yours, people have already given you it. It almost feels like they are trying to trick you into a false sense of security, but we are an experienced group now, so we don't fall into the traps of saying or doing the wrong things. There was definitely an issue after the gaffer's last game at Ibrox, in which we beat Dundee United. We went round the pitch with him and that could have been perceived as us saying we have won the League, but Coisty, fair play to him, went straight into the dressing-room and said we've got to be careful in how we play this and then he went into the press room to make that clear. It was almost like it was the moment he started managing the club. He nailed it and got the message across that it was a farewell to the gaffer, not a title celebration. Things like that are important because of the influence they can have on the way things are perceived.

We blew Kilmarnock away in our last game with three goals in the first seven minutes and eventually won 5-1. I lifted the trophy together with the manager. It was the right thing to do, just as it had been before with Barry. If anything, he should have been lifting the trophy himself on the last day but as captain you are the representative of the players and he wanted us to get credit, too. It was fantastic, a special moment for me. Coisty whispered to me that I had been a great Rangers captain and would go down with the rest of them. That was fantastic to hear. I am sure he had nice words for everybody on a day like that, but he said it and meant it, which was really good of him. Then we went back to Ibrox for the usual party with our families. I'd played 57 games including four internationals, actually five more in total than the previous season.

Rangers will miss Walter Smith, now that he has stepped down as manager. It has hopefully come across already in this book how highly I regard him as a manager and a man. I don't think people appreciate how hard he works and the master of his trade he is. The biggest thing for me is how good he is at analysing situations and predicting what's going to happen both for yourself and the other team, tactically he's always ahead of the game. He also puts the team first, he's not a showman. He doesn't do anything for effect, he does it to win games – that's his rationale first and foremost. He always says to me the key to being a football manager is to assess your players and set your team up to give yourself the best chance of winning. Recently, when he's not had the resources to bring in the people he would have wanted and liked to, he has set up his teams accordingly. He's definitely got a big respect for Italian football and a big interest in it. He likes the way they play. Personally, I am probably from that school as well. I think good defensive play is an art as much as good attacking play is.

Walter always gives you a feeling at Rangers that he's seen it before and that gives you confidence. He always talks in groups of games and gives you wee targets to hit all the time. Now and then, I like to ask him why he did certain things and when he explains it to you, it just makes sense. Football often is common sense and we try to complicate it. Every question you ask, you get an answer that justifies his decisions. He's got an acute perception of what the dressing-room needs. He will come in before games when we are sitting there and kick a board or throw a cup or kick a bottle. It doesn't happen very often, but when you are least expecting it and when he senses something in the dressing-room is not quite right and some complacency is creeping in.

He's humorous in how he treats the staff, the 'I am working with idiots here' sort of stuff. He makes it fun, he doesn't make anything seem too serious or important. That is his modus operandi within Rangers because the results matter to a lot of people and he feels if players get too much of a feeling of that, they become nervous and uptight. He will come in and say, 'Coisty, is that everybody in?', and Coisty will say, 'Yes, that's everybody in, gaffer', and then some-body will come in the door two minutes later and Walter will just walk away shaking his head. To play for Rangers, and Celtic, is a hard, pressured environment, you can't get away from that, and he feels he shouldn't make it any worse and that makes sense to me. Otherwise you would just be living in a pressure-cooker 24 hours a day and that can only last for so long.

He definitely ramps up the tactics for the European games. He works on that more, the shape of the team and so on. A lot of the time we are playing a different system. The dynamic is slightly different, but he always reinforces that we are still expected to win, regardless of who we are playing, whether it is Barcelona or any other of the great clubs we have faced in Europe. He never lets you get away with thinking, 'We'll take a draw here.' He always talks about the winning culture of the club and how we are expected to win. With the takeover rumbling on last season, you read and hear things in the media and you know it's there in the background, but he never brought it to the forefront or let us use it as an excuse. He makes you aware of it, he doesn't kid on it's not there. Nobody could ever complain about not being informed, but you are also made aware it's not an excuse not to win games or be successful. It's a fine line between what's information to help you and what's a get-out clause.

Taking over from him is a tall order for Coisty but one I am sure he is ready for now. I just get the impression that it's his dream job and Rangers being successful is the most important thing for him. The club's in his heart. It's not a personal glory thing for him, he's got a genuine feeling that he wants the club to do well and he's a winner. Everything he's done, he's succeded at. His football career was a success, his media career was a success, his time as assistant manager has been a success, so he's the kind of man that you expect whatever he's doing he will be successful at. He always tells you how he's won at cricket or table tennis or whatever else he plays.

He's got a quip all the time, one of the sharpest and funniest guys I have met, always listening for an angle and jumping on somebody saying something. He just loves life. That's the way he is and that will not change. I would imagine that when he is the manager there will be tense times and worrying times, but he will relax the atmosphere just by the nature of who and what he is. He has been over the course and distance with the manager as well and has seen a lot of situations and I would imagine he will still phone the manager, it would be silly not to use that resource. You could tell how much it meant to him in his career to win, how he always remembers the ones he lost, and that tells you everything about people. They just don't like losing and take it as a personal affront when they do. He's definitely got all the hallmarks to be a successful Rangers manager and I genuinely hope he is because of what he's done at the club and the esteem he is held in. He's been such a big part of Rangers' history. There's not been that many managers of Rangers through the years and I think it is an honour for him to join that illustrious band. I don't think anybody knows until you are in that position, 100 per cent pulling the strings, how it will feel. I am sure he's got his own ideas of how he's going to do it, but how it actually turns out depends on many factors. How much money is he going to have to spend? How many players is he going to be allowed to bring in? All these things will dictate how it's going to be. He'll make decisions, I don't think there's any doubt about that. I am sure he is more than capable of that. I think the players know that already. He will not suffer fools.

He will get plenty of support from the other staff at the club. We see them interacting and you can tell there's a good bond and dynamic. They get on well, they socialise and play golf together. They are all different, but they work well together and hold the gaffer in the highest regard. They will have a laugh, but you can tell he's the boss and they all look up to him. You can see that for yourself when they sit at the dinner table at the pre-match meal and they are all chatting away.

Kenny McDowall is very funny. He's been round the block with regard to his football, with the clubs he has played for and the stuff he's done. He's not had his career handed to him on a plate. Around the place him and Coisty are like a double act, like brothers. Kenny was working at Celtic and had a good name, a reputation of being a progressive, up-and-coming coach. I think it was perceptive of the gaffer appointing him as first-team coach, realising what the club needed and preparing for the future. When he first came in, he thought it was short term, for a year to 18 months, when he could hand the reins to Coisty. I am sure he started enjoying it and it became a bit of a work-in-progress for him, but I am also sure that given the state the club was in, he felt handing it over to an inexperienced manager would have been really unfair. To leave this big club in a state of disrepair wouldn't sit easily with him. We were all sure he was going to walk away last summer before his staff talked him out of it. I can believe that because they hold him in the highest regard and there was never one per cent a sense of animosity toward him. They were very much a team together and weren't waiting for him to go.

Ian Durrant scouts the opposition and potential signings. He's an all-rounder, who does bits of coaching here and there as well. He's always involved in the sessions and the boys enjoy his training. It's quick and sharp and you respect what kind of a player he was as well. He's funny about the place, with a cutting remark for everybody that can be pretty close to the bone. He's still got the banter of a player, he can handle himself in the dressing-room and gives as good as he gets. He makes me laugh just by looking at him sometimes. He's definitely got an interest in the younger players' development, he likes watching them play and he has a good eye for them. He's quite perceptive in that respect. I think the gaffer admires that and values his opinions on the game. That's why he sits next to Durranty in the stand sometimes because he thinks he's a good judge of the game and can see things happening that are relevant to the team and can help it. Maybe because of his injury, Ian started thinking about that side of the game before most players do – when their careers come to an end naturally. He was only 22 when he got injured – I couldn't believe that when I was reminded of it recently – and he was a top player.

There are also guys like Jim Stewart, the goalkeeping coach. Jim's a big gentleman and part of the team, very protective of his goalies and the gaffer as well. Very calm. I worked with him at Hearts, too, and he has just been on the Scottish circuit for a long time. With all the staff, you could almost feel this respect they had for the gaffer. He doesn't need to be protected but they would protect him if he did. Jim was part of his staff with Scotland before he returned to Rangers and so was Pip Yeates, our physio, who is another gent. We never had a fitness coach at Everton, but when he came back to Rangers, the gaffer brought Adam Owen in, on Kenny McDowall's say-so, I think, and he has been a key member of the staff, too. I don't think you can do without a guy like Adam at your club now with the game getting faster and more fitness-based all the time.

Jimmy Bell, our kitman, is a Rangers legend. Every time you go into Murray Park he's there. I think he started by driving the team bus but gradually his influence has increased and he's kind of fallen into the job of kit manager. He has a room at Ibrox full of all the old kits and it is like a treasure trove. I take the boys in and some of the shirts in there are incredible. All the balls and boots from bygone days. There is the trophy room and all that, too, but anybody I know enjoys going to Jimmy's room more. Jimmy is old school and he's got pride in the club, he's almost like its conscience, he keeps you on your toes. He definitely keeps people down to earth, there's no doubt about that. He's not happy about much, that's his nature and people perceive him as grumpy, but he's actually a really nice man when you get to know him. Within the camp there's boys he loves and will do anything for, Barry for instance, and boys whose lives he makes harder depending on how he perceives their commitment to the club. He stitched me up, literally, recently when he sent me out in a special strip with a message congratulating the royal couple on their marriage sewn onto it for our game at Motherwell. This was against the rules, and caused a bit of a stir, although I am told it later raised a decent sum for charity when it was auctioned off.

There's definitely a changing of the guard now at Rangers. The club has been in safe hands and the gaffer has made it his mission to ensure it stays that way. Hopefully, it is going into safe hands with regard to the ownership of the club, but with the management of the club, the bit he's got influence in, he's done his best. It's nice to think that will be the case. I also think it's important the fans respect what Sir David Murray did for Rangers. I think it goes with the territory that you won't be remembered fondly – maybe Jack Walker was at Blackburn, but that's difficult at Rangers with how definitive it is with regard to success and failure. He spent money with all the best intentions – how do you follow nine-in-a-row? When you are successful, you will think you can keep being successful and Dick Advocaat was a top coach who brought in top players.

It was the same with Chris Robinson at Hearts. He brought a major trophy to Hearts, which they hadn't had for 36 years, yet the fans really hated him and I think that goes with the position. Fans pay for a season ticket, but these guys put their life savings in, their family's money, and they don't come out with a profit. People think they are in it for the ego and maybe they are, but it's a big price to pay. They could have bought the best seats in the house and gone and watched without all the hassle so I am full of admiration for them.

Whatever happens there will always be a Rangers. I think an institution and football club like that, which means so much to so many people, and has the history it has, will always be there in some shape or form. You just want it to be at the level it deserves to be at, that's the biggest thing. The manager has done that in the last three or four years along with his staff. Probably for a couple of years before that it had slipped and he's got it back to a decent level. There's been periods in Rangers' history where that has been the case but none of them have been in the manager's time.

I have never been a fans' favourite throughout my career. I got a lot of Player of the Year awards at my clubs, but I was never really a player the fans sang about. It wasn't my style and it genuinely never bothered me, but at Rangers in the last couple of years I have been more aware they have an affinity for me, which is great. They sing 'We All Dream of a Team of Davie Weirs'. By picking up a couple of trophies you become a symbol, I guess, a figurehead, and you obviously get a bit of attention, but I have never been one for courting it or enjoying it. If anything, I am the other way and want to avoid it, but when you are captain of Rangers you can't avoid it, it goes with the territory and good or bad you are going to get it.

The fans also sing 'No Surrender, Davie Weir', you can hear them clearly, and there is no point skirting around it. 'No surrender' was a slogan used by Loyalists during the siege of Londonderry in the 17th century, although I had to check that. Some people will tell you it is a sectarian slogan and some will say it should be considered no differently than, say, 'Flower of Scotland'. That is the minefield you enter when you start to discuss the various songs and chants. Some are clearly sectarian, but some are less blatantly so and some aren't at all. I don't know enough of the history or care enough about it to get involved in those arguments, but I don't want to duck the issue either in this book.

The fanbase of Rangers is so large there is going to be a bad element and it is probably bigger than in the majority of other clubs because the fanbase is much bigger, but the vast majority of Rangers fans are great supporters and people with a big feeling for their club and they feel it is getting dragged through the mud with various issues. Some fans have brought it on themselves with their songs and behaviour, but it is over 100 years of history that people are trying to wipe out overnight and I don't think it's going to happen like that. To an extent, Rangers have become targets of the PC brigade, something I have no time for. When people outside Scotland, and particularly Glasgow, pass judgement they don't realise that Rangers and Celtic fans can have good-natured banter with each other. People have got this perception they are constantly fighting, that they simply can't live with each other.

That there's not any divided families. I know a lad well who is a Celtic fan and his dad is a Rangers fan. I get him tickets to go to Rangers games now and again and he goes with his dad, I am not saying he wants us to win, but people have got this great perception of Rangers and Celtic as a great divide and everybody hates each other. It is there, of course, but not to the extent that people think. If I bought into all that garbage would Kev Kilbane, who I played with at Everton and has over 100 caps for the Republic of Ireland, be one of the best friends I have made in football?

These people are the minority and it seems to me that they are dictating how everybody else lives right now. You can sing the songs with different words to the same tune and you would get the same feeling, but that wouldn't please some people. Those tunes have been going round that stadium for 50 to 100 years and to just take them out of the atmosphere is difficult. I think the Rangers fans get a bad press, a harder time than any other set of fans on this issue. The Manchester riot was partly due to circumstance. It was a quirk of fate, the accessibility and the number of people that went. It could have been a stadium for 100,000 people and they would have filled it with Rangers fans that night. I would never condone that behaviour, but the good-minded, sensible, normal Rangers fans are the ones who suffer and now face the prospect of the stadium being shut for European games. They get the vitriol. I am not blaming anybody else, you have to be responsible for your actions, but there has definitely been a campaign to try and vilify them and point the finger at the decent majority as well as the moronic minority. They are not so different to any other football fans and it feels like there has been a concerted campaign to try and persecute Rangers. Celtic fans get a hard time as well. There was a do in Kelvingrove Park for the Royal Wedding and there were more arrests there than at many Rangers–Celtic games, so is that an Old Firm problem? That's the nature of Glasgow. If you put 10 Glaswegians in a room, there will be a difference of opinion because they have all got one.

People always talk about us being the laughing stock of the world, but we're not. People don't see it like that. If anything, rightly or wrongly, the best thing to happen to Scottish football in terms of publicity was when Coisty and Lennon had their argument last season. I guarantee the TV ratings went through the roof for the next game. Sky loved it, the newspapers loved it. Like they say, no publicity is bad publicity. Scottish football is struggling and the number of people who wanted to speak to me about Scottish football after that was unheralded. Clever marketing people find out what your selling point is and then they promote it. They know people like arguments and controversy and God knows there is enough of all that in Scotland.

There are more stories down in England, more big clubs. So any single incident doesn't seem that important, it is just a small factor in the big circus, whereas up in Scotland it's the issue and will be the issue for the next three weeks. The media will get maximum mileage out of it and look at it from every angle, analyse and dissect it, and then we will all do it again next week. It is probably self-fulfilling to a certain degree now because people expect it.

Playing each other so often is a factor, too. The gaffer is well aware of that, he's seen it before and knows it is going to happen. We saw similar scenes, perhaps worse, with Real Madrid playing Barcelona four times very quickly in succession between the Champions League, La Liga and the Copa del Rey recently. You could put two teams that don't have a rivalry together that often and you would have grudges just by the nature of football. When you add in all the media attention and the high stakes, it is always going to be a powderkeg. It was the same the last time when we played Celtic twice in quick succession at the end of the season in 2008 and the games meant so much. Everything kicked off.

Better judges than me, the gaffer for instance, say Scottish football is not at a good level right now but I disagree. I think there is still a lot of good football played by a lot of good players. I think Rangers played great football in the last month of the season and I think Celtic played a lot of great football last season, too, as did clubs with less resources like Kilmarnock and Motherwell at times. I still think there are a lot of good things in Scottish football but it is governed by money. Decisions are made based on money and Rangers playing Celtic as many times as they can. It's not based on the development of football players or clubs, it is based on bringing as much cash into the game as they can. How it is spent doesn't matter, it is just bring in revenue. Take what you can, while you can. There's not a strategy in terms of what we are trying to achieve. Look at all these young lads who can't play in the under-18s at Rangers and Celtic because they are too old. There's not a reserve league so they can't play in that either and they are not getting a game on a Saturday. Rangers and Celtic need a team each in a lower league. That would solve a lot of problems. Barcelona and Real Madrid do it and, for me, it's a win-win situation, as it would also add to the lower leagues.

I played for Falkirk when we were struggling in the Premier League and couldn't get a crowd and when we were successful in the First Division and got big crowds. People couldn't get in the gates when we played Dunfermline in our promotion season, you couldn't get a ticket. So when people say Rangers and Celtic going to England would be the death of Scottish football, I say it could be the making of Scottish football. Hearts, Hibs, Dundee United, Aberdeen and Motherwell would develop as clubs if they had the chance of winning the League. Fans like being successful, and I think if these teams had a chance of winning the League and there was a possibility of European football or of getting into the English League as a result they would progress. I don't know the dynamics of it, but if there was a real reward for winning the League it could work. My point is that football fans like watching teams that win, people like to be associated with winners.

English football doesn't think it needs the Old Firm, but I don't think it appreciates what Rangers and Celtic would bring. I think they would add to it and make it a better product. It would create a greater interest, raise the standard, bring so many positives, but I can also see it from the standpoint of the Wigans and Blackpools and various other teams who are between the Championship and the Premiership. Rangers and Celtic would be fixtures in the elite, they would challenge the top five or six every year. There would be seven or eight good teams instead of five or six. Without a doubt, Rangers and Celtic, with time and the finances available, would challenge the present hierarchy. The Wigans and so on will never compete at that level. And you could argue that clubs like Hearts could as well in time, given the population of Edinburgh. I think there is a big argument for it with the fanbases they would bring to the party.

Epilogue

My father, my family, my future

MY DAD is my hero and always will be. I admire many people in football and have made many friends in the game, but he will always come first for me. Alzheimer's is a particularly cruel illness because you still have the person you loved but you have also lost them in a sense and are left in a kind of limbo. A big part of writing this book for me was that I wanted to speak about that because I think it is quite important that people who are in similar situations or worse situations understand that many families are going through what they are going through.

We are lucky now that my dad is in a good place and, touch wood, we are past the worst in terms of the effect it had on our family, but it is horrible to see a person change so much. I would describe my dad as your typical Scottish leader of the family. A proper moral compass, who would always want you to do the right thing. He was always concerned not just about himself but about the bigger picture, the state of the country and so on. He always moaned about the lack of industry because he was used to having his hands dirty and doing an honest day's work. He would say we have gone from an industry where we were building things, making things and inventing things to a service industry culture where we are just providing for other companies and countries. We have turned into a country where everybody is sub-contracting instead of contracting. Nobody is taking any responsibility for anything. He wasn't religious or preachy with me but he would go to church and he would go to his bed early and sometimes I would go in and see him praying, just sitting at the side of his bed. When I came in, he would quickly stand up to talk to me. I was in awe of him and I am still in awe of him. He is a good type of person.

I guess I am quite like him in that I am very family-orientated as he was and have started to have similar opinions about the world as I have got older. It is almost get what you can, while you can, and don't worry about the consequences. Dad was always the opposite. Anything you get, you have got to work for. If you tell a lie, it will come back and haunt you and if you are not nice to somebody then somebody will be not nice to you. He was a reader as well and he would take me to the library and encourage me to educate myself, but he wasn't like a teacher about it. He was, in my opinion, a proper, principled person, someone who feared God and feared his dad, who firmly believed in an old-school upbringing.

You probably know within yourself a relative has Alzheimer's before you admit what it actually is they are suffering from. It was very gradual with Dad. He would have bad days and then he would be better but it was horrendous to see him getting worse, particularly for Mum. She was living with it day in and day out and he wouldn't go to bed at night and things like that. He wouldn't go to sleep and was angry if she told him to come to bed. He didn't hit her, but there was a threat of violence all the time if she was trying to get him back to bed. He was frustrated and would get embarrassed about it as well. He would go for a walk and my mum wouldn't know if he was coming back. She would get phone calls from people she knew saying, 'We have found him' or 'We have seen David out walking again, is he all right?' It was very stressful for her.

Mum still goes and visits him every night and I have got to drag her away to come and visit us in England. Physically drag her. They lived in each other's pockets for so long and did everything together. The place my dad is in is only about ten to fifteen minutes from where they lived and it has been easier for Mum since he moved in there. It was hard for her to do that but we have been really lucky that the family doctors made sure he was well looked after and Mum has had great advice and support. Dad's ended up in a place where he's being well looked after.

I don't think there is advice you can give to other families dealing with Alzheimer's because I don't think you do deal with it, you just make the best of it you can. There's not an answer I am afraid, there's not a happy ending. It's cruel but you do get bits of humour with the illness itself, things Dad does or says that are inappropriate but funny. Sometimes he'll not speak and you'll walk out the room and he'll suddenly go, 'Thank God for that', or shout, 'Blast it', one of the catchphrases he had. He has been in there a couple of years now and there is a female nurse that looks after him that he has got a good relationship with. One day she came out and my dad looked fondly at her and Fiona, my sister, was in tears. She said Dad looked at the nurse like he used to look at her. That really upset her and I know exactly what she means. That's the person who cares for him, the one he has the biggest relationship with now and he's happy in his world there, in his environment.

When I signed for Everton my parents moved into Falkirk near my sister and out of Shieldhill. My dad always told me stories about his dad. He was the first person in Shieldhill to have a car. Dad was the oldest brother and the guardian of the younger brothers, Robert and Walter. I am sure he would be fighting their battles for them and so on. They go and visit him and that's the worst sight for me probably. Walter looks like him and is fully functioning and very bright. When I see my dad sitting there opposite him, that's when it kind of kicks in for me. It's quite sad. When I go in and see him on his own, I just treat him as he is. If somebody else is there of the same generation, you almost compare them, which is wrong, yet natural I think.

I wasn't really a great talker to my dad, but we were very close. I wouldn't phone my dad and speak to him, but he would always say, 'Do what you think is right.' His was the opinion I always valued most but I felt he trusted my opinion as well. I thought he was really clever, although I am sure everybody thinks that about their dad. My dad would read the *Herald* during the week and on a Sunday he would get the *Sunday Times*. He loved reading the papers. In Shieldhill, there was a pub called the Clachan and he wouldn't let me go into it. He always said to me, 'If I ever see you in that pub, you will be in big trouble.' I always wondered what went on in it that was so bad, but he just thought that was wrong, a young boy in a pub. He would never go in there. I was probably 25 before I went in, which tells you how much I respected him.

My older boys do remember Dad before he had Alzheimer's, but I would have loved them to have more time with him because he is brilliant with kids, absolutely brilliant with them. My sister's first son, Douglas, had a great relationship with him, which they have missed out on a bit. Dad was so family-driven, that was all he was interested in. He had friends and work colleagues, but his family always came first. When I was living in the flat in Falkirk he would be in and out every day, cutting the hedge, washing the windows, checking the oil in my car and probably checking up on me, too.

I always try to get a smile from him when I go in to visit. Even when I was aged 25 to 30, he'd always shake my hand. He had big hands and he'd squeeze your hand and hurt you. I do it to my kids now. It was to show he was still the boss, so sometimes when I go in I still shake his hand, but he has got no power in his now. He remembers that ritual but he can't follow it through. It's hard going in sometimes, it demoralises you. There's a book where you sign in and out which I don't use. I should, but I just don't want to feel like I am reporting for duty or it's a contest to see how many times you can go and see him.

As I said, my mum still visits him every night. Mum is more social and outgoing, whereas my dad was happier in his own company or with his kids. That was his kind of life. My mum worked in the bank, she worked in a hospital, she worked in places where she was interacting with people and she enjoyed it and still does, I think. She retired from the bank about 10 years ago. She worked in the TSB for ages in the High Street in Falkirk, so she knew everybody. When my dad was working, she brought us up with 'Wait till your dad gets home' warnings if we were playing up.

Fiona and I are not unlike Mum and Dad in that she is more extrovert than me. I met her in my final year with Falkirk, probably at a low point in my career. As I mentioned earlier, Fiona was friends with Tony Parks' wife, Simone, from cutting her hair, and she also knew the girl Jamie McGowan, another of my teammates, was seeing at the time. Our first conversation was as I was going into the toilets of the pub we were both in and she was coming out of them. 'Are you David Weir?' she said. 'Depends who is asking,' I replied. I was such a smoothie.

Seriously, for a young player there are traps and pitfalls out there, people have a perception of footballers, so you are going to be wary. You have got to take people as you find them and make a judgement yourself. I immediately liked that there wasn't any hassle or pressure from Fiona. She wasn't one of these girls who said, 'Why did you not phone me?' That just wasn't her style. She had her own business, which I also liked. She was a hairdresser and she worked hard. She was self-sufficient and had her own flat and I liked that, too. Fiona is a year older than me and I didn't have designs on settling down until I met her. We met in 1996 and were married in 1999. We were out together one day in Edinburgh, when I asked if she liked a ring and she said she did. We bought it and went back to Falkirk and Fiona sat with her gloves on until her dad came in from work.

When I first met Fiona, I was living with Tommy McMillan. Tommy lived in California, a village just outside Falkirk. There's Falkirk, then two miles to Shieldhill, then about half a mile further to California. Tommy used to own the pub between Shieldhill and California and we lived in this big house with four or five bedrooms. Tommy's mum and dad lived there for a while, too, and there was also me, Richie Vannett, a lad who played for Brechin who Tommy knew, and Tommy's brother, Colin, who is a really good guy as well. They just took me in and looked after me. I got a bedroom there and had a great time. Like back to the old days when I was living in America.

I probably spent half my time there and half at Fiona's. Tommy and I became friends when he came to my high school and he's the friend I have kept in touch with longest. He was quite bright and I think his mum and dad or a teacher guided him to what they perceived to be a better school, but he ended up not liking it and wanted to move back to where all the numpties were. We had similar humour, we just made a connection and didn't expect anything from each other and there was no jealousy between us. It would have been easy for Tommy to be jealous with his own football career. He was the blue-eyed boy. He was a midfielder and arguably the best player in the country in his mid-teens. He went to Dundee United and came through the system. They were the club to be at back then, with the best young players. He grew up with guys like Duncan Ferguson, Christian Dailly, Billy McKinlay and John O'Neil. Tommy was always perceived to be a really good footballer – he played for Scotland right the way through and joined Dundee United straight from school. He had a bit of everything. He had skill, he could score a goal and be aggressive as well, but unfortunately injuries stopped him realising his potential properly.

When I go home to Cheshire, Fiona doesn't speak about football to me, which helps me switch off. She likes football and is interested in it and she'll watch it with the kids, but she'll not transmit that to me. Obviously it's important to her and she wants me to win and she'll come and watch me. She was at Kilmarnock on the final day of the 2010–11 season and when I was Hearts she used to go through to games with my dad. When I was at Everton she used to go with the kids to a corporate box that the Dunn family, who were good friends to us, invited us to soon after I joined.

My career has always come first. Even when the kids were born Fiona would always get up in the night and feed them. She never gave me an excuse not to do well at my work and she never worried about moving. When I went down to Everton, I went down first and she was probably on the train every week to see me. I'd said to her, 'Come down, you don't have to work', but she would never assume she was coming to Liverpool with me and kept working. My career has never been a problem, it has always been a priority, and socially Fiona's very good, too, she mixes well with other people. There can be problems between players' wives and that's just a nightmare as it can have direct ramifications on your job. I just don't want to hear about stuff like that when I go home, and it has never been an issue for Fiona, which is a godsend.

We didn't really date as such. We would go to local pub with our own friends and then meet up, so it wasn't as formal as that. Maybe once a week we would go to the pictures or out for something to eat, but she was busy with her work and I was busy with mine, so it wasn't like we moved in together straight away or anything like that. She kept her place and I kept my place, although we were only about a mile apart. She was particularly strong after the burglary – a lot of people would have insisted that I moved back to England permanently or that we moved the family up to Scotland but she was strong about it. We made the house like Fort Knox afterwards but I am sure she still lay in bed at night, listening for noises with her heart pounding. She was prepared to put up with that because she felt it was the right thing for me to play for Rangers. Fiona doesn't think I would have lasted as long if I had come down to play at a lower level in England and we didn't want to go back to Scotland to live. It has been perfect for my age and our family. She knows I wouldn't be happy sitting around the house.

We've also had great support from Guy and Elizabeth, Fiona's parents. They often come down to visit us and help us out with the kids and they've been perfect in-laws because they help us make sure that Lucas, Jensen, Kenzie and Ruben don't develop any pretensions. I am determined to make sure they don't and I try to set the same sort of standards my mum and dad did with me.

Lucas, my eldest son, is eleven and probably quite like me, strong-minded and determined but not a big speaker. Not one for cuddling his mum or showing much emotion, not that kind of wee boy, but a real thinker, an intelligent wee boy, very deep and good one-on-one. If he's with friends of mine they enjoy his company, he's quite mature that way.

Jensen is nine now and he wakes up in in the morning with a smile and goes to bed with a smile. The kind of kid you would look at and get an immediate warmth from. He's more likely to be lying cuddling his mum than Lucas, but they are both football mad. Jensen just now wants to kick a ball all day, every day, that's all he wants to do, yet when he was younger he wasn't interested. Fiona used to worry about him because he wouldn't kick a ball. There are TV pictures from BBC or Sky of Jensen when he was three or four with his feet up on the chairs outside the box at Everton yawning his head off and the commentator mentioning it.

In contrast, Lucas was into football from day one. We have photos of before he could walk and I am holding his arms while he's booting this ball. They couldn't be any more different. Lucas is left-footed; Jensen is right-footed. Jensen is sturdy; Lucas is slighter but he sees a pass. You can pick faults saying that he doesn't run about enough, but I really enjoy watching him. He's got a football brain, or that's how I see it, and I like that. He's always been a striker, he's a good finisher and strikes the ball well. He hits all the free kicks and corners, he's just a natural in that respect. My pal, Gary, a jewel of a guy from Liverpool, always calls him Chris Waddle because he's a wee bit ungainly, left-footed, and goes past people really easily yet he looks lazy when you are watching him.

Jensen is bigger than all his pals. He can play a year up and he's played in Lucas's team and been fine. I see more of them and watch them closer than anybody. Jensen is more up and at them. He has improved so much, he's the one that people see and go 'Wow, he's a bit special.' He also plays as a striker just now but he could play anywhere. He's a natural athlete. He goes running with his mum if Fiona goes out for a jog and comes back and wants to go running again. That's the kind of boy he is. He's got big lungs and enjoys being outside. He always looks hot and like he's just been playing sport. Jensen's also got a tough streak. I think it originated from the two of them knocking lumps out of each other. They have both been mascots at Everton and we have good pictures of them on the pitch at Goodison.

Kenzie, my daughter, is seven now. Fiona was delighted when we had a girl but, over the years, she's developed into this wee sporty thing as well – tennis, dancing, and football is now the highlight of her week. She plays with the boys but she's one of the best players in the team. I have been to see her two or three times now on a Saturday morning. When the games are called off, Fiona is scared to tell Kenzie because she's absolutely devastated. In tears and all the rest of it, it's like the end of the world for her. The tennis club is at the bottom of the road and she goes down there twice a week, too, and she just looks like an athlete. A lot of girls don't look comfortable running but she does and she's quick. Kenzie is still the cuddly one. When she comes up and hugs you, she really hugs you. You have different feelings for a daughter as a dad and it's a different experience, but a very nice one.

Ruben, the youngest, is five and quite a character. Everybody that meets Ruben says he has been here before and sees things differently. He comes out with things and does things that you just wouldn't expect of a wee boy that age. He and Lucas were born on the same day, 1 June. He's different, really perceptive, and he sees things from a different angle. Very good with his words and clever. A lot of it will be down to having older siblings, but it really is more than that. He makes me laugh, it is funny just thinking about him. He just plays to the crowd. He's a handful, very demanding, and never shuts up. His party trick is to go and take all his clothes off if anybody is in the house. He's just started getting into football from not being interested but that was probably because the whole weekend and half the week, too, is about the other three's football teams. He's not been interested in it, but is starting to think he quite likes it now. He's certainly dragged along to it a lot.

There's not a feeling like the birth of your child, especially the first one. It blows your head off, it is a surreal experience. The more you have, the more you worry what could go wrong. Lucas came out and had strep B, Fiona was a carrier and he got it and had to have antibiotics. He was in hospital for a couple of weeks and I was in at the same time for an operation on my Achilles. You make the mistakes with your first one, every time they cry you feed them and all the rest of it and just create problems for yourself. We were never going to stop at one. Both of us agreed we wanted to have a bigger family, so we had Jensen. We found out Jensen was going to be a boy by accident but never told anybody and then we had Kenzie. I relate better to boys and know what to say to them but you have to be a bit more careful how you approach things with a girl and you are definitely more protective. Kenzie's not that kind of girl, she's not precious in the slightest. She likes her dolls and prams, but she is just as liable to be on her bike or scooter or kicking a ball about with the boys.

Having kids is definitely a good thing because when times are hard it gives you a reason to keep going and I am sure that's true of anybody in any walk of life. It gives you that kind of impetus if you are saying, 'Why I am doing this, why am I putting myself through this?' It gives you a reason to keep doing it.

Being away from them has been the biggest sacrifice of playing for Rangers and I beat myself up about it a lot. I will never get the time back with them, but I say to myself that I am probably there as many hours a week as if I was working somewhere else. You phone up and hear them screaming and Fiona saying Lucas or Jensen are playing up. You try to talk to them on the phone but you can't do it properly and it's not fair to them either. I now use the phone to do video calls with them but I do feel guilty, I feel like I have missed out on a lot and should be there for them more. I have done it for the right reasons, for everybody's good, but you go down and you are a 100 per cent there for a couple of days and then you are away again.

To start with, every time I left they were in tears and that was hard. You start by saying, 'Dad will be gone in an hour' and you leave just as they are going to bed, or you take them to bed and then leave, or you go in the morning when they are still sleeping. You learn how to get round it. Initially, I made a lot of mistakes that made it worse. You know that five minutes after you are out the door they are fine, but it was really hard, I felt sick sometimes when I left them, asked myself what am I doing when two or three of them were crying and I was driving away. It's not pleasant, but you realise it's the right thing to do or you think it is the right thing to do.

It was particularly hard with Ruben. I am really close to my kids, I am sure everybody says that, but really close to them. Up to the last year to 18 months, Ruben was always a mummy's boy and I couldn't argue because I wasn't there enough. The rest of them would always come to me first. I am not boasting about that, but Fiona would be on to them all the time and I would be the soft one even when I was there, probably the opposite of most families. But with Ruben he would always go to his mum. I have realised I have got to spend more time with Ruben because I have not had that full-on bonding I have had with the rest of them. Now, I know we have got a relationship that is at the same level as the rest of them but I was worried about that. It was definitely an issue for me and Ruben being Ruben he was capable of knowing how to wind me up about it.

I was at Everton when the kids were born and I was there all the time. I would take them to nursery, then pick them up, and the same with school. If they were playing football on a Saturday morning, I would take them, watch them, and then go to my work if it was a home game. I was full-on, but I loved it. I enjoyed waking them up in the morning, it was like Christmas every morning for me. I am ready to go in the morning, while Fiona likes a lie-in, but I loved all that and I went from doing it every day to doing it twice a week. It was particularly hard after the burglary and that's where Fiona deserves so much credit because she would have been worried out of her skin at what happened, as I would have been if it was me there alone. She has been a tower of strength for the family and me and has definitely helped me prolong my playing career.

When the end of my playing career finally arrived last season, I felt much better prepared for it than I would have six or seven years ago. For the last few years I have been working toward my Pro Licence coaching qualification. The courses have given me a new insight into the game and I have developed or renewed friendships with the people on them. At night, you sit up talking, planning the next day's sessions. It's almost like being in a dressing-room again but in a different format. It gets a lot of stick but I think it is essential if you want to go into coaching when you stop playing. And I couldn't have picked a better group to be part of as several former teammates like Scot Gemmill, Alan Stubbs, David Unsworth, Gary Locke and Scott Booth were on the same courses as me.

At Everton, I was the Professional Footballers' Association representative and I am now on its management committee and a trustee for decisions with regard to funding and where our priorities lie. Gordon Taylor, the PFA's chief executive, gets stick for his salary but I think that's just jealousy. He is worth every penny as far as I am concerned for the work he has done for footballers. Probably more than anybody else I have met in my life, I could sit and listen to him all day, he's a great speaker. He's been sensational for his members with the work he has done with regard to their rights, working conditions and things like football creditors always being paid first. Players in England get contracts to the end of June though the season finishes in May, which guarantees them another month's salary, and that's far from the case in Scotland. Then there's the amount of former and current players who have had help with issues such as drinking, gambling, drugs. So much of the work doesn't get publicised. My uncle Graham had bad knees and hips and the PFA paid the vast majority of his knee replacement and they do that retrospectively for former players and players in hardship. If anything, they probably do too much but that's because they have the funds to and because of the negotiating skills of Gordon and how well he's done in getting a share of the TV money. They pay players' wages when clubs go into administration, help the wives of ex-players who fall on hard times, they do a lot of good work.

I was determined to keep on playing for Rangers last season if I could, but then I was injured and couldn't regain my place in the team. I felt January, exactly five years after I joined, was the right time to move on and free up my salary for someone else.

Unfortunately, it didn't work out that way in the end as the club lurched into administration a few weeks later. Now liquidation looms for Rangers, which is an extremely sad situation for such a great club that means so much to so many people.

I briefly considered playing on somewhere else but when David Moyes offered me the chance to return to Everton as a coach, it was too good an opportunity to turn down – although I still sneak in the odd reserve outing when I can. Nothing will beat playing, but I hope coaching and perhaps managing in the future will come somewhere close. I am ready for a new chapter in my life.

Career Record

DAVID WEIR
Born Falkirk, May 10, 1970.

INTERNATIONAL PLAYING RECORD
Scotland: 69 caps. 1 goal.

SCOTLAND APPEARANCES

1997

1:	May 27	Wales (Kilmarnock) F	L	0-1
2:	June 1	Malta (Valletta) F	W	3-2
3:	Nov 12	France (St Etienne) F	L	0-1

1998

4:	Mar 25	Denmark (Ibrox, Glasgow) F	L	0-1
5:	Apr 22	Finland (Easter Road, Edinburgh) F	D	1-1
6:	Jun 16	Norway (Bordeaux) WCF	D	1-1
7:	Jun 23	Morocco (St Etienne) WCF	L	0-3
8:	Oct 10	Estonia (Tynecastle, Edinburgh) ECQ	W	3-2
9:	Oct 14	Faroe Islands (Pittodrie, Aberdeen) ECQ	W	2-1

1999

10:	Mar 31	Czech Republic (Celtic Park, Glasgow) ECQ	L	1-2
11:	Apr 28	Germany (Bremen) F	W	1-0
12:	Jun 5	Faroe Islands (Toftir) ECQ	D	1-1
13:	Jun 9	Czech Republic (Prague) ECQ	L	2-3
14:	Sep 4	Bosnia-Herzegovina (Sarajevo) ECQ	W	2-1
15:	Sep 8	Estonia (Talinn) ECQ	D	0-0
16:	Oct 5	Bosnia-Herzegovina (Ibrox Park, Glasgow) ECQ	W	1-0
17:	Oct 9	Lithuania (Hampden Park, Glasgow) ECQ	W	3-0
18:	Nov 13	England (Hampden Park, Glasgow) ECQ PO	L	0-2
19:	Nov 17	England (Wembley) ECQ PO	W	1-0

2000

20:	Apr 26	Holland (Arnhem) F	D	0-0
21:	Sep 2	Latvia (Riga) WCQ	W	1-0
22:	Oct 7	San Marino (Serravalle) WCQ	W	2-0
23:	Oct 11	Croatia (Zagreb) WCQ	D	1-1
24:	Nov 15	Australia (Hampden Park, Glasgow) F	L	0-2

2001

25:	Mar 24	Belgium (Hampden Park, Glasgow) WCQ	D	2-2
26:	Mar 28	San Marino (Hampden Park, Glasgow) WCQ	W	4-0
27:	Apr 25	Poland (Bydgoszcz) F	D	1-1
28:	Sep 1	Croatia (Hampden Park, Glasgow) WCQ	D	0-0
29:	Sep 5	Belgium (Brussels) WCQ	L	0-2
30:	Oct 6	Latvia (Hampden Park, Glasgow) WCQ	W	2-1 (1 goal)

2002

31:	Mar 27	France (Paris) F	L	0-5
32:	Apr 17	Nigeria (Pittodrie, Aberdeen) F	L	1-2
33:	May 16	South Korea (Busan) F	L	1-4
34:	May 20	South Africa (Hong Kong) Reunification Cup	L	0-2
35:	May 23	Hong Kong (Hong Kong) Reunification Cup	W	4-0
36:	Aug 21	Denmark (Hampden Park, Glasgow) F	L	0-1
37:	Sep 7	Faroe Islands (Toftir) ECQ	D	2-2

2005

38:	Mar 26	Italy (Milan) WCQ	L	0-2
39:	Jun 4	Moldova (Hampden Park, Glasgow) WCQ	W	2-0
40:	Jun 8	Belarus (Minsk) WCQ	D	0-0
41:	Sep 3	Italy (Hampden Park, Glasgow) WCQ	D	1-1
42:	Sep 7	Norway (Oslo) WCQ	D	1-1
43:	Oct 8	Belarus (Hampden Park, Glasgow) WCQ	L	0-1
44:	Oct 12	Slovenia (Celje) WCQ	L	0-1
45:	Nov 12	USA (Hampden Park, Glasgow) F	D	1-1

2006

46:	Mar 1	Switzerland (Hampden Park, Glasgow) F	L	1-3
47:	May 11	Bulgaria* (Kobe) Kirin Cup	W	5-1
48:	May 13	Japan* (Saitama) Kirin Cup	D	0-0
49:	Sep 2	Faroe Islands* (Celtic Park, Glasgow) ECQ	W	6-0
50:	Sep 6	Lithuania* (Kaunas) ECQ	W	2-1
51:	Oct 7	France (Hampden Park, Glasgow) ECQ	W	1-0
52:	Oct 11	Ukraine (Kiev) ECQ	L	0-2

2007

53:	Mar 24	Georgia (Hampden Park, Glasgow) ECQ	W	2-1
54:	Mar 28	Italy (Bari) ECQ	L	0-2
55:	May 30	Austria (Vienna) F	W	1-0
56:	Jun 6	Faroe Islands (Toftir) ECQ	W	2-0
57:	Sep 8	Lithuania (Hampden Park, Glasgow) ECQ	W	3-1
58:	Sep 12	France (Paris) ECQ	W	1-0
59:	Oct 13	Ukraine (Hampden Park, Glasgow) ECQ	W	3-1
60:	Oct 17	Georgia (Tbilisi) ECQ	L	0-2
61:	Nov 17	Italy (Hampden Park, Glasgow) ECQ	L	1-2

2008

62:	Aug 20	Northern Ireland (Hampden Park, Glasgow) F	D	0-0
63:	Oct 11	Norway (Hampden Park, Glasgow) WCQ	D	0-0

2009

64:	Sep 5	Macedonia (Hampden Park, Glasgow) WCQ	W	2-0
65:	Sep 9	Holland (Hampden Park, Glasgow) WCQ	L	0-1

2010

66:	Sep 3	Lithuania (Kaunas) ECQ	D	0-0
67:	Sep 7	Liechtenstein (Hampden Park, Glasgow) ECQ	W	2-1
68:	Oct 8	Czech Republic (Prague) ECQ	L	0-1
69:	Oct 12	Spain (Hampden Park, Glasgow) ECQ	L	2-3

*Denotes captain.
ECQ=European Championship Qualifier.
F=Friendly.
WCQ=World Cup Qualifier.
WCF=World Cup Finals.

Playing Record

Overall

P	W	D	L
69	26	18	25

* Weir claimed his first full cap against Wales, at Kilmarnock, in 1997 and his only goal in a World Cup qualifier against Latvia at Hampden Park in 2001.

*In 2002 Weir retired from international football following criticism from the then manager Berti Vogts. Although Walter Smith was appointed in 2004, David did not return to the field until March 2005.

*After claiming his 50th cap against Lithuania in a European Championship qualifier in 2006 Weir was inducted into the Scotland national football team roll of honour and is the seventh most capped player in Scotland's history.

*In August 2010 Weir was recalled to the Scotland squad at the age of 40 and became the oldest ever Scottish football international when he played against Lithuania on Sep 3 2010.

*In May 2011, Weir was inducted into the Rangers Hall of Fame, becoming the first player to receive the honour while still at the club.

*In January 2012, Weir left Rangers and, a month later signed for Sheffield United on a monthly deal

*Weir returned to Everton in late February 2012 as a coach with the club's academy. He featured for the club's reserves but has not play in the first team.

CLUB PLAYING CAREER

CLUB HONOURS

Scottish Challenge (B&Q) Cup Winner (Falkirk) 1993
Scottish League Division 1 Champions (Falkirk), 1994
Scottish Cup final Winner (Hearts) 1998
Scottish Premier League Winner (Rangers) 2009, 2010, 2011
Scottish Cup (Rangers) 2008, 2009
Scottish League Cup (Rangers) 2008, 2010, 2011
Scottish Football Writers Footballer of the Year (Rangers) 2010

CLUB PLAYING RECORD

			P (Gls)	SC (Gls)	SLC (Gls)	E (Gls)	O (Gls)	T (Gls)
1992–93	Falkirk	(Premier Division)	30 (1)	3 (1)	0 (0)	0 (0)	0 (0)	33 (2)
1993–94	Falkirk	(Division 1)	37 (3)	3 (0)	3 (0)	0 (0)	5 (0)	48 (3)
1994–95	Falkirk	(Premier Division)	32 (1)	0 (0)	0 (0)	0 (0)	0 (0)	32 (1)
1995–96	Falkirk	(Premier Division)	34 (3)	1 (0)	0 (0)	0 (0)	0 (0)	35 (3)
		Totals	133 (8)	7 (1)	3 (0)	0 (0)	5 (0)	148 (9)

			P (Gls)	SC (Gls)	SLC (Gls)	E (Gls)	O (Gls)	T (Gls)
1996–97	Hearts	(Premier Division)	34 (6)	3 (1)	4 (1)	2 (0)	0 (0)	43 (8)
1997–98	Hearts	(Premier Division)	35 (1)	5 (1)	2 (1)	0 (0)	0 (0)	42 (3)
1998–99	Hearts	(Premier League)	23 (1)	1 (0	3 (0)	4 (0)	0 (0)	31 (1)
		Totals	92 (8)	9 (2)	9 (2)	6 (0)	0 (0)	116 (12)

			P (Gls)	FAC (Gls)	LC (Gls)	E (Gls)	O	T (Gls)
1998–99	Everton	(Premier League)	14 (0)	1 (0)	0 (0)	0 (0)	0 (0)	15 (0)
1999–00	Everton	(Premier League)	35 (2)	5 (0)	2 (0)	0 (0)	0 (0)	42 (2)
2000–01	Everton	(Premier League)	37 (1)	1 (0)	1 (0)	0 (0)	0 (0)	39 (1)
2001–02	Everton	(Premier League)	36 (4)	5 (0)	1 (0)	0 (0)	0 (0)	42 (4)
2002–03	Everton	(Premier League)	31 (1)	1 (0)	2 (0)	0 (0	0 (0)	35 (1)
2003–04	Everton	(Premier League)	10 (0)	0 (0)	2 (0)	0 (0)	0 (0)	13 (0)
2004–05	Everton	(Premier League)	34 (1)	2 (0)	1 (0)	0 (0)	0 (0)	37 (1)
2005–06	Everton	(Premier League)	33 (1)	4 (0)	1 (0)	4 (0)	0 (0)	42 (1)
2006–07	Everton	(Premier League)	5 (0)	0 (0)	1 (0)	0 (0)	0 (0)	6 (0)
		Totals	235 (10)	19 (0	11 (0)	4 (0)	0 (0)	269 (10)

			P (Gls)	SC (Gls)	SLC (Gls)	E (Gls)	O	T (Gls)
2006–07	Rangers	(Premier League)	14 (0)	0 (0)	0 (0)	4 (0)	0 (0)	18 (0)
2007–08	Rangers	(Premier League)	37 (2)	3 (0)	3 (0)	18 (1)	0 (0)	61 (3)
2008–09	Rangers	(Premier League)	36 (2)	5 (0)	4 (0)	2 (0)	0 (0)	47 (2)
2009–10	Rangers	(Premier League)	38 (0)	5 (0)	3 (0)	5 (0)	0 (0)	51 (0)
2010–11	Rangers	(Premier League)	37 (0)	3 (0)	3 (0)	10 (0)	0 (0)	53 (0)
2011–12	Rangers	(Premier League)	0 (0)	0 (0)	0 (0)	1 (0)	0 (0)	1 (0)
2011–12	Sheff Utd	(League 1)	0 (0)	0 (0)	0 (0)	0 (0)	0 (0)	0 (0)
		Totals	162 (4)	16 (0)	13 (0)	35 (1)	0 (0)	231 (5)
		Overall Total	622 (30)	45 (2)	33 (2)	49 (1)	5 (0)	755 (35)

P=Played
Gls=Goals
SC=Scottish Cup
SLC=Scottish League Cup
E=Europe
O=Other
T=Total

Index